Mexican Lives

Also by the Author

Mexico in Crisis

Journeys Among Women: Feminism in Five Italian Cities

Mexican Lives

Judith Adler Hellman

The New Press
New York

Published in the United States by The New Press, New York.

Distributed by Perseus Distribution

Library of Congress Cataloging-in-Publication Data

Hellman, Judith Adler.
Mexican lives / Judith Adler Hellman.
p. cm.
Includes bibliographical references.
ISBN 1-56584-177-8
1. Mexico—Economic conditions—1982– —Case studies.
2. Mexico—Social conditions—1970– —Case studies.
HC135.H379 1994
306'.0972—dc20 93-40506

Book design by Laura Lindgren

Established in 1990 as a major alternative to the large, commercial publishing houses, The New Press is the first full-scale nonprofit American book publisher outside of the university presses. The Press is operated editorially in the public interest, rather than for private gain; it is committed to publishing in innovative ways works of educational, cultural, and community value that, despite their intellectual merits, might not normally be "commercially" viable. The New Press's editorial offices are located at the City University of New York.

Printed in the United States of America.

12 13 14 15 16 17 18 19

This book is dedicated to Andy and Rich

and to the Memory of

Edmundo Martín del Campo

10 July 1950 – 10 June 1971

Contents

Acknowledgments

Apart from my great debt to the people I interviewed and others whom, for a variety of reasons, I cannot thank by name, I want to express my gratitude to a number of friends and colleagues who supported this effort with their advice and encouragement: Hugo Aboites, Mariclare Acosta, Adolfo Aguilar Zinzer, Sergio Alcántara, Luisa di Aliprandini, David Barkin, Carmen Bueno, Maxwell Cameron, Maria Lorena Cook, Rolando Cordera, Susan Eckstein, Walter Ellsley, Fanny Engelmeyer, Emilio García, Adolfo Gilly, Silvia Gómez Tagle, Enrique González Tibursio, Gordon Hanson, Ingeborg Jones, Larissa Lomnitz, David Myhre, Frances Fox Piven, Richard Roman, Maria Luisa Tarres, Sidney Tarrow, Susan Tarrow, Ricardo Tirado, Pilar Valles, Edur Velasco, Ricardo Villapando, Wodek Wissotsky, Guillermo Zermeño Padilla, and Sergio Zermeño.

I am also grateful to Jorge Bustamante who invited me to the Colegio de la Frontera Norte as a visiting researcher, and I am deeply indebted to colleagues there who provided a crash course on the ways of the border, introduced me to the people I wanted to interview, and generously shared with me their own research findings. In particular I would like to thank Tito Alegría, Ana Barajas, Ana García, Alfredo Hualde, Jesús Montenegro, and Laura Velasco. Kirsten Appendini, Nancy Baumel, Carole Bender, Roberto Castro, Gustavo Del Castillo, Ricardo Grinspun, Cynthia Hewitt de Alcántara, Kathy Kopinak, Janet Sugarman, and Judith Teichman generously took the time to read parts of the manuscript and offered extremely useful feedback. Viviana Patroni was far more than an energetic research assistant; she was also an invaluable consultant and sounding board. Alda Lone, Jacqueline Selman, and Allyson Young committed themselves only to printing the computer discs, but they ended up reading the chapters as they emerged from the printer and they encouraged me enormously with their enthusiasm. I also wish to thank Dawn Davis, Don McMahon, and the staff of the New Press for their hard work and warm support. Finally, my husband, Steve Hellman, boosted my spirits immeasurably when I was in the field, provided his inevitably perceptive, provocative, and immediately useful comments, and rescued readers from assorted excesses I would otherwise have committed.

I also wish to acknowledge my debt to the Social Science and Humanities Research Council of Canada and to the Faculty of Arts, York University, for providing the grants of financial support and release time that made it possible for me to write this book.

A Note on Monetary Expressions and Calculations

In late 1992, in the middle of the research and writing of this book, three zeros were dropped from the peso: thus eleven thousand pesos (the minimum wage) became "eleven pesos" or, technically, "eleven New Pesos." This move by the regime only made official what had long been a popular form of expression. In speaking of sums both large and small, but particularly in the case of amounts over ten thousand pesos, most Mexicans had been saying "eleven pesos" to mean eleven thousand.

In the interest of simplicity, all figures in this book are expressed in New Peso terms. Thus, for example, the quota that street vendors pay to political bosses is expressed as three pesos per day, although at the time I began the interviews three thousand per day would have been accurate. Three New Pesos or three thousand old pesos remained roughly equivalent to one U.S. dollar throughout the period (1990–1993) covered in this work.

Introduction

Once Mexico was a country most Americans and Canadians thought of as poor. Those who traveled to Mexico could see this sad truth with their own eyes—or at least they could see it if they moved beyond the coastal resorts and the comfort of luxury hotels in the cities. Indeed, sometimes the poverty crept into view, even within the protected world of the tourist enclave.

Still, economists tell us that from the 1940s to the 1970s, Mexico was not so much a "poor" country as a "developing" one. In fact, in aggregate terms the Mexican economy grew impressively at an average annual rate of 6.5 percent. Economists insisted that this was an exceptional performance—one that many went so far as to call "the Mexican Miracle." Behind high protective tariff walls, a class of immensely wealthy industrialists emerged to accumulate vast fortunes as the Mexican economy expanded in size and complexity.

However impressive the overall growth rates may have been, these years of rapid economic expansion were also marked by one of the most unequal patterns of income distribution in the world. In 1958 the incomes of the richest 5 percent of all Mexicans were 22 times those of the poorest 10 percent; by 1980 the gap had more than doubled, and the rich enjoyed incomes 50 times greater than those of the poorest sector of the population.[1] Thus Mexicans themselves felt "rich" or "poor" according to their place on this scale of poverty and wealth. Even in 1968 when the regime decided to host the Olympic Games in an effort to demonstrate to the world that Mexico was a modern and prosperous country, Mexicans themselves—and many if not all the Olympic visitors—could see that this display was only an elaborate hoax. The pharaonic buildings and lavish sports installations notwithstanding, it was clear that relatively few Mexicans were rich or even well-off. Most were wretchedly poor.

Then one day late in 1976 word began to spread of an astonishing discovery. Under the luxuriant vegetation and off the steamy tropical coast of Campeche, Chiapas, Tabasco, Veracruz, and Tamaulipas lay billions of barrels of oil. As the dimensions of Mexico's petroleum resources became known, each new estimate of certain and potential reserves was higher. By 1978–1979, with only 15 percent of the country surveyed, Mexican resources were widely understood to run to 200 billion barrels. By 1980 proven reserves had reached 60 billion barrels, and many experts believed that Petroleos Mexicanos, or Pemex, the state-owned oil company, would soon uncover oil reserves greater than those of Saudi Arabia.[2] Estimates for the fields in the Bay of Campeche alone rose geometrically until it was clear that petroleum resources in this area would make the North Sea reserves look meager. A single oil field off the coast of Chiapas and Tabasco held reserves almost equal to those of the North Slope of Alaska.

It seems that the CIA knew the extent of Mexican oil wealth in the early 1970s, even before much of the Mexican political elite got wind of the facts.[3] But once the word spread and the news sunk in, the discoveries marked a break with Mexico's past. In no time Mexico had been transformed from the "poor man of North America" to a country holding the potential riches and political influence that control of energy resources brings. The oil stimulated a reformulation of Mexico's collective self-image and unleashed a wild spending spree.

Rich Mexicans consumed abundantly in the oil boom years. In addition to importing great quantities of foreign-made luxury goods, the rich raced to convert their pesos into dollars and get them out of Mexico and into either a Swiss bank account or a piece of real estate. Padre Island, Texas, became an upper-class Mexican enclave, while an opulent condominium development in Coronado Beach, San Diego, came to be known locally as "taco towers." While real estate purchases by upper-class Mexicans were concentrated in the American sun-belt states, European villas, chateaus, and chalets and resort properties around the world were also quickly snatched up by wealthy Mexicans. In addition to acquiring his own Parisian pied-à-terre, the president himself constructed a compound for his extended family, consisting of four marble mansions and a library filled with imported French Provincial furniture, all perched on a hill overlooking the main highway running west from Mexico City—clearly visible to anyone jostling along on a second-class bus below.

While the economic and political elite exported billions of pesos, the main concern for middle-class Mexicans was to spend their newfound wealth before inflation could reduce its value. Thus, they poured a large proportion of their increasing incomes into durable consumer goods: the houses, cars, electronic goods, and home appliances that transformed the character of middle-class Mexican life in the late 1970s. And, for the first time in large numbers, they began to spend their pesos abroad, not only on foreign-made goods but also on foreign travel. The family outing to Disneyland or the annual shopping trip to Houston, Miami, or Los Angeles became a fixed event in the upper-middle-class calendar.

As for the poor, given the unequal distribution of the fruits of development that marked the epoch of the "Mexican miracle," it is often said that peasants and workers did not expect their lives to improve as a result of the discovery of this new "national treasure." However, they probably did not guess that oil would bring them greater misery. Yet for many, if not most, it did. Between 1976 and 1982 inflation rose 100 percent, and, despite price controls and subsidies for staple foods, the real income of the lower half of the Mexican population declined sharply. Despite the optimistic projections, the oil boom did not create jobs because petroleum and petrochemical production are capital-intensive rather than labor-intensive activities. Moreover, in the gulf coast states the exploration, drilling, and construction associated with the oil boom brought about an ecological disaster: rich agricultural land and fishing grounds were lost, and the only new employment created for the local population was in temporary construction projects and prostitution.

While the private spending of the upper-classes and upper-middle-classes, if not of the poor, was unrestrained, the oil boom also precipitated a public spending spree. Despite promises of austerity and efficiency, the almost weekly announcements of the new and ever-greater oil reserves stimulated a spendthrift spirit in government that made limitations difficult to impose. By no means was all of this expenditure wasteful or ill-conceived. Much of the investment in key areas was carefully planned to prepare the way for the future economic development of the country. But with the expansion of Pemex, the construction of the new industrial centers and ports, and the flood of public revenue invested in rural infrastructure, education, and health, as interest rates rose, government spending soon exceeded earnings from oil exports.

How could the regime cover the costs of this spending? Oil revenue alone was insufficient, because at this point Pemex was investing more than it earned. And, as production declined in the countryside due to decades of neglect of peasant agriculture and rural labor shortages, Mexico, which had achieved food self-sufficiency in the mid-1970s, once again became a net importer of basic foods. Soon the cost of food imports greatly exceeded what Mexico could earn from all its exports.

To cope with this situation, the regime of President José López Portillo (1976–1982) borrowed abroad. Although in 1981 López Portillo set a ceiling of $5 billion on loans from foreign banks, using future oil revenues as collateral, he ended up borrowing three times that amount. Overall, Mexico's foreign debt increased eightfold during his administration.[4]

In large measure Mexico's indebtedness grew because foreign banks were keen to raise their stake in what they considered to be a good risk: a boom economy in a third-world country that featured high rates of return on investments and a long history of political stability. With the price of a barrel of oil moving higher and higher, seemingly with no end in sight, the feeling prevailed among bankers that they could not go wrong putting money into an oil-rich country like Mexico: banks were virtually flinging money at the Mexican government. With the major banking institutions leading the way, smaller private investors, too, were emboldened. And so the intense eagerness of foreign investors to get in on the action was a key factor in stimulating the overextension of Mexican spending, since credit was readily available to the Mexican government (as well as to private Mexican corporations) for almost any project they might propose.

Eventually, however, Mexican policymakers and foreign bankers both began to see that Mexican indebtedness to foreign creditors was spiraling out of control. Moreover, the dramatic rise of interest rates throughout the world further intensified the problem for countries like Mexico. But what was to be done? Some superfluous programs might be cut, but the government could not reduce its imports of basic foods. And in the same moment that Mexico was facing the problem of meeting these expenses, the price of oil on the world market was dropping as reduced demand and overproduction moved OPEC to cut its price. Mexico, although not a member of the cartel, was nevertheless forced to follow suit in order to remain competitive.

Given the sharp decline in oil revenues, the Mexican government continued to look abroad for foreign loans to cover its deficits. And foreign banks, having already overextended credit based on miscalculations of Mexico's future oil revenues, continued to renew loans—although now on much less favorable terms. By the summer of 1982 foreign indebtedness had reached a staggering $80 billion, of which $60 billion represented loans to the public sector. In mid-August it became clear that Mexico would be unable to meet its payments on the debt.

In a recent conversation, a Mexican friend recalled what he felt when the news of Mexico's colossal debt broke on the world.

> *It all seems like a half-remembered dream. It happened so fast. We were a "poor country," as we had always been, and then suddenly we were rich like sheiks, and then, not long after, we were poor again—indeed, worse than poor. We weren't just paupers, we were an international disgrace that threatened to destabilize the whole global system of finance.*
>
> *In truth, most people I know somehow weren't surprised when the bubble burst, when we awoke from that strange dream in which we were* ricos.* *Most of us hadn't really gotten used to the idea of Mexico as a rich county, not to mention the idea of Mexico as a politically powerful country to which the Americans, the Japanese, and the Europeans were coming hat-in-hand, asking for oil, asking for the chance to invest. For a little while we were rich and powerful, but now we were back to living in "cactusland."*

By the time the bubble burst even the most drastic emergency measures seemed modest in light of the dimensions of the economic crisis. First, the government froze all foreign currency accounts to prevent capital flight. Then, on September 1, 1982, in his final State of the Nation address, López Portillo announced the nationalization of all private Mexican banks, placing the blame for the collapse of the economy on these institutions and the speculators they served.

López Portillo's hand-picked successor, his minister of planning and budget, Miguel de la Madrid, inherited this crisis when he assumed office in December 1982. The new president had been informed, but not consulted by López Portillo when the latter

* See Glossary on pp. 233–34 for English translations of Spanish words.

decided to nationalize the private Mexican banks. Long a proponent of an "open economy," de la Madrid did not share his predecessor's enthusiasm for bringing the banks under state control or, indeed, for increasing greater state involvement in the economy. Therefore, although de la Madrid could not "denationalize" the banks, he could and did move to "reprivatize" what had become state holdings by selling to private stockholders shares in the banks and the industries they controlled. He also moved to relax all restrictions on the movement of currency into and out of the country and began negotiations to open the Mexican economy by bringing Mexico into the General Agreement on Tariffs and Trade (GATT). Morever, de la Madrid removed from forty-seven hundred items the price ceilings that López Portillo had imposed in order to prevent inflation from pushing these goods beyond the reach of most Mexicans.

Every aspect of de la Madrid's draconian program was reinforced by the demands made by the International Monetary Fund (IMF) as a condition for assisting Mexico in refinancing its foreign debt. In return for a $4 billion loan, the IMF required that the Mexican government impose an austerity program designed to bring about cuts in every area of state spending.

The austerity program of the early 1980s spelled an end to the last remnant of the "import substitution program" that was the foundation of the development strategy that had produced the "Mexican miracle." In place for more than forty years, this strategy proposed that a country like Mexico could produce its own manufactured goods, rather than continue to depend on goods imported at high cost from advanced capitalist countries, if it could attract foreign investment and provide domestic industrialists with the incentives and sufficient protection from external competition.

In the Mexican import substitution program, high tariffs and import licensing were designed to give Mexican entrepreneurs and their foreign business partners a strong competitive advantage over firms producing goods abroad. At the same time, the government used licensing to restrict the amount of internal competition with which a new producer had to contend. To further stimulate Mexican production, new enterprises were granted tax exemptions for periods ranging up to ten years and duties paid by manufacturers on the machinery and materials purchased abroad were rebated. The government also provided credit at rock-bottom rates of interest, and loans from foreign investors were guaranteed by a government bank established to fund private enterprise.[5] Further incentives for domestic and foreign entrepreneurs included extremely low taxes on interest earned from investment and on profits derived from production.

With the protection Mexican entrepreneurs enjoyed under the import substitution program, they had carried on since the 1940s at low levels of productivity. Small domestic industrialists had been able to survive only because they were shielded from foreign competition and propped up by an assortment of government subsidies. However, starting in 1982 with the debt crisis, these domestic industrialists found that, in their greatest hour of financial need, as the prices for their imported inputs spiraled out of sight, these aids were reduced or withdrawn altogether. Thus the austerity program brought about the collapse and disappearance of the least productive sectors of Mexican industry and, with those firms, the jobs of at least eight hundred thousand workers.

In Mexico people now speak of the 1980s as the "lost decade." Through these years, investment fell, production in some sectors came to a complete standstill, factories closed, and hundreds of thousands of workers were laid off. Oil exports declined, export earnings dropped, and, as a consequence, the foreign debt reached more than $100 billion by 1986. The peso continued to fall, and capital flight continued unchecked. Indeed, it is estimated that the total value of wealth stashed away in foreign accounts and property purchases overseas was greater than Mexico's entire foreign debt.[6]

Given all these trends, the living conditions of peasants and the working class deteriorated in both absolute and relative terms. Inequality of income distribution steadily worsened, and by 1986 almost two-thirds of urban households had incomes below the official poverty line. Even the official figures on unemployment show that joblessness doubled and, in rural zones, six million landless agricultural workers could find employment for only one third of the year or less.[7]

In particular, unionized workers suffered drastic cuts in real wages as consumer prices moved upward through the 1980s. By 1988 the minimum wage was worth only half its 1981 value, and by 1992 it had sunk to only 37 percent of what it had been in 1981.[8] At the same time, nonwage benefits such as subsidized transport, health, housing, and food and clothing supplied to the organized working class through government agencies declined as austerity measures led to cuts in social spending. In the process, the prices of goods consumed by low-income Mexicans, including the tortillas and beans that are still the staff of life for peasants and workers, rose steadily, with dreadful consequences for the overall nutrition of the rural and urban poor.[9]

The statistics that demonstrate these trends and transformations are easy to reel off. And it is not difficult to sketch the impact of a decade of economic crisis on broad masses of people and whole social classes. But what has it meant to individual Mexicans to live through these times? What was it like to travel in so short a period from a poor country living in the shadow of a rich and powerful one, to the prestige and influence of an oil-rich state, to the lowly status of a debtor nation?

What did these changes mean for the women and men in factories and for those trying to eke out a living from the land? What happened to government employees, teachers, and public health workers when cutbacks in spending drastically reduced jobs in the state sector, and they lost not only their salaries but also their benefits? What has it meant for Mexican industrialists to be protected—indeed, by their own assessment, "overprotected"—for forty years and then suddenly plunged into a world of competitive international capitalism? And what do these people think about the fact that the dramatic changes in their personal situation were largely the consequence of the decisions made by a government over which they exercise little or no control?

In 1990 I set out to see how Mexicans experience these changes in their everyday lives. I wanted to understand in concrete terms what it means to a worker to see wages frozen while inflation rises by 100 percent, and what poor people do when basic foods that have been subsidized and controlled by the government for as long as anyone can remember are suddenly "decontrolled." Poor Mexicans have never been able to count on receiving a fair share of the national income, but at least they could count on riding subways and buses for the equivalent of a few pennies and buying a stack of tortillas to see them through the day. In practical terms, how do poor people respond when these subsidies, this "social wage," suddenly disappears? How do they manage to put food on the table? In short, how do people survive?

I was also eager to understand what Mexican industrialists did when the economy suddenly opened to Asian imports and the austerity program summarily eliminated their subsidies. The neoliberal policymakers sitting in the ministry of finance may regard the "elimination" of the "weakest sector" of domestic producers as indispensable to any program designed to streamline the economy, but the industrialists who are at the receiving end of these radical policies very likely are not ready to roll over and die. What do they do? How do they respond? What are their strategies for personal and entrepreneurial survival?

The Mexican countryside is also slated for radical change as the regime of Carlos Salinas de Gortari (1988–1994) attempts to apply neoconservative solutions to the crisis in agriculture. Salinas has moved rapidly to put an end to the agrarian reform that, since the revolution of 1910–1917, has been the foundation of the "social peace" in rural Mexico. He has withdrawn government subsidies for agricultural inputs and price supports for agricultural produce, and he has removed most of the restraints that used to circumscribe the activities of multinational agribusiness corporations in Mexico. What will these changes mean for peasants and large landowners? How will they cope with the loss of government support to agriculture? Does the expanded activity of multinational food corporations hold out any promise for their future? Will the implementation of a free trade agreement with the United States and Canada improve their prospects?

To answer these questions, between 1990 and 1993 I carried out sixty in-depth interviews, all but two conducted in Spanish. These interviews focused not only on the current situation but also on the years of economic crisis since 1982. The people I interviewed were poor, middle-class, and rich, both rural and urban. I spoke with men and women in central Mexico, and others who live in or travel regularly to the border zone and the United States.

In addition to seeking out people who come from a broad range of economic situations, I explored two contrasting sets of responses that Mexicans had made to the years of economic instability and rapid change. I tracked down women and men who had joined with others to seek collective solutions to their personal economic problems—activists in neighborhood movements; trade unions; and manufacturers', industrialists', and landowners' associations. I also sought out other individuals who, for a variety of interesting reasons, had no involvement with any group beyond their immediate or extended family, but, rather, relied for their well-being or their very survival only on themselves and their kin.

The fifteen profiles presented in the book represent a cross-section of experiences, and come from open-ended, wide-ranging interviews. Of the men and women I interviewed, I chose to present those whose stories most dramatically and poignantly illustrate the range, detail, and intricacy of the changes underway in Mexico. From the many narratives I collected, I selected the accounts of those people whose lives were most clearly influenced by the shifts in the political, social, and economic environment. But in order to present a more complete picture, I also included the stories of a few Mexicans whose lives have remained relatively unchanged by these shifts—people who find themselves worse off and working harder to survive, but for whom the differences are of degree rather than of radical change.

This book tells the stories of fifteen Mexicans whose circumstances range from vast personal wealth to abysmal poverty. What links these people is that they are all subject to the influence of economic and political forces well beyond their control. These include broad changes in the global economy as well as policy choices of a government that came to office through electoral fraud and provides only a few, weak institutionalized mechanisms for popular consultation—not to speak of the stimulus of a free press. Together, these economic and political structures provide the framework within which these fifteen people struggle to survive or, in some cases, to prosper. The ways they grope to understand the forces that are shaping their lives, and the personal plans, plots, and programs they devise to face this highly uncertain future are the focus of this book.

What emerges in these personal stories is the remarkable flexibility, clear-headed thinking, ingenuity, and courage of people who take great risks to meet challenges they might wish had never come their way. Almost all that these Mexicans recounted about their situation is so straightforward and logical that it requires no interpretation from me. I have simply tried to retell these tales as they were told to me including, at the same time, enough of the sights, sounds, and smells of the scene so that the reader will have some idea of the stage on which these lives are played out. In the final chapter, I draw observations on the broad range of experiences represented in these personal stories and offer an overview of what they mean for Mexico's future. In the postscript the reader will also learn what I have been able to discover of the way in which the hopes, fears, and plans people shared with me in 1990–1992 actually turned out.

I have included in this book the stories of people who expressed a willingness, and in many cases, an eagerness to open their lives to others—specifically, to those who would read this book. In every case I have altered details to disguise the personal identity of the people who appear here. In a few cases, the individuals profiled are prominent in their particular field or have led such public lives as political actors that it was impossible to change their stories so as to make them completely unrecognizable to everyone. These people appear, as do the others, under invented names. But I also sought and received their permission to use the material they provided, with the understanding that I would not be able to guarantee them total anonymity.

In the course of the long hours of conversation that my fieldwork comprised, I was struck—as I have often been in the past—not only by the openness and generosity of those who were so ready to share their lives with me, but especially by the certainty expressed by so many of these people that to know more about others is to see them with greater sympathy and humanity. Of course, this view was a point of departure for me in my decision to write this book. But whenever my own conviction faltered, I was buoyed by the enthusiasm of the people I interviewed, for they were confident that it would be a very good thing if foreigners, especially North Americans, would come to know more about the everyday lives of Mexicans.

1

The City

3 A.M.: Lupe González

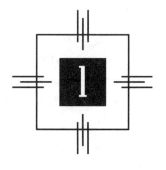

On Thursday, Lupe González's turn to draw water came at 3 A.M. Eighteen families in eighteen single-room dwellings share a single water tap in the courtyard of the *vecindad* in San Miguel Iztacalco, where Lupe lives with her second husband and six of their children. The tap runs nonstop, and each household has an assigned hour during which it is entitled to fill the oil drums from which to draw water for drinking, bathing, cooking, and household cleaning.

Her family's laundry is something that Lupe looks after on Mondays, when she washes and irons for two *señoras* who live in the Polanco neighborhood on the other side of Mexico City. These ladies pay less than the going rate for washing, which is five pesos (about US$1.75) for a dozen articles of clothing. But the *señoras* let Lupe use their water and hang out her family's clothing with their own in the fenced and padlocked area on the roof of their apartment building meant for this purpose. This is an arrangement that Lupe prizes because it guarantees not only the continuous and ample supply of water she needs for her laundry but also the security of a clothes-line less open to theft than in her own courtyard.

This morning Lupe's efforts were rewarded. Often, during the dry season, for no reason that the landlord or the local politicians seem ready to explain, there is no water for days at a time in the *vecindad* or, indeed, in the whole *barrio*. But this time water trickled from the tap slowly, but in a steady stream and Lupe managed to fill three drums and move them across the courtyard to her door on a small cart before her neighbor appeared to take her turn at four o'clock.

Bleary-eyed, Lupe returned to the bed she shares with her eldest daughter. She looked around the room to where the others lay sleeping: her husband with the two boys, and the other three girls in another bed. But Lupe never fell back to sleep. As she would later tell me in careful detail, going around and around in her mind were a series of problems she was trying to sort out.

For starters there is the matter of the *tanda*. When I ask her how it works, she explains that it is a kind of lottery. But in fact the *tanda* is more like a "forced savings club" than a game of chance. A group of people undertake to contribute a fixed sum to a common fund every week. In the case of Lupe's *tanda*, the weekly contribution is one hundred pesos (roughly US$36). On a pre-established schedule, each participant is entitled to collect the total pot. The *tanda* in which Lupe is involved has twelve participants, so she can expect to collect the jackpot once every three months. Although Lupe thinks of it as "winning a lottery," in reality, the only element of uncertainty the *tanda* holds is whether all twelve people committed to putting their pesos into the kitty will continue to do so after their turn to collect the twelve hundred peso jackpot has passed.

Lupe can only remember one occasion in which a participant in the *tanda* either absconded with the common fund or refused to contribute after receiving her share. She laughs at me but also looks a little hurt when I ask how she could be so certain: is it not self-evident that only a certain kind of person, a person who inspires confidence in others, would be invited to participate in a venture of this kind?

Lupe is now preoccupied with the *tanda* for two reasons. To begin with, she faces another three weeks in which she is obliged to contribute her hundred peso share. But in this same period, as she tells me, she anticipates some special expenses. She has to find money for books and school uniforms for the younger girls and meet the tuition fees for her eldest daughter's secretarial course.

In addition she is concerned about the fourth week in which she is slated to be the person who collects the jackpot. Lupe explains that she finds herself, in one fashion or another, committed to use this windfall in three different ways.

The first involves a scheme Lupe has worked out with her sister, Marta. The plan calls for Marta to take the twelve hundred peso payoff, hop a bus for Laredo, Texas, and return with an industrial sewing machine that a cousin purchased from her former boss, the owner of a sweatshop who is moving his operation to Taiwan. With this machine Lupe and Marta plan to position themselves to profit from the coming free trade agreement with the United States.

There are, however, a lot of intangibles and uncertainties in this plan. Do I know, Lupe inquires, if they are paying too much for the machine? I don't. After she discounts the cost of the bus fare, her sister's expenses, the packing and cartage of the machine, and the bribes to the border guards and customs officials, she reckons they will have US$200 to pay for the machine and related equipment. I say that seems reasonable to me. But what kinds of clothing, she wonders, should she make for North American women? Will I send her a fashion magazine when I return, as she puts it, *al otro lado,* "to the other side"? I say I will.

Lupe has not begun to work through the problem of marketing the clothing she intends to produce with the new sewing machine. This will be Marta's department. Marta has been to the other side.

She knows how to move around Laredo and the border region. But her experience was limited to a short and unhappy stint as a domestic servant. Lupe says she wishes that her sister knew more about the flow of goods over the border, about the appropriate amounts to pay in bribes, about wholesale and retail markets in Laredo, about a host of details that their *comadres* who have dealt for years in contraband used clothing would know. She wishes that I knew and could tell her more about what the treaty would mean for someone like herself living in a *ciudad perdida,* a "lost city" on the outskirts of the capital. However, for now, Lupe is focused on the production end of the plan, and so she is thinking about the *tanda* and the machine that the money could buy.

But it wasn't the sewing machine and all the unanswered questions associated with that scheme that kept Lupe from returning to sleep on Thursday morning. The problem was that there are at least two, perhaps three other ways in which she feels she may need to use the money she expects to receive in four weeks' time.

Lupe's oldest son, age twenty-one, left with a friend for the other side more than a month before. As far as Lupe knows, Jorge is working in Los Angeles and making good money. At least that was the plan. Lupe herself underwrote this trip, matching the four hundred pesos that Jorge had saved with eight hundred that she had put aside. A thousand pesos was earmarked to pay the *coyote* who would sneak Jorge across the border, she wasn't sure how. The rest was meant to support Jorge while he was laying low and looking for work.

The problem is that Lupe has received no word, let alone money, from Jorge since he crossed the border weeks earlier. Now her next two sons, José Luis and Ricardo, are preparing to join their brother in Los Angeles, but the plan is on hold. Lupe has promised them the funds they would need, a sum they calculate would be lower than Jorge's expenses because they count on their brother to look after them and find them work once they make their way across. They also plan to save on *coyote* fees by crossing on their own. José Luis favors the strategy by which a large group of Mexicans mass on the Tijuana side of the border and dash for the U.S. side running helter-skelter along Interstate 5, as cars speed by and the U.S. Immigration and Naturalization Service agents, the *migra,* pursue the slowest in the pack while the rest escape.

Ricardo is indifferent to the method they use, be it climbing the guard fence at night, burrowing under it, or running up I-5; he is ready to try any of the high-risk/low-cost techniques he and his brother have learned about from friends. Ricardo is optimistic: he assumes that if for each time they are caught by the *migra* and returned to the Mexican side they try again, they will eventually make it across. But a long stay in Tijuana worries him, because the border zone has the highest prices of any region in Mexico.

Lupe is waiting to hear from Jorge, but is not yet worried. She has no phone and a letter could take more than a month to reach her in a *vecindad* in San Miguel Iztacalco. What she is hoping now is that José Luis and Ricardo will postpone their journey and she can meet her commitment to fund them later on. For now, she is thinking about the sewing machine—and about the down payment on the new house.

The question of the deposit on the house is by far the most complicated of all Lupe's financial concerns. Two years earlier Lupe's sister-in-law, Elena, persuaded her to attend a demonstration organized by the Asamblea de Barrios, a popular urban movement that grew out of the mobilization following the earthquake that struck Mexico City in 1985. Initially formed by those left homeless in the disaster, the Asamblea outlived the emergency, expanded its membership, and is now dedicated to organizing slum dwellers around a broad series of issues and demands. By the late 1980s the Asamblea boasted a "Women's Commission" concerned with the widest conceivable range of women's problems, and it became involved as well in electoral politics, backing Cuauhtémoc Cárdenas, the opposition candidate for the presidency in the elections of 1988. But while it ranged beyond the housing issue, the Asamblea's efforts continued to focus on the demand for affordable houses for slum dwellers in the center city, and for the extension of urban services—potable water, sewer lines, electricity, schools, clinics, and bus lines—to poor people living in makeshift dwellings in the *ciudades perdidas* of the periphery.

Lupe attended her first demonstration, a march on the ministry of housing, in June 1989. From that point on she gave every bit of time she could spare to the movement. At first, she explained, her motives were uncomplicated and frankly self-interested. Elena had convinced her that the most militant activists are the ones who move to the head of the lists that the Asamblea presents to the authorities when demanding new houses. So Lupe made sure to be conspicuously present at every meeting, demonstration, march, and sit-in.

But in the course of this calculated participation, Lupe was, by her own account, transformed. "I started to work in the Women's Commission," she explained. "We composed a pamphlet on AIDS, we organized a convention for peasants, we worked on human rights violations."

> *I learned about politics. I even learned how to talk about sex without embarrassment. I learned so many things I never knew before. Most important, I learned how to deal with people, to talk to people. And now I know how to get more information out of the people who really know what's going on. I learned that only when we unite do we achieve anything.*

Even as Lupe's participation intensified and her consciousness rose, her family's name moved higher and higher on the list of those waiting for the chance to buy into a new government housing project on the southeastern edge of Mexico City's vast sprawl, about two hours by public transport from the city center. As the day approached Lupe knew she would have to come up with three thousand pesos as an *enganche,* or down payment, on the four-room house and prepare to meet mortgage payments of two hundred pesos a month.

When she first enrolled the family on the Asamblea's list, her plan was to ask each of her four grown sons to contribute five hundred pesos, to borrow a thousand from a *compadre,* and to sell some personal possessions—she never told me which—to make up the difference. But as the months rolled by, she realized that none of the four sons, except perhaps Jorge, if he were to find work in Southern California, would soon be in a position to contribute even this modest amount (then about US$180).

Just as the financial crunch was about to come for Lupe and her family, in the very month that their request reached the top of the list, they learned that all work had halted on the housing project because the contractor had absconded with the funds. He is now in prison, but for the time being the construction project is on hold. Thus Lupe is wondering if it doesn't make sense to channel whatever money she has raised for the down payment into one of the other projects.

Finally, there is one last financial demand that weighs on Lupe, and this she speaks about only with difficulty and embarrassment. It would be easy, she tells me, to get the wrong impression.

In July of the previous year, Lupe's younger brother, Alfredo, was leaving a late-night fiesta when he was set upon by three youths—glue sniffers and drugheads, by Lupe's account. They demanded that he hand over the leather jacket he was sporting that night. When Alfredo resisted, they tore the jacket from his back, threw him to the ground, kicked him in the ribs and stomach and, for good measure, sliced up his face with a knife.

Now Alfredo is badly scarred and cannot get work. During the period he was recovering from his broken ribs, he lost his job plucking and eviscerating chickens in a huge industrial *pollera*. And now, no one will hire him. As Lupe explains, potential employers take one look at Alfredo's scars and say no. They have him figured for some kind of bandit, *mariguano,* or pimp. Alfredo's only hope is the plastic surgery that the doctors at the Social Security hospital suggested could repair his face. But he is required to come up with more than two thousand pesos, because the operation falls under the category of "special surgery" and the IMSS, the Social Security Institute, will cover only half.

Lupe herself is unclear about whether the IMSS would pay the full amount had the injury been officially recorded by the police when it occurred. But, in any event, an official report was never an option that the family considered: they feared reprisals from Alfredo's three attackers who were members of a powerful and large *banda,* or youth gang.

So now Lupe is wondering if Alfredo still means to go ahead with the operation, or if perhaps it is too late to treat his face. It is hard to know, because Alfredo is depressed and won't address the issue with her. But if he wants to borrow the money, Lupe feels bound to give him what she can.

Her current situation, she tells me, reminds her of a time, a few years earlier, when she had a particularly good run of luck in the herb market where she works when she isn't washing laundry or busy at the Asamblea de Barrios. Lupe had done particularly well selling what she refers to as "Christmas spices" and she had just collected the jackpot in a *tanda*—and she was hoping to use these windfalls to pay for a technical course for Jorge. But Jorge had the bad luck of riding with a friend in a pickup truck that the *policía de tránsito* decided to pull over and ticket, alleging, as they do, some sort of traffic violation. When Jorge's friend could not come up with the money to pay the *mordida* that the police demanded, both men were clapped into jail and Lupe's nest egg went to pay the bribes to gain Jorge's release a week later. As Lupe explains, the transit police tend to prey on those traveling in beat-up pickup trucks, because they fall into a category that perfectly suits the police's pattern of extortion: these drivers aren't rich and powerful—if they were, they'd be tooling around in a fancy car, not a beat-up truck—but they can be assumed to have *some* money, otherwise they'd be hanging off the side of second-class bus rather than driving their own vehicle, however humble.

Lupe can't help but feel that however she spends the money from the *tanda,* it is important to act quickly, before her plans can be overtaken by some unforeseen misfortune. But she is uneasy with the idea of disappointing Marta, or of letting José Luis and Ricardo down, or of failing to aid Alfredo if he decides to go ahead with the operation. On balance, she thinks there is still plenty of time to put together the money for the down payment on the house, and it makes more sense to worry about that when the time comes. She figures the boys are not yet ready to leave for the United States, and for the time being Alfredo has said nothing more about a loan. It was 5 A.M., Lupe tells me, before she rolled over for what was, at best, another half hour of sleep before she had to rise to prepare the children's breakfast.

8 A.M.: *Sergio Espinoza*

At 8 A.M. Sergio Espinoza climbs into the passenger seat of his Mercury Gran Marquis and flips on the air conditioner. The early morning air is still chilly, but Sergio runs the air conditioner in his car—and the one in his home—day and night. He does this, he explains to me, to remove at least some of the poison from the air he is forced to breathe every day of his life—except on those weekends when he manages to get away from Mexico City to his home in Cuernavaca, an hour from the capital.

Sergio lives in the Bosques de las Palmas zone of the capital in what had been, until the oil boom years, a distant ring of hills and arroyos lying well outside the city. Now this parched, mountainous zone with its sage brush and scrub bush is laid out in winding streets, crescents, and cul de sacs on which large, multilevel houses—almost every one an architectural statement in its own right—spill over the uneven terrain.

Sergio can still remember the drive out of the city to these mountains from the downtown Colonia Roma neighborhood where, in the 1950s and 1960s, prosperous, upper-middle-class families like his lived in mock–Spanish colonial houses. Off they would go in his father's Buick, through the grand tree-lined Paseo de la Reforma, past the winged statue of Independence, past the fountain of Diana the Huntress, and through Chapultepec Park into the Lomas, or hills, where the richest revolutionary generals and the most corrupt politicians had built their mansions behind high wrought-iron gates. He can recall thinking, as a boy, that just past the generals' and the politicians' palaces the great metropolis of five million people in which he was growing up ended and a place he thought of as "Mexico" began: a rural country populated by poor peasants and Indians for whom he felt sympathy but with whom he shared absolutely no link.

Now Sergio's boyhood city of five million has grown to perhaps twenty million people—no one really knows. And the empty countryside between the Lomas de Chapultepec and the ring of mountains at the edge of the Federal District, has filled with houses, shopping centers, and, of course, auto traffic and pollution. To be sure, the capital has grown more dramatically in its other outskirts. The area called Netzahuacoyotl, just to the east of the international airport, which began in the 1950s as so many cardboard and tin-roofed shanty dwellings set in a dry lake bed, has become an incorporated entity of six million, with full urban services. And the roads south from Mexico City toward Cuernavaca or east toward Puebla and Tlaxcala are now populated by millions of other rural migrants and are served by two of the nine lines of the 160-mile subway system.

But, for Sergio, the most impressive manifestations of unregulated growth and urban blight are the ones that affect him personally. He tells me he feels bitter that the fresh, open air to which he brought his children in 1980 is now almost as poisonous as the atmosphere in the industrial and slum zones of the city.

As I sit in the climate-controlled comfort of the back seat of this luxury car, Sergio explains that the great irony of Mexico City's pollution is that it afflicts rich and poor alike. There is no exclusive neighborhood in which those who are better off can escape the prevailing northerly winds that sweep into the horseshoe-shaped ring of volcanic peaks around the capital. The wind pushes automobile exhaust, factory fumes, and dust laced with particles of fecal matter into the southern reaches of the capital, trapping these contaminants in the neighborhoods where the wealthy make their home. In elite quarters such as the Lomas or the Pedregal Gardens, and the best neighborhoods of the colonial villages of San Angel and Coyoacán, the rich breathe the same air as the poor: suffused with gases like nitrogen dioxide, sulfur dioxide, carbon monoxide, and ozone. Here contaminants reach levels four times the absolute maximum exposure limits set by the World Health Organization—two or three times worse than the smoggiest day in Los Angeles.

Sergio says that he is always staggered when he thinks—when he allows himself to think—that infectious diseases like salmonella and hepatitis, which in other countries are communicated by drinking water contaminated with sewage, can be caught by his own children just by sucking in a lungful of air. Sergio explains that he has felt intensely uneasy about this situation ever since he read a United Nations report, released in 1991. The report indicated that each day the five, possibly six million poor people living without sanitary facilities in the Valle de Mexico deposit roughly six hundred tons of human waste, which dries, pulverizes, and, picked up by the wind, blows throughout the valley. "Think of it," he says more to himself than to me, "six hundred tons of shit, flying around as tiny particles of dust!" And with this thought, Sergio resets the control on his Mercury to lower the air conditioning and close the air intake vents.

Seated next to Sergio, behind the wheel of the car, is his driver, Jesús Rodríguez, a sixty-five-year-old migrant from Oaxaca State. Deeply lined and gray, Jesús looks as *indio* as Sergio looks European. Jesús is diabetic and, although they have not discussed the problem, Sergio suspects the disease is affecting Jesús's eyesight—not a promising development for a person one relies upon as a *chófer*. Moreover, while Don Jesús (as Sergio has called the older man since he was a boy) was once considered by Sergio's father, Adolfo, to be a true mechanical genius, uncanny in his ability to repair a car with little more than pliers and wire, the computer-driven inner workings of Sergio's Gran Marquis are well beyond Jesús's technical knowledge.

However, dismissing Don Jesús, Sergio would later confide to me, is out of the question. The old man worked for Sergio's father for more than thirty years until Adolfo's death in 1984. And Sergio knows that Don Jesús relies on the steady if small income that he receives from this job to supplement his earnings from the taco stand he runs with his daughter and grandson in the Villa neighborhood in the north of the city, near the Basilica of the Virgin of Guadalupe. From what he understands of Jesús's personal situation, the old man is supporting himself and his wife, as well as their three daughters, each of whom has been abandoned with several children and no choice but to move with her children back into the family's two-room dwelling in a *vecindad* in La Villa.

As a boy Sergio was allowed to visit Don Jesús at the taco stand, which turned out to be two charcoal braziers mounted on a collapsible metal table set at the entrance to the *vecindad*. Sergio says that, as far as he knows, the operation is no more sophisticated or hygienic today. Then as now, Don Jesús had no refrigerator in which to keep the meat he bought in bulk once every three days at La Merced, the central food market of Mexico City. He kept it "fresh" by cooking it up immediately and then reheating it to "cure" the meat just before scooping it onto a fresh corn tortilla and smothering it with hot chilies.

Given Don Jesús's failing eyesight, Sergio tries to call on him as little as possible for service as a *chófer*. Instead, Sergio tries to employ the old man in other tasks. Most days Jesús is dispatched to banks or government agencies to wait on line to cash checks, pay bills, and pick up or fill out official forms. Luckily Don Jesús, who as a youth worked as a school master in his rural village in Oaxaca, can read with confidence and writes in a clear, legible hand.

This assortment of activities easily absorbs the full eight hours that Don Jesús puts in for Sergio before returning to his evening efforts at the taco stand. But, although Jesús Rodríguez is called upon far less often as a driver, by his own estimate he is still a man well rooted in the world of automobiles. And the contacts Jesús developed during his years as a *chófer*, and even earlier as taxi driver, stood his boss in good stead when the new antipollution regulations came into effect in 1990.

These regulations were meant to cut by 20 percent the pollution caused by auto emissions through the simple expedient of requiring each auto registered in the Federal District to "rest" one business day each week, determined according to the final digit on the car's license plate. At first, Sergio says, he complied with some enthusiasm: the policy seemed to him a small but important step to improve air quality. But, like virtually all other middle- and upper-class Mexicans, he quickly realized that he could not get by without his car on that day of the week when his auto would be ticketed if found on the road. His children had to be dropped at their private school, and his wife, Hilda, needed her car or she would feel a prisoner in her suburban home. And so, with genuine regret, Sergio joined the other Mexico City residents who managed to sidestep the restrictions on auto use. Don Jesús used his contacts to find an old, broken-down Chevrolet that he restored for Sergio to use on Wednesdays, when the Gran Marquis has to stay in the garage.

As Don Jesús drives Sergio down the Paseo de la Reforma toward his office, Sergio reflects on the irony of his situation. He cannot even consider dismissing the old driver, and yet only two years earlier he had shut down production in his factory, putting almost six hundred of his seven hundred workers out on the street. The difference, Sergio would later explain to me, is that he feels a measure of personal responsibility for Don Jesús precisely because he is in a position to exercise some control over the old man's fate. But Sergio emphasizes that he did not choose but rather was forced to cease production of the televisions, stereos, audio components, and other consumer electronics that his father and, later, he had manufactured for the Mexican market. He was compelled to do this, he says, by a series of policy changes that were all made over his head and behind his back.

To be sure, talk of Mexico's entry into GATT began at least a decade before it actually occurred—which, Sergio insists, was precisely the problem. For so many years the political leaders threatened to drop the protective barriers that provided Mexican producers with huge profit margins, often as high as three hundred percent, sometimes more. The *políticos* went on and on for so long about the need for domestic manufacturers to modernize and become competitive in the international market that it was difficult for middle-sized industrialists like Adolfo and Sergio to take these assertions seriously.

It wasn't that Sergio and his father doubted it would eventually happen. On the contrary, their reading of world economic events suggested that an end to protectionism was inevitable. But they didn't know *when* it would happen, and they had no personal contacts that might have enabled them to tap into inside information on this kind of policy. All of Sergio's friends from school had, like him, gone into business. He has often wished, he tells me, that some old buddy had risen to power as a *político,* someone he could phone up at the Ministry of Planning to get a tip, or at least some hint of warning of what is to come. But he was not so lucky.

Instead, Sergio says, when the economy opened he was ill-informed and unprepared. Above all, he felt powerless to influence the course of economic policy set by a political elite that was responding to political pressures other than those asserted by his sectoral organization, the Chamber of Electronics Industries, or even by CONCAMIN, the National Federation of Chambers of Industry, the umbrella organization that officially represents business and industrial manufacturing interests. Thus when the announcement came suddenly in 1986, and from one day to the next, the borders were thrown open to cheap Asian products, domestic manufacturers like Sergio were generally caught by surprise.

Sergio tells me that, in a way, he is glad that Adolfo did not live to see the factory he built in the early 1960s turned into a warehouse for imported goods, which in effect is what the plant has become. Where seven hundred productive workers used to turn out reliable television sets, stereos, and sound systems that Sergio and Adolfo were proud to distribute throughout the country under their own brand name, now a few dozen men ride around on forklifts, moving the boxes of finished electronic equipment that arrive from Korea, Taiwan, and Hong Kong. The unskilled workers' efforts consist simply of opening the packing boxes and assuring that nothing is broken or missing. The Research and Development department, staffed with highly qualified technicians, was once

Adolfo's pride. Now it researches and develops nothing at all. Instead, it focuses on meticulously testing the quality of imported products in order to guarantee that Asian-made goods sold under the company name can still carry its guarantee of quality and service, and Sergio hopes to win a government contract to test new electronic imports to see if they meet official Mexican standards. But the life of this enterprise as a productive unit is over.

It could not be otherwise, Sergio explains. A variety of factors make it unfeasible for him to carry on as a manufacturer. First of all, the Mexican suppliers of wood, glass, wire, aluminum, and other materials he needs for his manufacturing process have disappeared. Cheaper Asian imports quickly drove them out of business. To be sure, Sergio could purchase the less expensive Asian inputs and thereby lower his own costs of production. But his labor costs would still be much higher than those in Asia, and his productivity lower than that of the plants there.

Thus when Sergio calculated the 20 percent duty he would have to pay to import finished products from Asia as against the 15 percent duty he would pay on the raw materials and components, it made sense for him to shut down his own production and merely import, from his old Asian suppliers of components, the fully assembled electronic goods he used to make. As he explains,

> *Yes, I am paying an extra 5 percent to import the finished goods. But because I import, I don't have to worry about labor, about strikes, about turnover and all the other problems you have when you employ a work force. Let the Asians worry about it. Somehow their labor costs are much lower. Their governments help them to hold the price of labor down. And their governments also subsidize their inputs. Not like here in Mexico where everything that the state controls, like petroleum, natural gas, and steel, is more costly than in other countries, both poor and rich.*

When I ask Sergio what this means for the future, he says,

> *I can give you a basic equation that tells you all you need to know about the future of the domestic industrial sector: the price of an Asian product on sale in Mexico—with all the transportation and middlemen's profits figured in—is still lower than the basic cost of production of the same article manufactured in Mexico.*

However, Sergio's problems did not end with his decision to contract with his former Asian suppliers to produce his name-brand line of consumer electronics and ship them to Mexico for him to distribute. The opening of the borders in 1986 created other problems as well.

With domestic manufacturing firms closing down all over Mexico, the country is experiencing a colossal, nationwide going-out-of-business sale, with Mexican producers liquidating their inventories and driving down the prices of all products in the same field. Fortunately for Sergio, the problem of being undercut by former competitors who are closing out their line of products is only temporary. But the open border also gave U.S. manufacturers the opportunity to dump slightly damaged seconds, rejects, and reconditioned electronic equipment in Mexico in a way that had never before been legal. And this situation, which is likely to persist, will seriously cut into Sergio's sales.

Most damaging, however, from Sergio's point of view, is the new competition from the explosion of sales in contraband goods in the markets that have sprung up on every street corner and throughout the subway system—indeed in every open space where vendors can cluster and spread their wares. Sergio finds it infuriating that the regime turns a blind eye to millions of people selling what can only be smuggled goods on which the 20 percent duty has never been paid. It further angers him that the street vendors do not collect the 15 percent Value Added Tax (VAT) on their sales and pay no income taxes on their profits, not to speak of payments for the electricity they tap directly from the power lines running over their heads.

To be sure, many other Mexicans not only enjoy the bargains they can obtain by haggling in the street for a color TV, they also look with sympathy on the street vendors as poor people just struggling to get by. But Sergio insists that this sympathy for the "little guy" is misplaced. He is convinced that, at least in the sale of electronics, the sector is highly monopolized: only someone with big money can afford to smuggle whole container shipments of Sony Walkmen, Toshiba VCRs, and other high-ticket items that are for sale every day on the streets of Mexico.

The very existence of this so-called informal sector "sitting under the nose of the great economic modernizers and free traders who make up the current political regime" seems outrageous to Sergio, who sees himself as one of the few honest businessmen left struggling to make a living by honest work. And, as Don Jesús stops the car at the front gates of the factory, Sergio speculates on why the government permits this illegal trade to flourish.

Sergio says he never thinks of himself as a political person or as someone gifted at divining the political mind—but he has lived in Mexico all his life and understands enough to know that if the "submerged" or "clandestine" economy is thriving out in the open, it can only be because this suits the regime's needs. He asks me what I think is behind it. Is it the bribes that the *políticos* collect from the vendors, or that the street vendors can be controlled politically and forced to show up in the Zócalo to shout *vivas* on Independence Day? Or is this a concerted program to forestall unrest among the poor by bringing fancy consumer goods within their reach? Or is it simply a way to give employment to the hundreds of thousands who lost their jobs when factories like his closed down? Before I can answer, Sergio says he thinks that it is probably all of these reasons and, shaking his head, he climbs out of his car, holds the door for me, escorts me into his office, and flicks on the air conditioner.

8:30 A.M.: Miguel Ramírez

Miguel Ramírez moves deliberately as he loads his wares onto two small carts, *diablitos,* the "little devils" he uses to transport his goods from the two rooms he shares with his wife and four children in La Villa to the new Ferroplaza market. Miguel's routine for loading the carts never varies. Keeping the center of gravity low, he puts the two televisions at the bottom, the tape recorders, radios, clock radios, and Walkmen in the middle, and the electronic games, calculators, and wristwatches on top.

While Miguel's basic stock and his method of transporting his merchandise remain unaltered, everything else in his business life is dramatically changed—and not for the better. For the last five years, Miguel sold his electronic wares on a table he erected each day on the sidewalk of the Calzada de Guadalupe, the broad boulevard leading to the Basilica dedicated to the Virgin of Guadalupe, Mexico's patron saint. The Calzada is an ideal spot for commerce in any product: clothing, cosmetics, fruit, candy, tacos, or *fayuca,* the clandestine goods that Miguel peddles. Day and night, the sidewalks are crowded with the faithful on their way to worship, to redeem some vow made to the Virgin, or merely to see the mantle on which her image miraculously imprinted. Even though the new subway line running to the northeast corner of the city now makes it easy for worshipers to jump off at the Basilica station just to the side of the huge complex, most prefer to approach the church on foot, as in the past, walking along the Calzada de los Misterios until it turns into the Calzada de Guadalupe, which runs to the main gates.

When Miguel was situated on the Calzada, sales were always brisk. He would tap some electrical power off the wires overhead and run both his televisions, while a cassette player blared out the *rancheras* of Juan Gabriel or even a little Michael Jackson to please the passing crowds. People would stop, and people would buy. It was that simple.

When he was on the Calzada, Miguel was earning, as he puts it, between four and five *salarios mínimos* every day. That was a big step up from the single minimum wage he used to earn working as a driver for a soft drink company, or as a common laborer at a plastics factory. Miguel says that during his five years on the Calzada business went so well that he allowed himself to hope that the family might move from their tiny two-room dwelling into a larger place. Certainly he was determined that his children would go beyond the primary schooling that was all he had been able to complete before going out to work to supplement his own peasant parents' miserable income.

Of course, the prime position on the sidewalk of the Calzada did not come free or without some serious difficulties. Along with the other two hundred thousand street vendors in the capital, Miguel had to pay a daily "quota" to a political leader who, in return for this sum, would guarantee that Miguel could ply his wares unmolested by the police. If these guarantees failed, the political boss, or *jefe*—in this case Don Gerardo Gómez Sánchez—would extract Miguel from jail and, insofar as possible, compensate him for the merchandise seized by the police.

Miguel can't tell me for certain where his two peso quota goes once the money leaves his pocket. He thinks that Don Gerardo pays some of it directly to the Department of the Federal District, which has the responsibility of regulating commerce in the capital. For certain, he gives part of it to his lieutenant, Don Jacinto, who directly oversees the affairs of the street vendors in La Villa. And Miguel believes Don Gerardo keeps a portion of it for himself, both for personal needs and to pay bribes to secure the release of his people when they are imprisoned.

Because Miguel is located in a peripheral neighborhood, his quota is relatively low: two pesos per day, plus fifty pesos every three months as a "social fee," and another thirty-six per year to the Ministry of Finance and Public Credit for an identity card that gives him his *derecho de mercado,* his right to sell goods in a market. If Miguel were to shift to the center of the city, his payment to a political *jefe* could easily run him ten pesos per day, plus another fifty per week paid directly to the police, and another five every night to the subway guards for the right to store his wares in a secure area of the Metro—an extra expense he would incur if he were to sell anywhere but near his home in La Villa. Of course, the men and women working the central zone of the city earn more than Miguel does, and the vendors selling in the Tepito market at the very heart of the commercial district are rumored to take in the equivalent of eight minimum salaries, sometimes more. But the Tepito vendors must make assorted payments that are at least double those of the others in the *centro,* and the risks they face from thieves and the police—sometimes one and the same—are even higher.

Miguel doesn't think he is cut out to work an area like Tepito. He says he doesn't think his nerves could take it. As it is, he has been cleaned out by thieves twice: once at home and once at knifepoint at his stand on the Calzada. On another occasion a police *camioneta* pulled up, two uniformed characters emerged with pistols pointed, and his entire inventory was loaded into the van, never to be recovered. At least on that occasion, though, he was not arrested, and Don Gerardo came up with a nice loan to get him started again.

Overall, Miguel thinks that Don Gerardo and Don Jacinto do a good job and are sensitive to the needs of the vendor. He is satisfied with the way they keep too many people from selling the same products in the same market. Specifically, Miguel has the assurance that they will not allow another *fayuquero* to set up a stall too close to his own. Moreover, both Don Gerardo and Don Jacinto rose from origins as humble as his own, and, Miguel says, he finds it easy to talk to them. In fact, Don Gerardo sold Chiclets in the street from the age of four, and even though he now lives in a gracious colonial house framed by palm trees and purple jacaranda vines just off Insurgentes Avenue, he always receives Miguel and the other vendors in the organization with great courtesy when they call on him in his downtown office to seek his help, or come to his house off Insurgentes to pay their respects on his Saint's Day.

Don Gerardo, like almost all of the roughly fifty political chiefs who control the city's street markets, was long affiliated with the Institutional Revolutionary Party (PRI), the most recent name for the party that has controlled the state since the end of the Mexican Revolution. By paying his quota to Don Gerardo, Miguel became a member of the leader's organization, the Union of Market Merchants which was, in turn, formally affiliated with the CNOP, the PRI's Confederation of Popular Organizations. The creation of this kind of highly inclusive confederation enables the PRI to gather in the electoral support of people like Miguel—people who are not affiliated to the party as unionized workers would be, through the Confederation of Mexican Workers (CTM), or as peasants would be, through the official party's peasant organization, the National Confederation of Peasants (CNC).

The CNOP is by far the most heterogeneous of the PRI's umbrella organizations, incorporating people as diverse as physicians and street vendors. While the membership is varied, though, the role of the CNOP is essentially similar to that of the two other pillars of the PRI's power, the CTM and the CNC. Very simply, the organization is used as a channel for the distribution of patronage in return for electoral support.

Miguel himself can easily see the similarity among the three organizations. He remembers well when he was a boy living in a rural village on the Costa Chica of Guerrero State, not far from Acapulco, that the CNC would send trucks to his *pueblo* to collect peasants for the campaign rallies of PRI candidates. Everyone who attended the rally—men, women, and children alike—would receive ten pesos, a sum equivalent to a daily wage, plus a lunch of tortillas and beans, and sometimes even chicken *mole*. On election day, when the CNC leaders appeared in the village, they dealt out as much as fifteen or twenty pesos to each voter who dutifully put an "X" next to the name of the PRI candidate before depositing the ballot in the box.

Later, when Miguel worked in the plastics factory, he was affiliated with the CTM, and his union leaders made clear to him his responsibility to show up for rallies in the Zócalo, the Constitutional Plaza, and to vote the PRI line. As Miguel recalls, his participation then was virtually identical to what he was later called upon to do as a street-vending member of the CNOP. When a huge and enthusiastic crowd was required on Independence Day or when the president decided to address the masses from the balcony of the National Palace overlooking the Zócalo, Miguel would be assigned a number that corresponded to a square lettered in chalk in the immense plaza. He was then expected to appear in that specific space in the plaza to shout "*viva!*" at the appropriate moment, and have his name duly checked off on the list that his union boss carried around on a clipboard.

Because he knew the routine so well, Miguel was able to comply satisfactorily with the demands of membership in Don Gerardo's PRI-affiliated organization of street vendors. But then, in the 1988 electoral campaign, for reasons Miguel only partially understood, Don Gerardo left the PRI and went over to the opposition, choosing to support the candidacy of Cuauhtémoc Cárdenas. With this signal from Don Gerardo, Miguel felt free to become involved in the Cárdenas campaign and, for the first time in his life, not only voted but also worked as a poll watcher for the opposition party, the PRD, the Party of the Democratic Revolution. As he explains,

> *For the first time we had a candidate who was clean and honorable and who really cared about the common people. Cuauhtémoc Cárdenas was the son of Don Lázaro Cárdenas, the president who gave the land to the peasants and the petroleum resources to the Mexican people. And Cuauhtémoc stood for the same things as his father: for an end to corruption and an end to privilege for the rich.*

Although Cárdenas carried the Federal District handily and captured a majority in the Valle de Mexico—and, in all probability, won a plurality in the country as a whole—his electoral victory was denied by the ruling party that controled the levers of the electoral commission. In the postelection period, at Don Gerardo's urging, Miguel became involved in mass mobilizations to protest the electoral fraud that brought the PRI's presidential candidate, Carlos Salinas de Gortari, to power.

Miguel says that he will never regret following Don Gerardo into the *cardenista* camp. But Miguel's affiliation with Don Gerardo may possibly have been his financial undoing. In 1990 planners in the Department of the Federal District (DDF), the municipal authority of Mexico City, decided that the street market in the Calzada de Guadalupe was unsightly, a national disgrace, and probably a sacrilege as well. The police were sent to clear out the thousand street vendors who were established on the boulevard, and Miguel lost his place of business.

What followed, as Miguel explains it to me, was complex. Don Gerardo had abandoned the PRI, so his political clout was insufficient to halt the implementation of a policy that was economically disastrous for his people on the Calzada. He did what he could, but to no avail.

While Don Gerardo had suffered a loss of political influence, he nevertheless remained a *jefe* who controlled tens of thousands of street vendors—thus he was not without some resources on which to draw. In the end, he managed to secure for those who had lost their spot on the Calzada first choice on stalls in a new market under construction along what had once been the railroad tracks running in front of La Villa train station. Grabbing these places in the Ferroplaza market was a coup for Don Gerardo, since the stalls were supposed to be distributed without a trace of political favoritism, in a lottery open to any applicant. Don Gerardo was able to assure that one of the places was assigned to Miguel.

The development of the Ferroplaza was the Salinas regime's response to the political pressure exerted by shop-keepers and to the general criticism that the street markets were unhygienic, unlawful, and unsuited to a modern country about to enter into a free trade partnership with the United States and Canada. The Ferroplaza and other shiny new market areas constructed after 1988 were meant to get people like Miguel off the streets and enable the government to collect payments directly from them, thereby breaking the power of the political *jefes* who, in effect, rent public space for personal profit.

But the policy was not working well, and nobody knew this better than Miguel. All of the new markets are stuck in out-of-the-way places, especially the Ferroplaza built on the old railroad tracks that run through an area where, obviously, there is no traditional pattern of human foot traffic. The plaza, perpendicular to the Calzada de Misterios and the Calzada de Guadalupe, is an elongated area that leads from nowhere to nowhere else, and hardly anyone passes this way. Although Miguel turns up his TVs and blasts his *rancheras,* there are no casual passersby for him to attract to his stall. Under the circumstances, he is lucky to sell a few of the cheap and medium-priced items each day. Miguel's income has now dropped below what he used to earn in the factory.

The worst thing, from his point of view, is that only months after he and the other vendors were cleared off the Calzada de Guadalupe, the area was repopulated with other street vendors who were affiliated with a more powerful political patron than Don Gerardo. Short of switching allegiance to a different political *jefe,* Miguel has no hope of reinstalling himself on the Calzada. And even if he were to switch to the *priísta* boss who now controls spaces on the Calzada, Miguel explains that, as a newcomer to the organization, he would stand at the back of the line of those hoping to receive a good place on the street.

In the quiet of the early morning in the Ferroplaza, as he organizes his merchandise in the market stall he has been assigned, carefully placing the cheap watches up front and the pricey items in the back, Miguel describes the options he thinks he has.

A factory job is out of the question. Since the austerity programs put in place in the 1980s, the government no longer subsidizes beans, flour, sugar, coffee, soap, or any of the basics (other than tortillas) that used to be state-controlled. As a consequence, prices have risen to the point that no family can survive in the capital on a single minimum wage of eleven or twelve pesos, about US$4.50 per day. So the question for Miguel would not be to take a factory job but to find two or three such jobs for his wife and himself. In any event, Miguel doubts it would be possible to find three jobs, since so many factories have closed since Mexico joined the GATT in 1986.

No, Miguel says, he is certain that he wants to stick with commerce, but the question remains what to sell and where. Miguel thinks he should continue with *fayuca,* because he likes the goods he sells and he firmly believes it is impossible to sell successfully things one would not want for oneself. Besides, what are the alternatives? Food is a nightmare. To sit and watch his stock rot on the counter is more than Miguel can bear to imagine. And the competition in clothing, shoes, and cosmetics is, if anything, more intense than it is in *fayuca*.

Thus, Miguel hopes to continue selling electronic articles, but the monopolization of the sector by a few immensely wealthy middlemen in the Tepito is a major stumbling block. These are the only people economically powerful enough to bring in the container shipments of goods, legal and contraband, from the other side. The only way that Miguel can get hold of these goods is to travel downtown to the Tepito market each week and buy from these "wholesalers" whatever they are offering at whatever price they demand. Incredibly, the importers do not give Miguel wholesale rates for buying in bulk. He pays the same price for his watches, recorders, cassette decks, calculators, and the rest as any individual who strolls through the Tepito and picks up a single item. This is also the case for those dealing in foreign-made clothing, notions, cosmetics, candy, and luxury foods. The price to the peripheral street vendor is usually the same as the price offered to the individual customer. In fact, the profits for street vendors like Miguel who work in outlying neighborhoods come from charging ten to twenty percent above the price paid in the Tepito.

When I ask Miguel why his customers in La Villa don't buy the same items downtown at lower prices, he shrugs.

> *In general they're either too busy or too afraid to go downtown to the* centro *to buy these things for themselves. The Tepito can be a dangerous place because so much money changes hands down there. I take a personal risk, and so my customers are paying me a few pesos for the convenience and safety of shopping here in La Villa.*

So, despite the problems involved, Miguel hopes to stay with the line of goods he knows best. But he thinks his fortunes would improve if he could get out of the Ferroplaza and into one of the *circuitos tianguis*. A *tianguis*, the Nahuatl word for "market," is a special kind of street market that moves each day. Those vendors officially enrolled in the circuit appear once a week in each of seven neighborhoods, always in the same spot, thereby building a clientele of customers who count on the return of that vendor on market day every week.

Miguel thinks he would do well in a *tianguis,* but he has to count on Don Jacinto to get him into the circuit. However, Don Jacinto has obligations to the *tianguistas* who already sell *fayuca.* He cannot place Miguel until he can find a spot in which Miguel would not undercut the sales of another dues-paying member of the Union of Market Merchants. Miguel knows that this might take some time, so he is also thinking about the possibility of selling his goods in the provinces, along the routes he knows from his years driving a delivery truck for the soft drink company. But this alternative program, he says, would take some careful planning and enough money to buy a secondhand car or small truck.

For the present, Miguel's eyes are focused on the taco stand opening a little way down the passage from his own stall. The crackling sound of frying food reaches his ears, and the smell of *chicharrón* (pork rind), fried bananas, and fried tortillas waft over the largely vacant market toward Miguel. A cluster of food stands are slated to open in that area to form what the planners hope will be an attractive, hygienic "food court." Miguel hopes so, too. It seems to him the only immediate possibility of drawing a crowd to his sad, empty corner of the Ferroplaza.

2

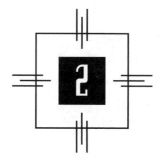

The Historical Background

Alejandra is an old friend of mine. She is now professor of history at the Autonomous National University of Mexico (UNAM). From the window of Alejandra's office I can look out over the vast university campus toward the library covered with Juan O'Gorman's mosaics depicting the history of Mexico from the precolumbian past through the struggle for independence and the Mexican Revolution.

Alejandra doesn't need the stimulus of these dramatic murals to get started on the subject of the revolution. For her the topic is both a professional focus and, more recently, a passionate, dramatic, and *very* contemporary controversy. In the summer of 1992, Alejandra explains, the Ministry of Education announced that it was about to publish new, revised history texts that would be distributed to all primary and secondary school children. On August 4, at a grand ceremony attended by the president, the then secretary of education, Ernesto Zedillo, released the new texts. Alejandra says that it is impossible to convey the sense of astonishment and outrage that the books inspired among scholars. Indeed, she says, "you don't have to be a professional historian to be incensed. You just need to know a little bit of Mexican history and feel even moderately attached to the truth to feel sick when you read these texts."

The books, Alejandra explains, rehabilitate Porfirio Díaz, the dictator whose oppressive rule sparked the widespread discontent and dissent that turned into the revolution of 1910–1917. The epoch of Porfirio Díaz, known as the *porfiriato,* began with Díaz's seizure of power in 1876 and endured for thirty-four long and bloody years, until the aged despot was ousted by the revolutionary forces in 1910. Ironically, the *porfiriato* resembles the administration of the present incumbent, Carlos Salinas, in so many ways that the current president has seen fit to sponsor a revision of the official texts that puts a new face on Díaz and turns him into one of the "good guys" of Mexican history. Alejandra says,

> *The real history of Mexico has become an embarrassment to the regime. So the ministry of education is inventing a new past, writing it up, printing it at public expense, and inflicting it on school children. Since the Salinas people are busy selling off Mexico—its industry, its resources, even its coastline—to foreigners, just as Porfirio Díaz did a hundred years ago, they are trying to redefine such activity as a public virtue, as an act of patriotism.*

This, Alejandra insists, is why Mexicans, who have been brought up on the myths and traditions of the revolution as the dominant shaping force of their national identity, are now being asked to swallow a version of Mexican history in which a dictator is rehabilitated as a hero of "modernization" and the true popular heroes of the revolution, Emiliano Zapata and Pancho Villa, have been demoted in status if not altogether ignored.

> *What does it mean when a new government comes to power determined to rewrite the past, erasing the aspects that give people a sense of national identity? Why has the accurate retelling of Mexican history become, in itself, a subversive act that undermines the*

program or grand "project" fostered by Carlos Salinas and his people?

When Alejandra poses these questions I am struck by just how central the revolution is to all that makes Mexicans feel Mexican. With all the cheerful talk of a "continental North America"—a North America that Canadians and Americans are beginning to think of as containing three, not two, countries—it is easy to forget the key historical distinctions among the three neighbors. In fact, Mexicans share a history that is very different from their neighbors to the north. The experience of the revolution not only defines Mexicans and distinguishes them from other North Americans, it also makes them different from other Latin Americans.

It is difficult to assess the impact of the changes and the challenges faced by the people profiled in this book without knowing something of the culture and history they share. Understanding what has shaped their attitudes and expectations and how they came to be in the economic condition in which they find themselves in the 1990s requires a journey almost one hundred years into the past. In short, without knowing something of the Mexican Revolution and its aftermath, it is very difficult to know how and why Mexicans think and behave as they do. In this chapter, then, I will sketch that history.[1]

The Porfiriato and the Revolution

Over the course of more than thirty years in power, Porfirio Díaz had his official portrait painted again and again: in each painting the dictator appeared less Mexican and more European. His grand projects for the beautification of the capital involved the construction of ornate Italian marble palaces on Mexican soil. So, too, his understanding of development required suppressing the indigenous and promoting all that was foreign. Through the last quarter of the nineteenth century, Díaz stimulated the modernization of

Mexico by throwing the country open to foreign investors. Díaz's success was such that, on the eve of the revolution, more than two thirds of all investment came from foreign sources.[2] Díaz invited foreigners to finance the construction of Mexico's rail system and offered all kinds of monetary inducements to reduce the risk to foreign investors. The penetration of foreign capital into the Mexican economy was so thorough that, by the early twentieth century, the banks were 94 percent foreign-owned, and electric power, most large mining enterprises, and the railroads were all controlled by foreign companies.[3]

Imposing a system of rigid political control, Díaz managed to persuade foreign capitalists that their investments would be safe in Mexico. But the social peace that was central to Díaz's strategy for making Mexico attractive to foreign capital was, of course, based on ferocious repression of the working class and the peasantry, as well as middle-class and elite opposition forces. And, naturally, such a policy created equally ferocious resistance to Díaz's rule. Revolutionary rumblings can be traced to the final years of the last century and reached a thunderous pitch among Mexicans like the Flores Magon brothers, who lived in exile in Los Angeles while plotting the overthrow of the regime. The earliest years of the twentieth century were marked by small-scale peasant revolts, violent labor struggles, and a famous strike by mine workers near the U.S. border in Cananea, Sonora. But the actual outbreak of hostilities did not come until 1910, when groups of northern landowners, resentful of their long exclusion from power and frustrated that the dictatorship provided them no institutional means by which to gain a share of political and economic power, allied themselves with the radical intellectuals who were calling for revolution, and rode into battle with their own ranch hands and peons as troops.[4]

Probably it is the inclusive, multiclass nature of the Mexican Revolution that has given this event the unifying power that has provided Mexicans with a national identity and a sense of national mission over the last seventy-five years. It was a war of just about everyone against the ultraprivileged few. Apart from the elites who were fighting to oust the narrow circle of Mexican and foreign capitalists in whose hands economic and political power had concentrated, the armies of the revolution also comprised middle-class people—clerks, teachers, professionals, small businessmen, owners of small- and medium-sized farms, estate overseers, and ranch foremen—whose economic aspirations were also blocked by Díaz's entrenched group. The mass base of the revolution was formed by workers, miners, agricultural laborers, peasants, cowboys, shepherds, mule drivers, cattle rustlers, bandits, and drifters.

The goals articulated by the revolutionary leaders were as diverse as the social classes participating in the struggle. Middle- and upper-class liberals called for political reforms to broaden the base of political participation, anticlerical legislation to curb the power of the Catholic Church, and nationalistic legislation to impose state control over foreign investment and ownership. They were concerned with putting an end to some of the more glaring abuses of the Díaz regime: forced military conscription, suppression of the press, the total neglect of public education, and the maintenance of order through the use of the brutal *rurales,* militias of mercenary soldiers.

While the call for social justice and democracy articulated by liberal politicians appealed to the mass base of revolutionary soldiers, the peasant and worker combatants had goals of their own. Workers were concerned with winning the right to organize, adequate pay and job security, the abolition of the company store, guarantees of decent working conditions, and other basic labor rights. Peasants, who made up the vast majority of the Mexican population in 1910, made demands that varied according to their work and their relationship to the land. Agricultural laborers who worked for wages on commercial estates had grievances that closely resembled those of workers—demands for higher pay and better working conditions. Sharecroppers and renters wanted land of their own; they wished to be free of the obligation to return to a landlord in cash or kind a large proportion of their produce. And those peasants who were tied to traditional estates, the *haciendas*, sought relief from the burdens of debt peonage. Finally, the Army of the South, a guerrilla force that fought under the leadership of Emiliano Zapata, a peasant turned horse trainer, was comprised of *campesinos* who were fighting for the restoration of traditional village lands that had been usurped and turned into commercial agricultural estates by members of the Díaz clique.

Together these were the social classes that made the revolution against the old regime, which, sclerotic and decayed after so many years in power, fell to pieces more quickly than anyone would have predicted. Only a year after the fighting began, Francisco Madero, head of the moderate, reformist faction, took office as the revolution's first president.

But Madero proved incapable of controlling the forces that had been unleashed in the fight against Díaz. A weak-willed, inconsistent idealist, Madero was unable to provide firm leadership or to reconcile the contradictions between conservatives and radicals within the revolutionary movement. With the support of the U.S. ambassador to Mexico, the deposed dictator's nephew, Felix Díaz, and two co-conspirators assassinated Madero and seized power in a counterrevolutionary coup that lasted eighteen months. The counterrevolutionaries were, in turn, driven from the national palace by the strongest of the revolutionary generals, Venustiano Carranza, a conservative landowner from the north. And another six years of bloodshed followed as Carranza's appropriation of leadership of the revolution was challenged by the radical forces of Emiliano Zapata in the south and Pancho Villa in the north.

In all, the revolution ravaged the Mexican countryside for more than a decade. Even today, it stands as the bloodiest conflict ever witnessed in the Western Hemisphere, and, until the recent years of carnage in Cambodia, it was the most violent revolutionary struggle ever fought in terms of the proportion of population lost: in 1910 Mexico counted a population of only 14.5 million people, and as many as 1.5 million Mexicans lost their lives over the next decade. The appalling death toll on the battlefield, the lack of medical care for the wounded, and the routine execution of captured soldiers all contributed to this staggering figure. Moreover, for nearly a million noncombatants the revolution brought death by starvation, disease, exposure, or execution. Villages were burned or flooded by government troops, crops were destroyed, and peasants taken hostage or summarily shot as examples to their fellow villagers. Thousands fled across the border into the United States never to return to their native land. When the 1920 census appeared, a total of eight thousand villages had completely disappeared from the map of Mexico as a direct result of the revolution.[5]

When the bloodletting came to an end in the early 1920s, the veterans returned to their villages and towns to find that there was not much left to come home to. The Mexican economy was in shambles and thousands of miles of roads, bridges, and railroad track had been blown up or torn out. The telegraph and telephone systems as well as public utilities were so seriously disrupted that they had to be completely reconstructed.[6] Mining, the most important industry in Mexico before the revolution, was now in decline. Production of all staple crops, particularly beans and corn, was down to about half of the prerevolutionary yield. As a result of the severe disruption in cattle raising and agriculture, food prices soared, and each day hundreds of peasants and urban poor who had survived the armed phase of the revolution died of malnutrition.[7]

After more than a decade of fighting, the old order had been overturned and a series of governments—some reactionary, some conservative, some moderately progressive—had followed in rapid succession. But the great masses of Mexicans were economically no better off than before the revolution. The "triumph of the revolution" did not alter their low status, because the peasantry and working classes were not the sectors that emerged victorious from the struggle. On the contrary, the gains made by peasant armies like those led by Zapata were undermined or neutralized by the manipulation of politicians who represented the aspirations of landowners, industrialists, and the middle class. At the end of the conflict a ruling coalition had emerged, composed on the one hand of the new elite of revolutionary generals, industrialists, and businessmen who had prospered during and immediately after the revolution, and on the other of members of the old landowning oligarchy who had become aware that they could pursue their prerevolutionary interests and preserve much of their prerevolutionary status by declaring their adherence to the new regime. Thus, even though the workers and peasants were the principal actors in the revolutionary drama, and even though it was mostly their blood that was shed, there was no point during a decade of conflict when peasant troops or workers' battalions, fighting under peasant or working-class leadership, were able to seize and hold national power.[8]

Looked at in a certain way, the revolution was a terrible defeat for the people who gave the most: the peasants and workers who lost their homes, their paltry possessions, and their lives. But, while the peasants and workers derived very little *immediate* benefit from the revolution, they later received immensely important benefits in the form of legislative guarantees. The goals of the popular forces that participated in the revolutionary struggle were written into a new constitution of 1917, which became the enduring legacy provided by the revolution to the worker and peasant combatants.

The Revolutionary Legacy

In November of 1916, even before armed hostilities had ended, Venustiano Carranza convoked a constitutional convention in the central Mexican city of Queretaro. Carranza's draft for the new constitution was a conservative document, but in the give and take of the constitutional debate the *carrancista* delegates were forced to make major concessions to the *villista, zapatista,* and other radical elements at the convention. The final document, ratified in 1917, showed the clear influence of the radicals. The constitution severely curtailed the power and influence of the Catholic Church, provided for an active role for the Mexican state in the economy, and laid the foundation for revolutionary education in the schools. Most significantly, in Articles 123 and 27, the document provided the legal underpinnings for the radical transformation of the status and condition of the working class and peasantry.

Many of the characteristics that make modern Mexico distinctive among Latin American countries can be traced directly to Articles 3 and 130 of the constitution, which stripped the Catholic Church of its political and economic power. The legislation confiscated church property, denied the clergy the right to vote or discuss politics in public, and even forbade nuns and priests to appear in public in clerical garb. Significantly, Article 3 deprived the church of the key role it had played in education. This change opened the door to a system of state education that, in the postrevolutionary years, was flooded with idealistic, left-wing teachers who carried the most radical version of the message of the revolution into the most remote corners of the country. These *maestros* and *maestras* undermined the conservative village priest's control over the lives of rural Mexicans and socialized generations of peasants and agricultural wage workers in a radical *agrarista,* or agrarianist, ideology that called for land for the tiller, here and now.

Of course, the anticlerical provisions did not go unchallenged in the postrevolutionary era, and this period was replete with church-led revolts against the central authority of the new revolutionary regime, culminating in the Cristero Rebellion in the late 1920s. But notwithstanding outbreaks of resistance that lasted into the 1930s, the constitution broke the immense power of the Catholic Church as a conservative actor in league with the landholding oligarchy and other reactionary elements. Today in Mexico, even casual tourists may notice that many of the state-owned museums, libraries, archives, and other public buildings they visit were formerly churches. To be sure, popular local saints are often venerated with the most passionate enthusiasm, and the cult of the Virgin of Guadalupe is deeply meaningful to Mexicans of various social classes. However, formal, regular observance is relatively low in comparison to other Latin American countries, and the Catholic clergy—whether conservatives or progressive, liberation-oriented nuns and priests of the kind who have had great influence in South and Central America—is generally much less of a presence in the everyday lives of Mexicans than in the lives of other Latin Americans.

In addition to Articles 3 and 130, the radical forces also managed to insert Article 123, which was the most progressive piece of labor legislation anywhere in the world in 1917. The article established the power of the state to intervene in labor relations in order to promote conditions favorable to the workers, and it guaranteed the right to organize and to strike—for public service workers, as well as those employed by private enterprise. It established a minimum wage, an eight-hour workday, and employers' liability for work accidents. Overtime was carefully limited, and every worker was guaranteed a weekly day of rest. All wages were to be paid in legal currency rather than merchandise or credit at a company store. Workers were entitled to a share in the profits, and three months' severance pay was due to any worker who was laid off. Well-defined limitations on child labor were set, and the principle of equal pay for equal work was established. A provision for maternity leave and limits on physical labor for pregnant women were also included in the legislation. The article also stated that "a social security law is considered of public utility, and shall include disability insurance, life insurance, insurance against unemployment, sickness, accidents and the like."[9]

The radical group responsible for drafting the progressive labor legislation was every bit as determined to provide both the constitutional principles and the mechanism through which the peasants could take possession of the land for which they had fought. In a series of statements that would later become central to the assertion of Mexican nationalism and the right of the Mexican state to control the activities of foreign capital, Article 27 of the new constitution established the nation's ownership of all land and water resources, all forests, minerals, and other products of nature. In Article 27, the radicals were able to lay down the conditions for the expropriation of private land holdings. The key passage states:

> The nation shall at all times have the right to establish regulations for private property which the public interest may dictate, such as those regulating the use of natural resources for conservation purposes or ensuring a more equitable distribution of public wealth. With this end in view, the necessary measures shall be taken to break up the large estates.

In addition to restricting land ownership on the part of the church and foreigners, Article 27 provided for the restoration of land to peasants who had been despoiled of their communally held properties before the revolution and the distribution of land to "any group of peasants who lacked sufficient land and water." These grants were to be made from the expropriation and distribution of the *haciendas* of the landed oligarchy.

Overall, the constitution adopted in 1917 provided labor legislation that, even today, seems advanced as well as the legal basis for the widest-scale land reform program ever attempted in Latin America. To be sure, it would be decades before the guarantees provided in Article 123 or the promises held out by Article 27 would become a reality, even for a fraction of the working class and peasantry. The lag in enforcement of Article 123 was due, above all, to the fact that it was too advanced in relation to the backward industrial structure of Mexico in the 1920s and 1930s. And once these labor guarantees were eventually enforced, they would benefit only the minority of Mexican workers formally organized in trade unions. As for the provisions of the agrarian reform, it would not be until the late 1930s, during the administration of the progressive Lázaro Cárdenas, that large-scale distribution of land would begin in earnest.

Notwithstanding the lag between the formulation of these principles in the constitution of 1917 and their implementation decades later, Articles 123 and 27 were, and continue to be, critically important to the masses in the countryside and the cities. Apart from establishing a vigorous role for the state in the control and distribution of natural resources in the public interest, the articles provide for active involvement of the state in securing basic minimum living conditions for every Mexican citizen. The text of Article 123 explicitly refers to the need to establish a social security system. And Article 27 sets up the mechanisms not only for the distribution of land to the landless, along with the water and agricultural inputs necessary to make that land productive, but also for the distribution to rural Mexicans of social goods such as potable water, electricity, health care, and education. Together, these articles establish the foundation for the later development of an extensive network of social welfare supports. These include government hospitals, public housing, recreational facilities, state-subsidized basic foods, price supports for subsistence farmers, and a range of other benefits that provide a safety net for at least those segments of the population that, together with their families, qualify for assistance by virtue of their membership in trade unions or their status as land reform recipients.

Today the Salinas regime, bent on promoting a free market economy and free trade with the United States and Canada, views these social guarantees as an impediment to the kind of programs it would like to implement. According to its calculations, Mexico's competitive advantage should lie in its abundance of cheap labor and a minimum of state intervention in the economy. Salinas's economic team assumes that investors are not going to close down factories in the United States or Canada in order to rush down to Mexico to pay a full range of social security contributions to Mexican workers. And the fact is that in some of the better-organized Mexican industries, payments into pension funds, workmen's compensation, health insurance, and other benefits may double the cost of labor over the minimum wage that foreign investors expect to pay when they calculate the expense of production in Mexico. Salinas's planners assume that if the organized working class in Mexico continues to be protected by the federal labor law, based on Article 123 of the constitution, foreign investors may simply take their dollars to other "offshore" locations where labor is cheaper and social security virtually nonexistent.

Under the circumstances, Salinas's neoconservative policymakers face a tough problem precisely because, as every Mexican schoolgirl and schoolboy knows, these social commitments and the nationalistic principles of control over foreign ownership of Mexican land, resources, and property represent the legacy of a decade of turmoil and bloodshed. It is little wonder, then, that the Salinas administration determined that these aspects of the revolutionary tradition had to be de-emphasized if not erased completely from the school curriculum.

Ironically, the Salinas regime has been highly selective in its use of the revolutionary heritage. Some key elements have been discarded like so much excess baggage. Yet those in power today, like their predecessors, continue to identify themselves as the Institutional Revolutionary Party and to base their claim to political legitimacy on that same revolution. Precisely because the system of political control employed by Salinas and his predecessors grows directly out of the revolution, the peculiarities of the contemporary Mexican political system can only be understood by looking at that critical period of Mexican history when hostilities ceased and the postrevolutionary power stuggles began.

The Official Party

The end of the armed phase of the revolution opened a period in which the major revolutionary generals scrambled for power and wealth, competing with one another for state governorships and the presidency. General Carranza clung to power from 1916 to 1920, when he was driven from office by a military coup led by two of his former allies, Alvaro Obregón and Plutarco Elías Calles. These two generals gave the job of acting president to one of their cronies, who remained in the National Palace only six months, just long enough to stabilize the situation so that he could oversee the election of Obregón. Obregón served until 1924, when he was succeeded by Calles, who governed another four years and sponsored the amendment of the constitution to permit the reelection of Obregón. Obregón was reelected, but he was assassinated before he could reassume office. Drawing a lesson from this experience, Calles declined to stand for reelection and instead contented himself with running the country from behind the scenes while a series of three puppet presidents occupied center stage.

It would be easy to view this period simply in terms of the clash of giant egos, individual rivalries, and personal squabbles writ large with the use of armed troops still loyal to their old revolutionary commanders. But the period in which Carranza, Obregón, and Calles held sway can also be seen in broader terms, as an epoch in which the strongest leaders to emerge from the revolution, men who represented the interests of the northern landowners and industrialists, worked to consolidate centralized state power. They did this by asserting the preeminence of national over regional or local power; that is, the authority of the president over hundreds of local and regional strongmen, or *caciques,* who ruled whole sections of the republic like personal kingdoms.

The device that Calles thought would best provide an institutional framework to centralize rule and solve the ever-troublesome question of presidential succession was a political party. Calles himself introduced the idea of a new "official party" that would incorporate within a single, inclusive structure all the diverse groups then vying for political power: the militant *agraristas,* labor leaders, military strongmen, regional bosses, industrialists, commercial landowners, merchants and others.[10] In September 1928 Calles announced his proposal for the National Revolutionary Party (PNR): it was to be a loose coalition of already existing regional and special interest parties with a structure flexible enough to permit the coexistence of the remarkably varied assortment of groups that collaborated in its formation.

From a weak coalition held together principally by the forceful personality and political clout of Calles, the PNR evolved gradually toward institutionalization.[11] From this time on, however, the person who would shape the features of the party and set its course was Lázaro Cárdenas.

The Cárdenas Regime

When the orange, green, and white sash of office was draped across the chest of Lázaro Cárdenas, few realized that the inauguration of this young general from western Mexico would mark a definitive break with the past. Cárdenas had come to the presidency through the familiar route of military service and political loyalty. At sixteen he had left his native Michoacán and walked halfway across the country to join the forces of General Calles. As a soldier he rose quickly though the ranks, and by the age of twenty held the post of lieutenant colonel; at twenty-seven, he was a general. Calles remembered him as a loyal and dutiful officer, and accordingly, after the revolution he appointed Cárdenas to serve as governor of Michoacán.[12]

Cárdenas's record as governor marked him as progressive within the Calles camp. He initiated a serious land reform program and pursued a variety of social reforms, which earned him the respect of the progressive forces within the PNR. At the same time, however, Cárdenas managed to retain his legitimacy as a loyal *callista,* in part by standing by Calles when the chief's control over national politics was threatened by military coup in 1929. Thus in 1934, under pressure from the most left-wing elements within his broad coalition, Calles selected Cárdenas for the presidency.

In all likelihood, Calles expected to manipulate Cárdenas as he had the other three presidents he had placed in the National Palace—but Cárdenas had other plans. By 1936, the two had broken publicly over the fact that Cárdenas refused to suppress the strikes that were spreading across the country as workers, encouraged by the new president's pro-labor sympathies, demanded the full rights guaranteed to them by Article 123.[13] At the same time, Cárdenas encouraged the organization of peasant leagues and petitioning committees to press the demand for the immediate resolution of the "agrarian question." If the peasants would formally articulate their call for land, Cárdenas was prepared to respond with the full authority of his office, distributing land on an enormous scale under the provisions of Article 27.

Naturally, these moves did not go unopposed by Calles or the conservative forces within the ruling coalition. But as Calles felt his power slipping away and regrouped to attack the man he had placed in the presidency, Cárdenas outmaneuvered him by organizing a popular militia comprised of tens of thousands of workers and peasants trained to defend his government against coup or insurrection.[14] The backing of armed peasants and workers gave

Cárdenas the security to press forward with his program. And when the inevitable confrontation with Calles came in 1936, Cárdenas was able to order the ex-president's expulsion from Mexico along with other prominent *callistas* who had been implicated in the plot to overthrow the Cárdenas regime.

With Calles gone, Cárdenas was free to pursue his program. Essentially, this consisted of the implementation of the radical provisions of the constitution of 1917. While Cárdenas was perceived by many (especially in the United States) as a socialist, his policies were, in fact, piecemeal reforms rather than revolutionary transformations. He accepted the division of Mexican society along class lines and viewed his task as one of "conciliation" among conflicting classes in the interest of "national progress."[15] Far from building socialism, Cárdenas's reforms were calculated to improve the conditions of peasants and workers enough to establish social peace, the climate of political stability that would permit capitalist development to proceed in Mexico.

To consolidate the support he needed, Cárdenas set out to strengthen peasant and labor unions and to reorganize the official party in a way that would reinforce the relative position of the peasantry and working class. The first step was to draw peasants out from under the domination of labor unions and establish them as a separate political force within the party.[16]

His next step, in December 1937, was to dissolve the PNR and call for the formation of a "new " revolutionary party, the Party of the Mexican Revolution (PRM), in which peasants and workers would each have their own official sector, as would the military and the organizations of the middle classes. In this way Cárdenas anticipated that the interests of the masses would be safeguarded by members of their own class who would be elected to public office on the official party ticket. By increasing popular influence within the political system, Cárdenas hoped to build a base of support for the land reform program and the nationalization of the railroads and the petroleum industry that he would carry out during his administration.

In this arrangement, competing class interests were supposed to be reconciled *within* the framework of a single political party. In place of direct class conflict, the popular masses and elite interests would compete for influence within the party's nominating committees. Each group would push to have more of its representatives placed on the party ticket—an achievement that, in a one party system, guarantees election.

Ultimately, for poor Mexicans this arrangement proved disastrous. To have popular representation organized from the top down is one thing when the person directing this procedure is a progressive like Cárdenas who is imposing generally decent and committed people on a bewildered and disoriented working class and peasantry. It is quite another when the progressive period ends, the regime becomes consolidated, and the progressive leader is replaced by a conservative.

Once Cárdenas was gone, the peasant and labor sectors of the official party, the National Confederation of Peasants (CNC) and the Confederation of Mexican Workers (CTM), evolved into pure mechanisms of control. In the CTM, the rhetoric of class struggle was abandoned in favor of an ideology that championed "national unity" and a line that stressed collaboration with government and industry to hasten the economic development of Mexico.[17] From this period on, the CTM was plagued by *continuismo,* the tendency of leaders to perpetuate themselves in office.[18] With officers imposed from above, the union's rank and file found itself powerless to remove and replace leaders guilty of bad management or abuse of power. The lack of internal democracy within the labor sector was exacerbated by the fact that the old-guard CTM leaders drew ever-closer to management and government as they became a moneyed elite in their own right. Given the links between union bureaucrats and big business and government, the official labor movement gradually lost its strength and influence as a potentially independent interest group, and as a consequence, the economic and political bargaining power of the workers declined sharply. Over time the role of union leaders was totally transformed: rather than bargaining for concessions to labor, they worked to assure labor support for the government. As this process accelerated, the more militant labor unions in the confederation—the petroleum, mining, and railway workers' unions—dropped out of the CTM for a period of time.

The CNC also featured a rigidly hierarchical structure in which peasant leaders were responsible to the official party bosses who appointed them rather than to the peasant base. Thus, it is not surprising that CNC leaders, if possible, have been even less militant and less responsive to their constituents than the CTM leadership.

When Cárdenas organized the CNC, he anticipated that grouping landless peons, sharecroppers, renters, agricultural wage workers, owners of small land parcels (*minifundistas*), and recipients of government land grants (*ejidatarios*) in a single organization would strengthen the peasantry in relation to other forces in Mexican society. He believed that millions of peasants united in a single confederation would prove strong enough to challenge the power of the landholding class. Through the CNC, Cárdenas set out to break the political influence of the great landowners by creating an alternative network to replace or offset the patronage traditionally provided by the landowners. To do this, Cárdenas sought to institutionalize a patron-client relationship through which government goods and services would come to the peasantry in return for the peasants' loyal adherence to his own regime.

As it turned out, the presidents who succeeded Cárdenas through the 1940s, 1950s, and 1960s looked to groups other than the peasantry for support. As a consequence, the loyalty of the peasants became marginal to the government, although government support continued to be crucial to the peasants who had come to depend on the state, above all for agricultural credit. But lacking a militant leadership to press for their interests, peasant needs came to have very low priority in the development strategies of those who held power.

In the end, the peasant and labor sectors never had the influence within the party that the other groups enjoyed, not even after the military sector was eliminated with the reorganization of the PRM into the Institutional Revolutionary Party (PRI) in 1941. The official party developed into a mechanism intended not to represent, but to control the organized working class and peasantry. Thus, it is not surprising that the strategies that guided Mexican development after 1940 were so damaging to the interests of these groups which still comprise the bulk of the Mexican population. Not only organized peasants and workers, but Mexicans of various social classes have become alienated from the official party, the regime in power, and the policies that regime has promoted. Just how great that sense of alienation has become is evident in the personal accounts that follow.

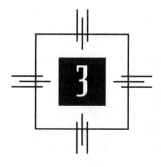

3

Two Women, Two Strategies

9 A.M.: *Josefina Valenzuela*

Josefina Valenzuela carries the map of the Metro in her head. On the day we talked in the kitchen of the apartment she cleans on Tuesday mornings, the subway system was comprised of nine lines with a total of 106 stops and another two lines under construction. I spread the Metro map on the kitchen table in front of me. Without looking, Josefina could tell me the stations and corresponding pictograms that would decorate any route I might select. She recited with pleasure the stops with Aztec names such as Pantitlán, Mixihuca, Cuitlahuac, or Tezozomoc, and those with evocative Spanish names such as Salto del Agua (Waterfall) or Indios Verdes (Green Indians). She also described the graphic symbols that identify each stop for the benefit of illiterate riders who can't read the station signs. "For La Merced," she explained, "you look for the symbol of six little fruits piled on a crate, which shows it is a market. For Lázaro Cárdenas you look for a locomotive, because the stop is named for the train station, which is named for the ex-president." Most important, Josefina could tell me exactly how to get from any point in the city to any other point. The itinerary she suggested was not always the most direct, but it was assuredly the cheapest way to make the journey.

This, Josefina explained, was one of her specialties. Anyone, she said, could go from San Pablo Xalpa just north of the Federal District to Coyoacán in the southern reaches of the capital by taking two *peseros* (minivans) at the outset, riding the length of one direct subway line, and then paying the fare on another two *peseros* to reach her final destination. But this, she emphasized, was a far more costly option than the one she would choose. Josefina's preferred route required that she change subway lines and go some distance east only to come west again. However, it cut out the extra minivan fares at both ends, and this represented a savings of more than two pesos in each direction. The subway ticket, at this point, still cost only thirty centavos or just under a dime and, of course, once inside the Metro, Josefina noted, "you can ride forever on a single fare."

Josefina has priced out every step of her travels around the city, just as she calculates her purchases and carefully budgets the time she needs to juggle the cleaning of two apartments each day, and three on Friday. She was lucky, she explained to me, because her work came on the basis of recommendations from her employers to their friends, and all of these people live within a few miles of one another in the southern zone of the city. The proximity of these houses and apartments permits Josefina to put in a full six hours in one place and then scurry over to another house to clean, cook, wash, mend—whatever is necessary—for another six hours.

Josefina lives in the heavily industrialized northwestern zone of the Valle de Mexico, just over the line that separates the Federal District from the State of Mexico. In this region, squatters' settlements crouch between major industrial complexes. Here the smoke from factories and the giant state-owned oil refinery in Atzcapotzalco mixes with the toxic waste produced by small-scale, family-based "informal" production of ceramic tiles and bricks baked in kilns fueled with old tires and sawdust soaked in kerosene. The boundary between Josefina's neighborhood and the Federal District is marked by the Rio de los Remedios. Josefina can remember when this river was blue and sparkling; now it is black with sludge and contains such high levels of industrial waste that gas bubbles escaping from the lower strata make the surface water "boil" like a devil's cauldron. Occasionally the surface of the Rio de los Remedios catches fire.

Josefina rises every day at 5:30 A.M. and prepares Teresina, her twelve-year-old, for school, mixing the girl a *licuado* of fruit and milk—one of the luxuries that Josefina works extra hard to provide. For her own breakfast Josefina prepares tortillas and beans, and she wraps more tortillas to take to work—although her employers often urge her to help herself to whatever leftovers she may find in the refrigerator. Thanks to her employers, Josefina eats a bit of meat several times a week. Most of her neighbors are lucky to eat meat, fish, or poultry even once a week.

Josefina sets out for work at six, sometimes a little later. Her departure time depends on the luck she enjoys any particular morning in getting to use the toilet and the water tap in the courtyard of the *vecindad* she shares with eight other families. She always hopes to be on her way by 6:15 to beat the flow of secondary-school students who generally set out at 6:30, jamming the few buses that travel the route between her *barrio* and the subway.

It infuriates Josefina that the government sells transport passes that are supposed to be good for unlimited access to the subway and municipal buses but then, doesn't provide nearly enough buses in the outlying districts. She describes to me the frustration she feels when, after waiting for ten or fifteen minutes at the stop as a small group gradually swells to a good-sized crowd, the bus finally arrives. Even at a distance Josefina knows if she has any hope of getting on. After 6:30 the bus is not merely full but is exploding with passengers, with several students standing on the back bumper and clinging to the top of the bus, another half dozen spilling out the door, and others seated on the open windowsills with their legs inside the bus and their torsos plastered against the outside of the vehicle. On mornings like this, Josefina is forced to spend extra money to take a *pesero,* or *combi,* one of the freelance private minivans that ply the same route to the subway, charging almost twice the fare charged for the bus.

Josefina's trip to work normally takes somewhere between one and a half to two hours, an average commuting time for working-class Mexicans, the vast majority of whom live in settlements on the periphery of the Federal District. Indeed, as a result of the 1985 earthquakes, which destroyed some of the oldest housing in the heart of the city and forced some of the poorest people out of the colonial buildings behind the Zócalo, where they had lived for generations, into the furthermost reaches of the Federal District and the State of Mexico, even more working-class Mexicans must commute three hours in each direction. For the millions of Mexicans like Josefina who put in a twelve- or thirteen-hour workday, the six hours spent traveling to and from work leaves them only four or five hours to eat and sleep. This is why, Josefina explains, she often sees folks asleep standing up on the bus. But Josefina tries never to doze on the bus, whether standing or sitting, especially at night. She is afraid she will be robbed of her day's wages, which she carries pinned into her skirt pocket under the red-and-white checkered apron she wears at work and at home.

When Josefina reaches the subway terminal she is greeted by the smell of donuts frying, tamales steaming in their banana leaf or corn husk wrappers, and simmering caldrons of *atole,* the sweet corn-meal drink that some of the commuters use to fortify themselves for the workday ahead. Eating from stands in the street is something Josefina views as a luxury beyond her budget, so she makes her way quickly past the food stalls. She then threads her way among the human carpet of peddlers who arrive at dawn to spread their wares in every open space of the broad esplanade in front of the station, as well as in the tunnels, on the pedestrian bridges, and in the corridors leading up to the turnstiles. Here she joins the hundreds of people who slowly inch toward the trains that leave the station at a rate of one every ninety seconds. The train pulls in, the doors open, the crowd surges forward completely filling the car in a matter of seconds, the doors close, the train pulls out, and another takes its place. At rush hour some cars on the most crowded lines are reserved for women and children, an arrangement Josefina much prefers. "It's bad enough," she says, "to be packed like cattle, without having your body smashed against the bodies of strange men who are grabbing a little feel here and there, when they are not actually picking your pocket!"

On her morning journey, Josefina is unlikely to encounter beggars, musicians, or peddlers, because the subway is too crowded for these people to make their way from car to car. When she returns in the evening, however, Josefina often picks up a bargain offered by those who hawk their merchandise up and down the aisles of the subway cars, and she always gives a few centavos to the blind. Josefina also digs into her pocket for the musicians, blind and sighted, who jump into the car and sing a spirited *ranchera* or a ballad accompanied by harmonica or guitar. She says she sees these people as less fortunate than herself and feels bound to give them something. "Besides," she says, "some of the *músicos* play and sing beautifully. I like to hear a nice song on the way home from a day of work."

In terms of transport, Mondays and Thursdays are Josefina's most complicated days. I can barely keep track as I trace my finger on the map while she describes the trip from Cuatro Caminos to the Metro Portales, and from there in three *peseros* to Ixtapalapa, and then to Coyoacán for her afternoon shift. But for Josefina the calculations are straightforward:

> *Altogether I clean five places. Two I clean twice a week, and the other three I clean three times, which is why I have an extra house*

> *on Friday. On Monday I am running back and forth between the two farthest points. This is a problem because, to save time, I take three* combis*, which adds up to an extra peso and a half. But fortunately, these people pay well. I make nineteen pesos in the morning and the other* señora *pays me twenty pesos in the afternoon.*

Josefina says that the people for whom she has worked the longest pay her the lowest wage (seventeen pesos) for the six hours she puts in. The wage was established years ago when she started working for them, and she finds it difficult to come right out and ask for more—especially when they have recommended her to their friends.

> *Tuesdays and Wednesdays I work in houses that are only a short bus ride apart, and these people all pay me twenty pesos for the six hours. Thursdays I am running again from Miguel Angel de Quevedo to Ixtapalapa. But then Fridays, I spend only three hours on each place, and I can walk from one to the other. In fact, one apartment is two floors above the other. The best part is that they pay me fifteen pesos, just for the three hours! Saturday I go back to the houses I cleaned on Tuesday.*

On Saturday night, as on week nights, Josefina returns between 10:30 and 11 P.M. She stops at her mother's house to collect Teresina, who spends every day after school and all of Saturday with her grandmother. The two of them then walk straight to their room in the *vecindad* and remain indoors.

> *We have to stay inside because Friday and Saturday is when people get paid, so there are lots of* borrachos *running around drunk, shooting off pistols and picking fights. There are also people smoking marijuana and sniffing glue. It's not a good time to find yourself out on the street with a little girl of twelve.*

On Sundays, Josefina cleans her own one-room house, washes and irons her own laundry, and prepares a meal for Teresina, her mother, and herself. Sometimes, to make a little extra money, she brings home some mending or ironing from the people she works for during the week. Once in a while, when she's feeling flush, she takes Teresina to the movies.

As we talk in the kitchen, Josefina has been preparing a large casserole of *chiles rellenos,* hot green peppers filled with ground beef, tomato, and onion. She now sets the ceramic pot on the stove to simmer, washes the counter and her hands, and turns her attention to a pile of shirts and blouses waiting to be ironed.

As she irons, she explains that her work today is a world away from the earliest employment she found as a new immigrant to the city. Josefina's family came to the city from Puebla in the 1950s, when they built a shack out of cardboard and hammered-out tin cans on open land to the west of the capital. After three years of primary education, Josefina left school to work for the five- and ten-centavo tips she could earn returning empty garbage cans from the curb to the doors of middle-class houses. She next worked delivering tortillas, followed by a stint plucking chickens. At the age of eleven she was placed as a full-time, live-in servant in the home of a middle-class couple in Polanco, where her main responsibility was caring for an infant. As Josefina puts it, "In this house, every ugly thing that can happen to a servant girl happened to me."

> *The* señora *used to hit me if I made a mistake. I remember once I put a white sock in with the colored wash and it turned blue, and she really whalloped me for that. Sometimes her husband would yell at her and, when this happened, she would walk into the kitchen and slap me hard on the arm or the face and call me stupid. The* señor *was kinder to me, but when the* señora *wasn't around he would call out, "Josefinita, come here, I need you," and then he would grab me and try to touch me.*

Josefina spent three years in this position until, on a visit to her family during her annual week off, a neighbor promised to help her find work stitching seams in a trouser factory. After her years as a domestic servant, Josefina experienced factory life as the ultimate form of personal liberation.

> *After the house in Polanco, it was like a dream to work in the factory. It was as if I had been in prison, and now I was released. There was a supervisor on the floor who watched over us at the machines. But after a while, I realized that he had hundreds of workers to watch, so he couldn't possibly be looking at me every minute. We had a contract, and this meant they couldn't beat you or fire you without a reason. And there were other young people all around, and the young men would say things to us to make us laugh and they would invite us to fiestas to dance. In fact that's where I met my ex-husband. I was fifteen and he was sixteen.*

I ask Josefina if she would prefer factory work to the kind of domestic service she does now. She responds that it is not an option she considers because she cannot afford to work in a factory.

> *Supporting myself, paying the rent, and providing food for my mother to cook for herself and Teresina when I am at work absorbs everything I earn. Five days a week I take home thirty-seven to forty pesos, and on Fridays, forty-five. That's around four minimum wages. The most I could earn in a factory would be one and a half mimimum wages. We just wouldn't make it.*

Josefina also points out that the kind of domestic service she performs now bears no resemblance to her experience as a live-in maid.

> *You have to consider what kind of person would hire an eleven-year-old child to mind an infant. When you think about it, you*

are not surprised that such people would beat that girl and lock her away in the house.

The people I work for today are different. It's nine years now that I have worked for Señorita Gloria, and the rest of the people are really all her friends and her friends' friends. They are modern and cultured people. I get all kinds of new ideas from talking to them or listening to them talk to each other. Most important, for them, I am not a "servant." I am an employee who cleans, someone who comes and goes and has a life apart from theirs. Of course, I am older now, too. But they address me as "usted," *and they speak to me courteously. Best of all, Señora Isabel, whose house I clean on Wednesdays, spoke to her husband, Señor Guillermo, and he listed me as if I were one of the workers in his factory. This means that he makes payments for me so that now I am registered with Social Security and can go to the doctor or the hospital when I need to.*

I ask Josefina how it is that, bringing home almost four minimum salaries, she is still forced to take in washing and mending to supplement her income. She explains that she can cover the basics with the wages she takes home from cleaning, but all the extras—schoolbooks, school uniforms, medicine, Saint's Day presents, and so on—come from the work she puts in on Sundays. Given that the cost of living is rising steadily, I try to get some sense of how Josefina plans for the future, how she copes with inflation. She tells me, "The only thing I can do is work harder. But I am in big trouble now because prices keep rising but there are still only twenty-four hours in a day."

At this point, Josefina laughs, puts down her iron, and looks over at me, shaking her head:

Right now I work six days a week, twelve hours a day, and when, for some reason, I have to get my hands on extra money, the only thing I can think of doing is to bring home laundry and wash and iron until two or three in the morning. But, at some point, even I have to go to sleep!

The problem is I don't see anything else I can do. For certain you can't sit around waiting for political parties or political leaders to rescue you, to change your life. You can only do that for yourself. And the only way you can do that is by working harder. The only way my life could change is if somehow I could find a way to work harder.

I ask Josefina if she thinks political activism can ever change a person's life, and I talk a bit about the popular mobilizations in which people like Lupe participate. She just looks at me and shakes her head once more:

Yes, a neighbor of mine told me about the Asamblea de Barrios. But the way it works is that you have to go every day to demonstrations and meetings and sit-ins and after you do this for a year or so, they put your name on a list and you get a house. I can't get involved in this kind of thing because I work every day and on Sunday I have to look after my own cooking and cleaning.

My comadre *says that if you join the party of Cuauhtémoc Cárdenas they can get you a house or a better job. But there, too, you have to go to all the demonstrations and you have to stand up and speak at meetings, and when they see that you are one of their people they place you in a job. Now, this is a very good deal for people who have no job, because they have the time to attend all the events, and then they get a job or a house. But I already have a job, so I can't participate the way you have to.*

Although she lacks the time for political participation, Josefina says she has always voted in elections, and as each electoral campaign proceeds, she tries to avail herself of whatever give-aways the PRI is offering.

During the campaign the PRI always comes around and makes promises: they give you a free haircut, *or they bring in a doctor to examine all the* children, *or they set up a registry in the market and everyone who wants to get married can get married for free, or* they *give you a shirt or a few pencils or a soda pop to make you vote for the PRI. The PRI knows how to be nice to people for a week or even two days before the elections. But then, after the elections, things are always worse than before.*

I always used to vote for the PAN, which they say is the party of the rich and the priests. But I would vote for the* panistas *as my way of getting back at the PRI. In the last election, I voted for Cuauhtémoc Cárdenas because I think he is a sincere man like his father, Don Lázaro. But when he won the election, the* priístas *wouldn't allow him to take office because he wasn't one of them.*

As Josefina describes to me the trickery and deceit—the stolen ballot boxes, the uncounted ballots, and all the maneuvers that cost her candidate the presidency—she folds the last of the starched white shirts she has ironed. Very solemnly, she asks me if I grasp that these practices are always part of Mexican elections. I reassure her that even abroad, people are aware of the electoral fraud that is practiced by the ruling party in Mexico. I tell her that the 1988 elections were especially well covered in the international press. She says, "that may be the case, but there's plenty that you'll never know, that they try to keep even us Mexicans from knowing."

You know the big oil refinery in Atzcapotzalco that the president shut down in March of '91 because of the pollution it created? They made a big deal out of it, and the president even won an award from some international organization because he closed the refinery. Well, guess what—it's not really shut down. I pass that

---

* Partido de Acción Nacional (National Action Party), a right-wing party.

refinery every morning on my way to the subway and I see workers going in for the morning shift and a cloud of smoke hanging over the plant.

To tell you the truth, none of this surprises me, because I know that we live in a world of lies. If there is a terrible accident on the subway, you never read about it in the papers, because they don't allow the reporters to write about it. I once saw the police breaking the cameras of photographers who were shooting at the scene of an accident at the Metro station Etiopia. If they could have kept the earthquakes a secret from the world, they would have. This is why I have no confidence that the people in power tell us the truth. I see their lies with my own eyes.

At this point I realize that Josefina will have to rush through the rest of her chores to avoid being late for her afternoon job. I quickly ask her what name she would like me to use when I describe her life in my book. She says I should use her own name, and that I should put in her address as well. She laughs and says,

I live an honorable life and everything I've told you is the truth. I've got nothing to hide. So, there's no risk for me in anything I've said. I'm not like the priístas, *you know. I've got nothing to hide.*

10 A.M.: Conchita Gómez

At ten o'clock on Tuesday morning, Conchita Gómez is working alongside three other women she refers to as her *compañeras*. They are clearing away the remaining crumbs and spilled milk from the breakfast they have fed to hundreds of children at the Mujeres en Lucha (Women in Struggle) breakfast program. Shortly they will begin to peel and slice the vegetables and cut the meat for the immense pot of *pozole* that they will prepare for lunch at the communal kitchen.

Conchita says that if anyone had told her ten years ago that her life would one day revolve around block committees, popular assemblies, women's commissions, and a communal kitchen, she could not have disputed this prediction: she simply would not have grasped what they were talking about. In fact, back then, she understood so little of what collective activities entailed that she carefully avoided those who were involved. "I completely accepted," Conchita admits, "the notion that a woman has no business anywhere outside the walls of her house unless on her way to work, and then, only if absolutely necessary."

> *You have to understand, I was a very ignorant and repressed person. I was afraid to leave my house to go to the corner. I saw the women who were involved in the collective efforts at best as busybodies, or even as women of questionable repute, and I criticized them and gossiped about them behind their backs. It was only the extremely precarious economic situation in which I found myself that brought me out of my house and into the organizations in which I am now active.*

Conchita's political involvement has now become so intense that her day always begins at the Women in Struggle Cooperative and often ends in the same room at a meeting of one of the groups in which she is active—the women's committee, the cost-of-living commission, or the health committee. Conchita rises at six, splashes water on her face, and wakes her eldest daughter, Inez, who gets the younger children up and readies them for school. Conchita then walks the three blocks to the cooperative, where she prepares the milk, cookies, and sweets (caramel or marzipan) that the cooperative serves to the roughly four hundred children who turn up each morning. Conchita's status as a volunteer in the cooperative entitles her to free lunch and dinner for her family—food that she carries home from the collective kitchen in two blue-and-white speckled enamel pots. As long as she can assure her children of these three meals per day, Conchita tells me, she feels her time as a volunteer is well spent.

At the urging of the other *compañeras,* Conchita takes me outside to sit in the sun on two straight-backed chairs in front of the one-room structure that serves as kitchen, dining room, and meeting hall. We are at the top of the *cerro,* the hill, on which the eighty thousand inhabitants of San Miguel Teotongo have constructed their modest houses, and we are looking down on what Conchita refers to as the *áreas verdes.* These "green areas" look parched and brown and treeless to me, but they are clearly a source of pride to her. As Conchita's description of the organization of San Miguel Teotongo unfolds, it becomes evident that the green areas represent the triumph of a twenty-year struggle of poor and powerless people against the combined forces of real estate speculators, political bosses, corrupt government agents, and an indifferent central administration.

Conchita, who is now in her late thirties, was brought to Mexico City as a child from a village in the state of Morelos. Even today, she remembers very clearly the beauty of her hometown near Cuautla. She describes how the adobe houses with thatched roofs were framed against the mountains and the intense green of the vegetation after a rainfall. She remembers picking wildflowers in the fields, and she still recalls the yearly round of festivals culminating in the three-day celebration of the village's patron saint.

But Conchita also remembers that, as a child, she often ate only one meal a day, and that meal always consisted of tortillas and *frijoles,* or beans. Her father, Tomás, could not raise enough food to feed nine people on the six acres of land he received in the agrarian reform. When Conchita's mother, Luz, realized that she could no longer feed her family on the corn and beans Tomás produced on this tiny parcel—even in a year of abundant rainfall—she decided that, like millions of other peasants, they too had to set out for the capital.

In this period, Conchita's uncle worked as a custodian in a large greenhouse on the outskirts of the Federal District. It was in a corner of this structure that Conchita's parents and six brothers and sisters camped out for their first year in the city—circumstances in which they made do until their presence was discovered by the owner of the greenhouse. Next, the family moved to a *ciudad perdida* on open land near the road to Puebla. Here Tomás and Luz built a rough shelter from scrap wood and other materials they collected along the roadside. This crude dwelling was their home until Conchita's parents, working as street peddlers, finally put together the down payment for a house lot in San Miguel Teotongo, a community comprised largely of migrants from Teotongo, Oaxaca.

Luz and Tomás had no idea that they would become part of a broad mass movement when they handed their down payment to the *fraccionador,* the developer, who was selling house lots on the steep slopes of a hill near the Mexico-Puebla highway. Like the thousands of other settlers who purchased their lots from Alfredo Castillo Neira in the early 1970s, Tomás and Luz believed that the land was Castillo's to sell.

In reality, the entire *cerro* was *ejido* property, that is, public land given in trust by the government to a group of landless peasants who had successfully petitioned for a land grant. Unfortunately for the peasants, the land they were granted lacked water and, therefore, was not arable. For this reason, it stood parched, barren, and empty. Without question, though, the legal rights to the terrain belonged neither to Alfredo Castillo Neira nor to the PRI-affiliated *jefe,* Candido Mendéz, with whom he was in league. Rather, it belonged to the *ejido* community called, ironically enough, Los Reyes La Paz. As it turned out, there would not be much "peace" for these "kings," or for anyone else over the next two decades, as the settlers in San Miguel Teotongo struggled to gain legal title to the land they had purchased in good faith.

Conchita says that mobilization for collective action soon became a permanent way of life in San Miguel, at least for an active minority of the settlers. Not only had unscrupulous speculators sold lots they did not own to credulous rural migrants, but it soon emerged that it wasn't even clear whether the hill on which the migrants had set about erecting permanent structures lay in the State of Mexico or across the line in the Federal District. Thus, along with the question of land deeds, the jurisdictional status of San Miguel became an issue of great importance, because the settlement's official location would determine which administrative entity should be petitioned and pressured to gain urban services for the expanding community. Under the circumstances, Conchita explained, much of the early organizational effort went into the push to gain recognition for San Miguel Teotongo as an urban zone within the Federal District—the administrative entity that had, by far, the greater resources.

Along with these questions of property rights and legal recognition, the settlers in San Miguel faced forms of exploitation so severe that Conchita says even the most timid and apolitical migrants like her parents were drawn into mass action. Not content with selling property they did not own, the speculator and his associates found that the physical isolation of the settlement and its lack of water gave them an opportunity to squeeze more money out of the lot owners. Employing his own force of armed thugs, Castillo imposed a monopoly on transportation, the supply of building materials, gas for heating and cooking, and even drinking water, which was trucked in and sold at vastly inflated prices. Conchita explains that Castillo was able to maintain this level of control because his henchmen ensured that only the buses and trucks he owned or licensed were permitted to ply the road that wound its way up the hillside of San Miguel.

To be sure, none of these problems was unique to San Miguel. On the contrary, these abuses are typical of the situation confronting millions of recent migrants and more permanent settlers in the lost cities in every corner of the Valle de Mexico and, indeed, in every major urban center throughout the republic. During the decades of mass emigration from the countryside, as the population of Mexico City grew by one thousand migrants a day, and the smaller cities tripled, quadrupled, and quintupled in size, *ciudades perdidas* sprang up in every square meter of unused land, whatever its status or ownership. Along the railroad right of way, under the high-tension pylons that crossed the city, in gullies and gulches and on the black lava rock of ancient volcanic flows, newcomers built their shacks and shanties wherever others did not already occupy the ground. And wherever the squatters settled, petty tyrants—*caciquillos*, "little *caciques,*"—appeared on the scene to charge them protection money, bully them into paying "rent," or sell them water, electricity, or other services the state would normally provide. The power of these *caciquillos* was reinforced by the fact that they often pledged loyalty to the PRI and, if allowed by the state to dominate and exploit their small territory, they were committed to gathering the newcomers' votes for the official party.

In this respect, Conchita points out, the people of San Miguel were no worse off than millions of other Mexicans. What set San Miguel apart from other shantytowns and lost cities was that, along with migrants fresh from the countryside, a sizable portion of the population was made up of factory workers. "A bunch of these people," Conchita says, "had been involved in union activity. They knew what it was to organize and because of this, it was more difficult for Castillo to frighten them." Moreover, by the time the Unión de Colonos, the Settlers' Union, was formed in 1975 to deal with Castillo's abuses, the organizers could also count on receiving technical and legal advice from a group of students from the Department of Economics of the National University—militant students who were determined to move their struggles for change off campus and into society.

Castillo's response to the threat to his control, Conchita notes, was typical of the way in which *priístas* operate. He countered the organization of settlers by forming his own "settlers' union" complete with assemblies, committees, and the trappings of democratic participation. He even managed to buy off Manuel Urbano, one of the central figures in the Unión de Colonos, luring him into the pseudo-union with promises of a share in the profits of his operations in San Miguel. In the end, however, the maneuver did not work. Conchita explains that "people were not fooled and, in any case, the 'real' Settlers' Union had already taken root in the community. Even more important," she says, "is that watching Manuel Urbano, a man many people had respected, switch sides for personal gain taught everyone a lesson." After this incident, the Settlers' Union was characterized by a decentralized structure and a lot of rotation in positions of responsibility.

Conchita says that when you start to think about the incredible number of battles fought and won by the union over the years you either feel triumphant or totally exhausted. She cautions me that some of the other *compañeros* who were active from the start might give me an even longer list. However, everyone would agree that the first undisputed success was the rent strike of 1974. The union managed to convince the settlers to refuse to make further payments to Castillo. Even Luz and Tomás joined the others in withholding their payments to the *fraccionador*.

After the triumph of the rent strike, the mobilization for recognition of San Miguel as part of the Federal District became the union's main goal. Conchita thinks that this effort really represents a more impressive achievement than the strike. "The rent strike," she notes, "called on people *not* to do something—something that was convenient for everyone not to do."

Even my parents were willing to go along with not paying Castillo the money that, in any case, he didn't have coming to him. But the mobilization for recognition by the Federal District was something positive that you had to do, and you wouldn't believe how many meetings and marches and sit-ins in government offices and delegations had to be sent before that effort came to anything.

The classification of San Miguel Teotongo as part of the Federal District was a key victory, Conchita explains, because it opened the way to breaking Castillo's power. Once San Miguel gained the official status of an urban settlement within the district, the community could pressure for the water, electricity, sewers, bus lines, schools, and clinics it needed. With these public works in place, the control that a *cacique* like Castillo exercised though his monopoly on services would be undermined.

It was important to challenge Castillo's power by every available means because, all through the 1970s, he continued to sell house lots to unsuspecting recent migrants. This, Conchita explains, is why the "Alternative Urban Project" was so crucial. In the mid-1970s the students helped the union draw up a plan for the development of the community. "There on the map, in green, were the '*áreas verdes*.' These were sections of land that had not yet been sold off by Castillo." It was critical, Conchita says, to keep Castillo from selling these areas as house lots, otherwise no open spaces would remain for the use of the community as a whole. "How could we have the schools, clinics, recreational areas, bus shelters and other features that we hoped would soon be supplied by the Federal District, if there was no space left to put them in?"

Thus, even as the organizational attention of the Settlers' Union turned to the problem of mounting the marches, sit-ins, and demonstrations that are the standard and most effective means to pressure government agencies to provide public services, the struggle against Castillo continued by other means. Conchita recalls,

This was well before I became involved, but I still remember how the activists seized Castillo's water trucks and the gas tanks and the buses he owned and they held these vehicles and their drivers hostage for two weeks. In the end, Castillo conceded the victory to the union, and he was forced to bring his charges down to reasonable rates. He was frightened, too, because by this time the union had in place a system of "People's Courts" where usurers and rip-off artists of any description were tried for their offenses.

*These courts are still active and they are used to deal with anyone—*pesero *drivers who overcharge, saloon keepers, drug dealers—anyone who threatens the well being of the community. As late as the early 1980s,* pesero *drivers were still being kidnaped in San Miguel and held until they signed papers promising to drop their rates to a fair price.*

The Settlers' Union was now on a roll. Its members had wrestled successfully with the speculator and the politicians who sustained him, and they now found that the forms of organization that had served them in their struggles to gain legal title to their land and recognition for their community were also useful in pressing for services. One by one the appropriate government agencies were targeted and lobbied, and step by step the settlers in San Miguel gained the paved roads, water and power lines, public markets, municipal bus route, and schools and health services that turned this "lost city" into part of the formal grid of urban centers within the Federal District.

For Conchita the most remarkable aspect of the process she described to me is the way in which an organization founded by men and built by men was gradually taken over by women. "Look around," she said to me, "and you will see that it is really we women who are running the show now." Conchita thinks that women have become central to these struggles because their daily lives are affected so immediately by the lack of public services.

We all, men and women alike, suffer if the closest municipal bus line is a half hour walk down the hill to the highway. But it is the women who cook and clean and care for the children, so it is we who notice the lack of water or electricity or schools. It is also the women who are here in San Miguel Teotongo during the day to carry out the activities that everyone decides on at night.

Conchita's involvement began slowly, when her husband, Fernando, left for the United States. In the first few years after he emigrated, Fernando returned for a few weeks at Christmas, even though each visit home brought with it the problem of getting back across the border into the United States. Finally, Fernando no longer returned for an annual visit, although he continued to send money to Conchita. It was at this point that Conchita learned from a cousin who worked as a farmhand in Watsonville, California, that Fernando now had another wife and family on the other side.

Fernando had never been happy about Conchita's participation in the Settlers' Union, an involvement that had developed during his long absences from home. He was particularly irritated by her increasing activity in the Women in Struggle Cooperative. For her part, Conchita explained her involvement to Fernando in strictly practical terms.

I told Fernando that the food I received for free from the cooperative was what we lived on, that we couldn't get by on what he sent us. But the truth is, the more I got to know them, the more I liked working with the other compañeras *and* compañeros. *I liked the feeling of being able to count on people beside my own family, especially when—as it turned out in the end—I couldn't count on Fernando at all.*

In fact, apart from the food that she brings home from the cooperative, Conchita relies not on the occasional check Fernando sends to his children from California but on a business she has developed for herself in San Miguel Teotongo. Conchita specializes in lady's underwear, which she sells to her neighbors from a stock she keeps in the bedroom of her two-room house. In much the same fashion as Miguel, the *fayuquero,* Conchita travels downtown to the Tepito district in the center of Mexico City (a good hour and a half from San Miguel) to purchase a stock of merchandise, which she then resells at a profit in this peripheral community. As she explained to me,

> *The bras and underpants usually come in packages of five or six. I pay something like three and a half pesos per item, and I sell them to my neighbors for five or six pesos. It's worth it for my customers to buy from me here because they can purchase just one bra or pair of panties at a time, and I let my customers make two or three payments on the item they buy. They can stretch their payments over a few weeks if they like. Most important, they can try on the underwear at my house, which is why they prefer to buy from me instead of in the street market.*

Once every three weeks, Conchita purchases three dozen underpants and three dozen bras in assorted colors, styles, and sizes. "Something for everyone," she says. When I ask her if she has sizes big enough to fit someone like me, she laughs and then looks me over carefully and says,

> *You're not* "big," *you're tall. That's different from being big. You're tall because you're well-nourished. That's the difference between women here and* norteamericanas *or* canadienses. *We get to be fat because we go our whole life without eating proper food.*

When I ask her if she thinks she can change this situation through the cooperative breakfast and lunch program she says,

The food cooperative is only a start. Ordinary people here in Mexico are not going to be well nourished until we have a government that works for everyone and not just for the rich. I had more hope when I thought that Cuauhtémoc would become our president. But although most Mexicans voted for him, the PRI just wouldn't turn over power to anyone else, so their candidate, Carlos Salinas, took office, just as if he had won the most votes.

Conchita explains that in order to concentrate on the issues closest to the real needs of the people of San Miguel, the Settlers' Union has a policy of maintaining a distance from all partisan politics, and, officially speaking, it remained scrupulously neutral in the elections of 1988. But it is hard for her to imagine anyone, among all of her neighbors, who did not vote for Cuauhtémoc Cárdenas. And when the returns came in for San Miguel Teotongo, the vote for Cárdenas was so overwhelming that here, as elsewhere in the Federal District, the PRI conceded the defeat of its candidate. In fact, it was not in the cities but in the countryside that the electoral commission "caused the dead to rise." In the most isolated rural areas more votes were registered for the official party than there were people living in the electoral district.

San Migueleños were very active in protesting the electoral fraud, Conchita explains:

We participated in all the demonstrations in the Zócalo after the elections. The funny thing is that now the priístas *have finally noticed San Miguel Teotongo and have started to respond to the demands we have been making all along. Last month the president himself came here with all his people, with flags and banners and streamers in the national colors—and, of course, the television crews—to announce that PRONASOL,* his own special solidarity program, was finally going to dig us some real sewers.*

---

* Programa Nacional de Solidaridad (National Solidarity Program).

Conchita and I are still seated on the hill overlooking the open space, the "green area" where Salinas made his speech—the same spot where, three years earlier, Cuauhtémoc Cárdenas spoke to the largest crowd ever assembled in San Miguel. Conchita tells me that she worries about the effect that Salinas's speech had on the community.

> *I know that some of my neighbors were taken in. They were impressed by the flags and the loudspeakers and, above all, that the president had come to our community. My* comadre *said to me, "Conchita, isn't it nice that the president is giving us these things!" I tried to explain to her that it's our right to have potable water and sewers and other services, that the government is supposed to give these things to all citizens, not just to people living in fancy neighborhoods. But I don't know if she understood. I don't think she believed me.*

4

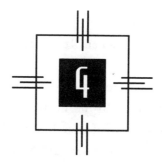

Getting By in the Business World

12 Noon: Rubén Ergas

It is only noon, and the big meal that Mexicans normally enjoy at midday is still three hours away. But Rubén Ergas is hungry now because he has been going nonstop for almost seven hours. He has been in motion since 5:30, when his brother and business partner, Daniel, collected him from his house in the Lomas district. They next picked up their sister, Sarita, and the three headed for the lake in the center of Chapultepec Park. Here they stretched, warmed-up, and ran two five-kilometer circuits.

Rubén says that Sarita is the best runner of the three. She has the perfect build and the right mind-set for long distances. But all three run with enthusiasm and, at present, Sarita and Daniel have dedicated themselves to assisting Rubén in his training for the New York Marathon. Over the next six months, they will run in Chapultepec—sometimes around the lake, and sometimes straight uphill to Carlotta's Castle. Gradually they will increase their time and distance from twenty to seventy miles per week, until they peak in November just before the race. Then the three of them, their parents, spouses, and children will fly to New York and stay in the Plaza Hotel for a week of shopping, tourism, and training, culminating when Rubén crosses the finish line in Central Park.

The Ergas family is intensely close, and Rubén says that he thinks this best explains why he is still in the textile business. "Any straight economic calculation I could have made after the opening of the economy in 1986 would have led me to get out, as fast as possible. But it's difficult to turn your back on a business that has been passed along to you by your father and grandfather."

Rubén's grandfather was the legendary Isaac Ergas who came to Mexico from Damascus in 1907. One family story has it that Isaac arrived in the New World unable to read or write, but knowing only how to sign his name and calculate numbers. Another version of this history says that he knew how to add but not subtract. Cousins of Rubén's from another branch of the family told me that Isaac spoke not a word of Spanish but knew Ladino, a Spanish dialect, dating from the fifteenth century, that became the lingua franca of the Sephardic Jews in North Africa and the Mediterranean. Rubén thinks that Isaac probably arrived in Mexico speaking only Arabic and some French. What everyone agrees upon is that Isaac left the Middle East on a boat that he thought would carry him to New York. Landing in the port of Veracruz on the Gulf of Mexico was, from Rubén's point of view, only a happy accident.

When Isaac discovered his mistake, he regrouped, invested his scarce capital in a stock of clothing and set out to peddle his goods from Torreón in the north to Tehuantepec in the south. Ergas family legend recounts that Isaac sold shirts to the wife of Porfirio Díaz for an orphanage she patronized and, with the outbreak of the revolution, sold trousers to Pancho Villa's troops and lace dresses to the generals' ladies. In fact, it seems that Isaac sat out a good part of the revolution in Paris, returning only in the 1920s. By this time he was already prosperous enough to set up what was then Mexico's largest textile factory.

Isaac became and remained one of the leaders of the textile industry. He was among the first Mexican entrepreneurs to import machinery from Europe, and he became a pioneer in the use of synthetic fibers, moving rapidly from his traditional production of cotton cloth to acetate, polyester, and finally acrylics. By the time he died in 1976, at the age of ninety-six, he had developed enterprises that integrated every step of textile production from the spinning of thread, through the distribution of finished bolts of cloth to garment manufacturers.

Rubén explains that his own involvement in the family business began even before he entered primary school. Rubén's father, Jacobo, would bring his son to his textile plant where Rubén first learned his addition and subtraction counting spools of thread. Working afternoons after school, he learned every phase of the operation—production, sales, and bookkeeping—from the ground up. At the age of nineteen, after attending only two weeks of university classes, Rubén dropped his formal studies to work full-time.

> *I have no specialized training other than what I've absorbed working all my life in this business. I think it was a good preparation for work and also for life. I plan to do the same for my sons. They can study or train for any job they like. But from the age of thirteen or fourteen, I am going to insist that they come here to work after school. This is important not only because it will give them a career, if they decide to continue in this business, but also because it will teach them how to manage the fortune that has come from three generations of fathers and sons who have worked hard to create something. This is different from the kind of training a person gets in a university.*

Until Mexico entered the GATT in 1986, Rubén, his father, and brother ran a textile factory that employed between seven hundred and eight hundred workers. Located north of Mexico City in the state of Querétaro, the operation was integrated to produce everything from the thread to the finished cloth. But the looms and other equipment were old, and a huge investment would have been required to modernize the operation to bring it up to internationally competitive standards. Rather than invest to update the factory, they sold out and, like Sergio Espinoza, began to import what they had previously produced.

I am seated in Rubén's office, which is only an alcove in what looks more like a giant warehouse than a downtown office building. The structure itself dates from the 1920s and is located in an area that, before the earthquakes of 1985, would have been described as the old business district of Mexico City. Some of the upper stories of this and surrounding buildings were damaged by the quakes and now stand empty. The financial and corporate headquarters that once clustered in these buildings, making the area a kind of Mexican "midtown Manhattan," have moved elsewhere. But at street level, the sidewalks bustle with shoppers moving in and out of the retail and wholesale outlets that still make this neighborhood a center of popular commerce and a point of attraction for small merchants. It is here that Miguel comes to buy his electronic goods, and Conchita her stock of underwear.

As I look around the room at both unfinished and brightly dyed bolts of cotton, acrylic, polyester, denim, and worsted, Rubén describes to me the decision he made with his father and brother to get out of the production end of the textile trade. He explains the move in terms of the size and structure of his family's firm. The majority of textile producers, he notes, are family-owned companies. The textile industry in Mexico was dominated first by Spanish and French, and later by Lebanese, Syrian, and Jewish families. Whatever changes have been set in motion by government policies, these family-owned companies have generally responded with their own capital, not that of foreign investors. This has been the case as well for Rubén, Jacobo, and Daniel:

When we saw the total uncertainty of the period immediately ahead, we felt we had to get our money out and find something else to do with our capital. Once we could see how things were going to shake down in the textile industry, we figured we would reinvest in something else and, maybe, go back to manufacturing.

Like Sergio Espinoza, Rubén acknowledges that the protectionist policies in place in Mexico from the 1940s provided manufacturers like himself with high profits on articles of low quality. And, like Sergio, Rubén was shocked by the suddenness and speed with which the policy was reversed. Rubén says he was surprised not so much because of the impact of the opening of the economy on people like himself but rather because of the effect it had on employment. He says that he always thought that, whatever the cost, the government used protectionist policies to create jobs. He always understood this to be the keystone of the strategy to maintain social and political stability. This is why he was unprepared for the dramatic shift: tariff barriers were dropped, many domestic producers went under, factories closed, and workers were in the street. But even taking into account the loss of employment for hundreds of thousands of workers, Rubén believes that what he thinks of as a dose of bitter medicine was necessary to bring Mexican industry into a competitive position. He says,

How many people worked in the textile industry in Mexico? Maybe 170,000 in this period. And, of course, not all these 170,000 jobs were lost or will be lost. But in order to save the jobs of 170,000 textile workers are you going to stick with a policy that means more costly clothing for seventy million Mexicans? That's the real question, because the fact is, before the government opened the economy, it was more expensive to buy a pair of jeans here in Mexico than on Fifth Avenue in New York.

But even as he accepts the need for an open, competitive policy, Rubén tells me that he is not entirely sanguine about the effects of the *apertura*. He says the opening served—on paper at least—to lower inflation and encourage the importation of high-tech machinery.

> *But what you really find is that all kinds of goods are coming into Mexico to satisfy demands that range from computerized looms to Milky Ways. The problem for Salinas is to figure some way to control this, because the country is not producing enough to pay for all that it is consuming. What's more, we're still producing low-quality goods at relatively high cost. This is something that can't be changed overnight. Hopefully, what's going on now is that industrialists are investing in ways that will eventually permit Mexican manufacturers to produce first-rate goods efficiently. But it's taking time—much longer, in fact, than the government thought it would.*

"Personally speaking," Rubén says, "my father, brother, and I were not rocked by the *apertura*. We weren't worried about being left with nothing to do." He explains that the first, most obvious step for them to take was to sell their antiquated factory. Once they got their capital out of the factory, they were left with sufficient resources to focus on imports. They then extended large amounts of credit to people who, before the *apertura*, had been the customers for their own cloth, and they started to import from Asia what they used to produce, using the distribution network that they already had in place.

To give me an idea of how well the new import business is going, Rubén shows me the figures for the previous month when they imported US$3 million worth of goods from China, Taiwan, and Hong Kong: denim, polyester suiting, unfinished rayon, and dyed and printed rayon. Bolts of this particular shipment are stacked against the walls around us. On average, Rubén says, they do about US$2 million of business each month. He explains that the key to their success has been that they have a streamlined, high-volume, low-cost operation.

> *Our overhead is very low. This building, as you see, is old. But we own it, so we have no rent to pay. We have a minimal staff and split most of the work among my brother, my father, and myself. We use our own money to extend credit to our clients. Thus, we calculate the cost of the article, plus the 20 percent duties we pay to import the cloth, plus 8 percent for the customs agent, and then we add in transportation costs.*

Rubén explains that they take a very low mark-up and count on selling what they have imported within ninety days to get their money back.

> *Right now, there's a huge quantity of contraband coming in. But we import different things than the* contrabandistas, *precisely in order to sidestep that whole problem. We are importing very cheap cloth, and we much prefer to pay the import duties than to fool around trying to smuggle stuff into the country. At least that's our situation—that's how we work. I know my father would rather close the company and move into another line of activity than get involved in the kinds of payoffs that you have to make to import without paying the proper duties. It's risky and it's foolish.*

Rubén says that they found it remarkably easy to establish the links they needed in Asia, although the family had no business connections there before 1986. "For us, doing business in Asia has been an amazing experience. We've really learned a lot."

> *Overall, the Asians have impressed us with their acumen, their energy, and their approach to business. Of course, this is not the case everywhere. There are times when we are trying to work out*

some kind of deal in China and we feel like we are talking to a wall. I mean, we find ourselves and the Chinese salespeople in a state of total mutual incomprehension. But in Hong Kong or Taiwan, you connect with people and they really come through. You send them a fax in the morning and that afternoon you have their reply. It's very easy to open a letter of credit, to establish a price, to close a deal. They keep their management costs really low because everyone in the operation seems to be walking around with all the detailed information in his head.

Comparing his experience dealing with businesses in the United States and in Asia, Rubén finds that U.S. firms are encumbered by multiple layers of bureaucracy and higher managerial expenses.

When you call the U.S., you dial and you get the receptionist, and then you get put on hold and then—buzz, zap!—you get transferred to the marketing department. You talk to one person, you want to confirm prices, and he says, "OK, but I've got to check with the director." You're back on hold. Then—buzz, zap!—you're transferred again to another department and have to begin your order all over again. No one has the authority or the information to make a decision on his own, to quote you a price on his own authority.

When you deal in Hong Kong or Taiwan, all the people you talk to seem to have all the information and authority they need. They don't have to check on prices and get back to you. They quote you a price and delivery date right away and then they stick by that commitment. Even when negotiating with the biggest Taiwanese and Hong Kong companies, you see the same thing. Everyone is sharp. Everyone knows what he's doing.

Given his current links to Asian suppliers, what worries Rubén most about the ongoing free trade negotiations with the

United States and Canada is the possibility that the agreement will come to regulate Mexico's commerce with Asia. Since most Mexican textile producers are not moving immediately to modernize their operations, 80 to 90 percent of the textiles used in the Mexican garment industry are cheap imports from Asia. Rubén explains that the way the treaty has evolved, a garment manufactured in Mexico can be sold as a "North American–made garment" only if it is made with Mexican, Canadian, or U.S. materials from the yarn or thread on up. Thus, it will not be possible to bring bolts of cloth from Korea or Taiwan, cut and stitch a garment in Mexico, and export it duty-free to the United States or Canada under NAFTA.

> *In order to rescue the Mexican textile makers from being undersold by Asian competitors, our Chamber of Textile Industries pushed hard for this stipulation. The American negotiators went along because, for their own reasons, they also don't want to see Mexico used as a conduit for the dumping of cheap Asian goods in the U.S. market. They don't want Asian goods to enter the U.S. as components in Mexican-finished products.*

Rubén doesn't see this outcome of the trade negotiations as a bad thing in itself. But until NAFTA is signed *and* implemented, he finds himself in an unclear situation. Should he continue to build his import business, counting on being able to supply Mexican garment manufacturers with Asian cloth? Or should he return to manufacturing, positioning himself to profit when the doors of free trade finally swing wide open?

Rubén warns me that it is exceedingly difficult for anyone—even someone who started at age four counting spools of thread in his father's textile plant—to weigh all the options available in textiles and apparel. "Right now," he says, "it's hard to see how the negotiations for the treaty are going to work out because there are, literally, hundreds of different categories of goods to be defined just for the textile industry, not to mention all other sectors."

> *What's more, we also don't know how the American manufacturers will read their opportunities. Take the case of denim. Before 1986, when Mexican industry was protected, Mexican jeans makers absorbed every last yard of denim produced in this country, whatever the quality and whatever the price. They had no choice, because the tariffs made it prohibitively expensive to import better material from abroad. Once the economy opened, the price of denim fell to less than half of what it had been, and a much better quality cloth started to arrive from the U.S.*
>
> *Once the free trade agreement is in place, American firms like Burlington or Swift, companies that produce really good denim will bring quality material into Mexico duty-free. At that point, Mexican garment makers are going to demand high-quality cloth. What's more, they'll move to automate their production because, once you're working with good fabric, it's a lot more efficient to turn most of the production over to machines. Then if Wrangler or Lee comes in, the Mexican consumer will begin to demand these brands, especially if these companies carry out a big publicity campaign geared to the Mexican market. At that stage, Mexican jeans makers who can't produce the quality of Wrangler or Lee, will have to look for another market to peddle their goods. But who's going to buy their stuff? Central Americans?*

This, Rubén explains, is the irony of the present situation. If Mexican manufacturers want to export, they will have to produce a product as good as the American brands. Although Mexico has cheap labor, Mexican manufacturers will increasingly move toward the automated forms of production that are used to make high-quality textiles in the United States and Canada. In the end, only those Mexicans with enough capital to build large, highly automated, integrated textile operations are going to be able to produce for export. The others will cease operations because their quality is too low to compete with the United States and Canada in the higher end of the market, and Asian manufacturers can produce a lot more efficiently at the lower end.

All of this, Rubén explains, is pushing his family in the direction of returning to manufacturing. Rubén believes that the level of ease and success they have enjoyed with imports will not last because the mechanics of importing are becoming more complex and difficult every day. Previously a container shipment took three weeks. Now there are more delays and complications and more restrictions on imports. As new regulations are put in place, his family's company is in increasing danger of being brought up on charges of "dumping" Asian goods.

When Rubén describes to me the logic that has propelled Jacobo, Daniel, and himself to invest in the construction of a new textile plant, he comes back to the theme of family and the three generations. He readily admits that the decision has as much to do with the memory of his grandfather as the careful analysis of market trends and the prospects for change under NAFTA. It turns out that I have arrived on the very day that the three of them are to fly north to the capital of Durango to close the deal on the purchase of land for the site of their new factory. It is evident that they are excited to be starting up again in textile production. The move to the open spaces of the northern desert will be a new frontier for the Ergas family, as it is for countless other Mexican manufacturers who are relocating outside the central Valle de Mexico and away from the increasingly congested border zone.

The Ergas family has decided to produce denim with their own management and financing, but with foreign technology. The plant will be built in Durango because it puts them geographically closer to the U.S. market. The factory will be six hours from the border, and when the new four-lane highway under construction is completed, travel times and transportation costs will drop even lower. A railroad line runs along the back boundary of the property, facilitating the arrival of the cotton fiber they will import directly from U.S. gins. Durango is also attractive to them because labor is relatively plentiful in this northern state. Moreover, although Durango lies in a desert region, the water table in the area is high, so the water that is essential to denim production can be tapped from shallow wells. Most important, the governor of the state, anxious to stimulate industrial development in this comparatively poor zone, has promised the Ergas family a range of facilities, tax breaks, and other incentives that make the location attractive.

> *We're starting at ground zero with this factory. We bought a piece of land on which we'll construct a thirty-thousand-square-meter plant, of which fourteen thousand square meters will be air-conditioned. The factory will be totally pollution-free because the air conditioning will filter out all dust and lint. The water we need for the production process will be purified and recycled. We're bringing state-of-the-art machinery from Switzerland, Germany, Japan, and the U.S. We're working out a system that will depend less and less on human intervention and more on computers. When the factory is finally up and running, you're going to walk into the place and think that you're in Switzerland.*

For Rubén, the difference between this new plant and the factories his family once owned is vast.

> *The factories that we used to run were entirely geared to the domestic Mexican market and were conceived to turn out cheap goods. We were cost-cutting at every stage. Obviously, today you can't proceed like that because the market for second-class fabric has disappeared.*

Rubén hopes that the new plant will also be a model of successful labor relations. He tells me that no one in his family has had any serious labor troubles since the late 1930s, when the workers seized and occupied his grandfather's factory at the height of the labor militancy that marked the administration of Lázaro Cárdenas. In recent years, his dealings with the union have been particularly smooth. The trick, Rubén says, is to follow the federal labor law to the letter and to pay precisely the sums stipulated in the contract.

Rubén says that they intend to develop the new enterprise in three stages. At first they will have three hundred workers producing cloth. Next, they will bring in more machinery and automate more of the process. In the final stage, with roughly nine hundred workers, they will also manufacture jeans and other denim wear. Right now, Rubén explains, there are quotas in place on jean exports to the United States. But Rubén figures that by the time he is ready to produce jeans these quotas will have disappeared with the signing of NAFTA.

For now, Rubén says, his focus is on buying the land, constructing the plant, and purchasing the machinery. At this point his family is not looking for foreign partners, but will bring in technicians and experts in denim from the United States and have them train the workers and run the day-to-day operation of the factory. Once the family moves to the production of denim clothing, they will look for U.S. partners because marketing jeans requires specialized knowledge.

As Rubén explains to me the strategy his family hopes to pursue in their new enterprise, he is gathering his papers for the trip to Durango, responding to a series of telephone calls, reading the fax messages that have arrived during our talk, consulting with Daniel, who has the car waiting to take them to the airport, and eating a sandwich. He says to me,

I keep thinking it's a lot easier to run the New York Marathon than start up a business like this one. You may not know how long the race will take to run, but at least you know where the finish line is.

1 P.M.: *Bernardo Navarro*

When Bernardo Navarro describes the ineptitude of the government planners whose policies he holds responsible for the destruction of whole sectors of the Mexican electronics industry, he struggles for the right words and switches to English, perhaps to distance himself a bit from the emotions he feels. This is a painful topic for Bernardo, who counts among President Salinas's closest advisers several boyhood friends, school chums and present-day close acquaintances. "I know a lot of these guys," he says:

We all studied together at the one of the private universities, the Universidad Anahuac. Some of these are guys I've known all my life. And I know they are honest and well educated, unlike most of the politicians who were in power before Salinas came to office. But that doesn't mean that they knew the correct approach to restructuring the economy. The fact is, you don't build a skyscraper from the twentieth story down.

I am seated in the boardroom of Bernardo's corporate headquarters in Mexico City. On the walls surrounding me are framed photos, laminated certificates, and awards that chart Bernardo's progress as a leader of his industry, a course that culminated when he was elected head of the Chamber of Electronic Industries in the late 1980s. From that point on, whatever Bernardo's personal situation may have been, he has felt obliged to speak out publicly to denounce what he considers to be a string of ill-conceived, half-baked policy initiatives that have all but wiped out the consumer electronics sector of the industry and unnecessarily damaged the computer, telecommunications, and scientific electronics areas as well.

Bernardo's official responsibility has made him extremely sensitive to the inadequacies of the liberalization policies put into place by President Salinas—far more so than he would have been simply on his own account. With respect to his own firm, Bernardo explains, he had a clear strategy to rescue his enterprise from disaster.

Bernardo comes from a prosperous family of industrialists. His father grew rich in food processing and marketing, and Bernardo's parents were able to provide him with the most solid personal foundation. Growing up in the upper-class Polanco district of Mexico City, Bernardo received a first-rate education at the best private schools. An American business associate of his father arranged for him to attend a year of junior high school in the United States to polish his English. Weekends and holidays were spent at his father's food processing plant in a neighboring state, where he acquired a variety of skills ranging from the mechanical to the managerial. It was here, for example, that Bernardo says he learned to drive a truck when he was still so small that he had to sit on cushions to see over the steering wheel. Finally, Bernardo notes, his family and his privileged education gave him a wide circle of economically and politically influential contacts.

But Bernardo is quick to underscore what he considers the central fact of his biography. His father was a self-made man and he, too, was determined to succeed on his own. For this reason, Bernardo explains, he rejected the opportunities that awaited him in his father's business, turned his back on the family enterprise, and set out instead to answer a series of "help-wanted" ads. The jobs he found through this channel carried him from one managerial position to another, from accounting, to sales, to personnel work in an assortment of industries: mining, rubber, and finally, electronics. But the dominant theme for Bernardo was always personal independence:

> *My parents gave me the means to do things, but I wanted to start from scratch. I looked for work on my own and was determined to live on what I earned. It wasn't easy, because my father had a lot of money, my father-in-law had a lot of money, but when I started out, I was just a poor employee in a large firm.*

Thus, unlike Rubén, whose personal and business lives are totally intertwined and tied to his extended family, Bernardo has rejected family links—in business, if not in his personal life—and has relied, instead, on a very different kind of survival plan. His strategy is based on specialization and foreign partnership.

Bernardo manufactures consumer electronics, a field that has been smashed by the opening of the economy. However, his business occupies a specialized niche in this area. His production is geared to the performance market: he turns out cartridges, microphones, speakers, amplifiers, and recorders so refined that—he assures me—outfitted with his equipment, I could launch myself in a career as a rock star, whatever the actual characteristics and quality of my singing voice might be. He explains,

> *I gear my production to a low-volume, highly specialized market where I don't have to face too much competition. I have an advantage because I have technical knowhow that not everyone shares. Obviously, this is not a strategy that can work for everyone, but it works well for me.*

Thus, compared to most of the other manufacturers in his industry, Bernardo's enterprise was rooted in relatively solid ground when the Mexican economy was thrown open to international competition. Making specialized goods that no one else in Mexico, and only eleven other companies in the world produce, gives Bernardo a reasonable chance to compete in a global market.

Moreover, Bernardo enjoys another, even greater advantage over many others in the electronics field. When the *apertura* was announced in 1986 he found himself in a position already reinforced by foreign contacts and capital. More than a dozen years earlier he had sought and found Japanese partners. Working through a Chicago-based "facilitator"—a U.S. businessman who specializes in brokering such relationships—Bernardo hooked up with a large performance-equipment manufacturer who provided him with technology in return for the opportunity to establish a base in Mexico. This Japanese company was one of the most important manufacturers of transducers, the device that changes mechanical vibrations into electronic beams. Its owners were seeking to gain a foothold in Mexico, a goal they accomplished when Bernardo sold them a 49 percent share in his company. Thus, unlike Sergio Espinoza or Rubén Ergas, or so many members of his own association, Bernardo did not need to halt production or to suddenly start seeking foreign investors or outlets for his product when the economy opened. These connections were already in place.

In describing to me the nature of his interaction with his foreign partners, Bernardo explains:

> *To this day, this has been an excellent relationship, better than many marriages. In sixteen years we have not had a single serious disagreement. We have our facilitator, Mr. Samuel, who lived many years in Japan. He brought us together, brokered the original agreement, and still works with us as an intermediary. When I have a problem with my Japanese counterpart or his partners, I call Mr. Samuel and tell him "look, these guys are doing something I don't like." I yell and carry on, and probably when he*

talks with the Japanese he translates this as something like "Bernardo is a little troubled because you have not sent this or done that." God knows what they say back to him. But when he calls me, he is completely calm and constructive, as if this was exactly how the Japanese responded. We developed this system, and it's worked and we've been very successful with it.

Of course Bernardo was not completely immune to the dramatic effects of the opening. Like others, he was forced to make a series of adjustments in his operation. Bernardo had to convert a work force that had been manufacturing complete products from parts he produced in Mexico into an assembly operation using components shipped to him by his Japanese partners.

Much of what we used to produce we are now importing from other plants around the world that are owned by the Japanese parent company. It used to be that no matter how much it cost, we produced the parts in Mexico. But that was when we were protected. I used to employ 180 people and now it is down to 80 or 90.

When Bernardo explains these changes to me, he insists that in whole areas of this operation he is not showing a profit. He is carrying on, he says, in order to retain his employees.

I want to keep my girls working because it has been very expensive to train these girls and I don't want to lose them. So, in order to pay their salaries, I take on some assembly jobs. About thirty or forty of my girls are really nonproductive for me, but I don't have the heart to tell them all, "goodbye, go away." These people have worked for me a long time, so I have a certain commitment to them, in spite of the restructuring we are undergoing.

I should also say that these girls are excellent workers. All my people here work faster and produce better-quality goods than their counterparts in Japan. It is something my Japanese partners always comment on when they visit my plant. The Japanese engineers come here and take photos of little modifications that the girls have invented, that they've created out of a hair pin or a paper clip. They are always finding ways to improve the process. They're flexible and innovative, and that's why I hate to put them out of a job.

Bernardo allows that the assembly work also provides an advantage in that it permits him to offer new products to his clients. "Using my sales force, I am able to approach my customers with a broader line. In fact," he says, "we've been able to grow and profit from the introduction of these new items that we only assemble from parts."

Having made these short- and middle-term adjustments, Bernardo finds that five years after the opening of the economy, he is in good shape to face an uncertain but in some respects promising future. However, while Bernardo was relatively well positioned with his Japanese partners to launch an increasingly internationalized operation, this clearly was not the case for most of the members of the industry he represents. And this is the problem that preoccupies him as we speak in his boardroom:

Becoming active in my industry's association really required the reversal of the attitudes I had built over a lifetime. I was a businessman, the son of a businessman, and I was accustomed to viewing other guys in my field as "the competition." It's a great honor to be chosen by the others to represent their interests, but it meant I had to learn to think in terms of the needs of the most vulnerable branches of my industry, not simply in terms of my own entrepreneurial survival.

Bernardo says that when the government summarily announced the opening of the borders, "it is not an exaggeration to say that there were grown men who cried. I mean we literally wept to consider the situation in which we found ourselves. Believe me, I spent many sleepless nights."

"There was no way to plan for the opening because we had no warning," Bernardo tells me. Not only did the regime move without consulting the official representative organizations of industry and business, but these chambers and associations weren't even given advance notice of what was to come. "Can you imagine," Bernardo says to me,

> *One Sunday I am waterskiing near Cuernavaca on Lake Tequesquitengo with my friend, who is a minister in the government, and our sons, who are also big buddies. Of course, he knows that I am serving as the head of the chamber and I'm responsible to a large membership of electronics manufacturers. He doesn't say one word to me about the changes that are in store. The next morning I have to read in the newspaper that tariffs on finished electronic goods from Asia have been dropped to 20 percent.*

The problem, in Bernardo's view, is a lack of experience on the part of the relatively young corps of advisers who surround the president.

> *I have built my connections in Asia for a long time, and I understand how things work in Asia. But Salinas's guys have no hands-on experience with the Asians. They just want to follow what it says in the textbooks: you know, you have to open the borders because that's what the formula tells you to do.*

The tragedy, as Bernardo sees it, is that the planners never really thought through the consequences of their policies. Moreover, they didn't want to consult the people who would be affected because they figured that these industrialists "would just scream."

Well, we would have screamed. But we also would have been able to offer some suggestions on how to phase in an open economy without destroying a whole industry. With a little more discussion and planning, the borders could have been opened, the economy could have been streamlined, and so many domestic industrialists would not have been ruined.

Bernardo insists the *apertura* was so poorly planned that it was not only small firms that were affected. The multinational electronic giant, Phillips, used to have three thousand workers in its Mexican operation, all supplied by local Mexican producers. With the opening, Phillips shut its Mexico City factory, moved to the border region, and started up a *maquila,* an assembly plant, that put together parts brought into Mexico from the United States and elsewhere around the world. "As I see it," Bernardo says, "we lost Phillips for Mexico, or at least we lost Phillips as part of the integrated, industrial base of Mexico."

Bernardo is also critical of what he calls the "triumphalism" of Salinas's economic planners:

They keep proclaiming in triumph that "we are over the hump," that we have put the debt crisis behind us. I hate when I open the newspaper and I read interviews where they are announcing that we are over the hump. This claim has no basis in reality. A debt crisis is over when you've paid off your debt.

Another thing that worries me is that their figures don't check with mine. I'm not talking about the personal tabs I keep, but the figures we have on production through the Chamber of Electronics. When the sixty-eight presidents of various chambers of industries sit down together at CONCAMIN and we report to one another on our sectors, and fifty-nine of the sixty-eight say their industry is in terrible shape, you don't expect to hear the political guys proclaiming that everything is great and we are over the hump.*

* Confederación de Cámaras de Industria (Confederation of Chambers of Industry).

Bernardo says he appreciates that the positive gloss is intended to inspire confidence on the part of both domestic and foreign investors. But he feels that the exaggerated assessments often have a dampening effect:

> *Sometimes I don't know who these guys think they're kidding. I go to a meeting where we have five Japanese executives, some Mexican businessmen, and two guys from the government. Things don't go especially well, and at the end of the meeting, the Japanese—very polite, as always—get up and say, "very well, we'll try again next year," and they walk out. But when we leave the meeting, the government guys give a press conference saying that things went great and that Japanese capital is flowing into Mexico so fast you can't count it, and that we can expect, I don't know how many billions of dollars of investment during the next year.*
>
> *I ask myself: Was I at another meeting? No, I was at the same meeting and that's not what I heard, because that's not what the Japanese said. The fact is, Japanese capital is not coming into Mexico, it's flowing into Europe or it's going elsewhere in Asia, to Singapore or the Philippines. That's what's really going on.*

While all of these problems—the policymakers' shortsightedness, their triumphalism, their lack of candor—trouble Bernardo, he is most worried about the effect of the *apertura* on employment, and he sees the shutdown of so many factories as destabilizing. "If we take the twenty-five thousand jobs that were lost in the electronics industry plus all the jobs that have been lost in other domestic manufacturing sectors," he explains, "this adds up to a very large number of people with nothing to eat." Bernardo says he finds this extremely dangerous. He tells me, "this is why you see so many socialist parties that have a following in Mexico."

I ask Bernardo where he thinks those who lost their jobs in the *apertura* have gone. Like Sergio Espinoza, Bernardo assumes that they are the same masses of people he sees peddling goods on the streets and subways. However, Bernardo markets a specialized product and, unlike Sergio, does not have to compete directly with street peddlers who undersell him. Nonetheless, Bernardo also views the informal sector as clear evidence of the policy failures of the regime and a great burden to people like himself:

> *The informal economy is a drain on all legitimate businessmen, because it is growing rapidly and it uses all the infrastructure that the formal economy provides, without contributing taxes or fees to support that system of services. And this underground economy is not limited to street vendors. We have whole "micro-industries," little family-based workshops, that are not registered with anybody and run purely on power tapped illegally off high-tension wires.*

Although Bernardo is proud of the inventive genius of his own workers when they improve the production process with hairpins and paper clips, he is a bit more ambivalent when he talks to me about the capacity for innovation displayed by the informal sector workshops. "If you ride out about ten kilometers on the road to Puebla," he says, "you'll see thousands of wires that people have hooked up to the energy grid that brings power into Mexico City." These people, Bernardo explains, use the electricity to run their sewing machines and power tools, and they produce all kinds of goods on small family assembly lines. The goods are then marketed on the streets by the informal sector "sales force." In Bernardo's view, the failure of Salinas's planners to anticipate the growth of the informal sector or offer alternatives to the people who fill its ranks is evidence of the confusion of *técnicos* who draw their economic solutions from textbooks without considering the "real-life" outcomes of their programs.

At this stage I can only ask Bernardo what programs he would put into place if he were directing economic planning for Mexico.

Without hesitation he replies that he has no short-term solution to the problems that have created the informal sector. But his vision of a broad economic strategy is clear enough: he sees his own experience with his Japanese investors as a model for the kind of partnership that would be a workable response to Mexico's need for capital and advanced technology. The answer, he thinks, is neither exaggerated protection nor a complete free for all. The trick is to find the right balance between an open economy and protection of the country's own citizens. In terms of specific policies, the ideal, he believes, is for the government to encourage joint ventures between Mexican and foreign entrepreneurs.

Bernardo is not, he assures me, an economic nationalist. "You have to remember," he says, "that business has no nationality."

> *I would rather open a factory near my home, in a country that I know because it is easier and logical for me to start up a business in Mexico than abroad. But if tomorrow someone tells me about an attractive investment in Japan well, I don't know, I might invest. I wouldn't have any problem investing money in the United States or Canada. I have seen where some Mexican has opened a factory in Taiwan. Others have invested in Spain and France. I admit, when I first see this I ask myself, "Why is this guy investing in other countries instead of Mexico?" Well, the answer is because he has business opportunities there, and that's the way business reacts. And to try to think otherwise is absolute nonsense.*

I ask Bernardo if he includes nonproductive investment in the same category. Does he approve of the Mexicans of his social class who have exported their capital, putting it into Swiss bank accounts or foreign real estate? He replies,

> *For me this is not an unpatriotic act. I think it's normal that a guy who has made some money and feels that his patrimony is insecure*

in his country will want to protect at least part of his patrimony so that he can count on it in any emergency. If you want to provide your family with some comfort in life, you have to be sure that you have at least enough to put bread on the table in the future.

I'm not talking now about some of the notorious people who stole money from Mexico and stashed it away in secret bank accounts abroad. That's another story. That's stealing and that should be punished. But I don't see anything wrong with taking care of your patrimony. We all do that. You have to protect your money in whatever way you can.

To be sure, Bernardo's belief in the absolute right of those with money to protect their resources is tempered by some sense of social obligation:

If you live in Mexico and you make money in Mexico you should give something back to this country. But if someone crazy comes into office who wants to take everything away from you, confiscate property, nationalize the banks, impose extortionate taxes, make you give up what you've earned, well, that's another story.

This, Bernardo insists, is what happened in Mexico under the presidencies of Luis Echeverría (1970–1976) and José López Portillo (1976–1982) in what business people often refer to as the "tragic twelve years." Bernardo recalls:

It's not easy to forget when someone steps on your toe. I remember when suddenly all U.S. dollar accounts could only be paid out in Mexican pesos at a new exchange rate established by the government. The government stole from us what was ours! And this was not the only thing that happened to our money. They tell you, "we're not going to raise taxes," and the next day you open the newspaper and taxes are way up.

Bernardo insists that middle-aged industrial executives and entrepreneurs like himself have gone through "fifteen years of lies."

> *These experiences have left a scar, and I think it is overly optimistic to think that because we have a guy like Salinas in power who seems to be nice, everyone's going to forget about what happened before. That's not what's going to happen. Business is not conducted that way.*

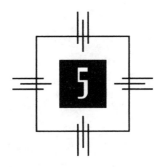

5

Agriculture and Rural Development

At 2 P.M. I am sipping coffee in the central courtyard of the Sanborns Restaurant in the House of Tiles, a beautifully preserved colonial building in the heart of downtown, just a block from the marble Palacio de Bellas Artes and the Alameda Park. I never come to Sanborns without thinking that it was here that Emiliano Zapata and his troops came to refresh themselves on the day they took Mexico City, riding on the capital from their stronghold in Morelos. It seems the *zapatistas* could not convince themselves that they really held the capital until they had taken coffee at the bar at Sanborns.

I, too, am never convinced that I am really in Mexico until I have come to Sanborns, although the spot has fallen from favor with others and no longer seems to be the setting for the power breakfasts and power lunches that once drew politicians from all over the city. I am here not to talk about power but to chat with an old friend, Eduardo, an anthropologist I know from my first years of fieldwork in Mexico. I am hoping he will help me make sense of the current changes in agricultural development policy that promise to radically alter rural Mexico.

"Let's face it," Eduardo says. "The history of rural development policy in Mexico has always boiled down to a conflict between two sets of competing objectives." On one side are those who think that Mexico can modernize only if land is concentrated in the hands of the farmers who are best able to produce efficiently. For the people who hold this view, "most efficient" always means the large-scale private agricultural entrepreneurs. They insist that only large, commercial landowners can produce food in volumes sufficient to feed the growing urban population, with a surplus left over to sell abroad to earn foreign exchange. It's not surprising, he says, that they see the original revolutionary commitment to the *campesinos* as an impediment to development which should be abandoned.

On the other side, Eduardo notes, are the so-called *campesinistas,* among whom he counts himself. Researchers like Eduardo have figures that show that given the same inputs, the small peasant and the large landowner can produce with equal efficiency. Eduardo says that virtually every empirical study ever carried out shows that with the proper organization and sufficient credit from the state, peasants who intensively cultivate small parcels of land can feed themselves and produce a decent surplus for either the national or international market.[1] In short, small peasant farmers—both land reform recipients (*ejidatarios*) and those holding small private plots (*minifundistas*)—do more with the few resources at their disposal than do the large landowners. Under the circumstances, *campesinistas* have always insisted that the commercial farms should not be favored on the grounds of their presumed superior productivity; instead, more state support should be given to the smallholding peasants.

"Life would be a lot more simple," Eduardo tells me, "if all there was to the debate between *campesinistas* and 'modernizing technocrats' was some disagreement over measurements of efficiency and productivity." But mixed into the discussion is another, even more passionate disagreement over the question of social welfare and what, in Mexico, is always referred to as "social justice."

Eduardo says, "whether we follow the course of the debate in the 1930s, in Cárdenas's time, when two thirds of Mexicans were still on the land, or we look at the issue today, when less than one third of the population still lives in the countryside, the central point remains the same." If viable economic alternatives can be created in the rural zones, then the monstrous growth of the capital and the other major cities could be halted or slowed. The major impulse for rural exodus would be gone, and peasants could remain where it is assumed they would genuinely like to be—in their villages. If rural Mexicans could attain at least a minimum level of well-being by working the land, and if social services like schools, health care, water, and electrical power could be extended to them in the countryside, the overtaxed social infrastructure of the urban areas would be alleviated.

Eduardo emphasizes to me that the debate is not an abstraction. It comes down to a question of pesos and centavos and where they will be allocated. The "modernizers" want to channel state support to private commercial agriculture, while the *campesinistas* argue in favor of reinforcing peasant agriculture and peasant life through land reform and social expenditure in rural Mexico.

When I ask Eduardo where he thinks emphasis will be placed by the current regime, he reminds me how public policy on rural development has swung back and forth on the issue, but overall, the trajectory has mostly been in one direction: a move away from support to the peasantry in favor of large-scale enterprises. He says that to understand how policy has shifted over time, it is important to go back all the way to the revolution and to the administration of Lázaro Cárdenas and the large-scale land reform he carried out.

Agrarian Reform under Cárdenas

Land reform was one of the explicit goals of the Mexican revolution. The incorporation of agrarian reform legislation into the constitution of 1917 represented a great victory for peasants and paved the way for a series of agrarian laws promulgated during the 1920s and 1930s. The legislation provided for the gigantic *haciendas* to be seized, in the name of the nation, and parceled out in smallholdings to individual peasants. These *ejidatarios* could work the land and pass it along to an eldest son. However, they were never free to sell or rent the land granted to them because it always remained "common property" given over to individuals for their use, but never to be "possessed" in the sense of private property.[2]

While the agrarian laws sat on the books for almost two decades, it was not until Lázaro Cárdenas came to power in 1934 that large-scale land distribution began in earnest. The Cárdenas land reform was spectacular, not only because he distributed close to forty-five million acres in five years but also because of the type, quality, and location of the land he gave out. In the twenty years that had elapsed since the revolution, Cárdenas's predecessors had distributed less than nineteen million acres consisting almost entirely of arid, nonirrigated, steep, rocky, and infertile land lying far from roads and markets. Large productive estates were not touched: the holdings of powerful landowners were left intact and their economic and political power was not diminished by any of the token agrarian reformist gestures made during the 1920s and 1930s.

Cárdenas's approach to the land question was radical. He expropriated and distributed highly productive, choice land, almost all of which was already under cultivation in modern, economically efficient estates. In order to establish a firm foundation for the *ejidos* that were to be formed out of the land parcels distributed to peasant petitioners, Cárdenas organized most of the *ejido* holdings into farming collectives, and he set up institutions designed to support the land reform program and aid the new land recipients in their struggle to break the old patterns of dependency on large landowners. The collective form of agriculture featured a number of advantages: it maximized the use of scarce irrigation waters; it facilitated the use of expensive agricultural equipment, as well as the harvesting and marketing of the crop; and finally, it permitted the peasants—long used to executing fairly specialized tasks on the *hacienda*—to continue to work in specialized teams, smoothing the transition from *hacienda* to *ejido* agriculture.[3]

Cárdenas also established a variety of supporting institutions to aid the newly landed peasantry. The National Ejidal Credit Bank was set up to provide credit, technical assistance, and supervision to the collective *ejidos* and to guide the *ejidatarios* in organizing their own internal administrative structures. In addition to the bank, Cárdenas oversaw the creation of agricultural-technology schools designed to train the new *ejidatarios*.

Although in their first years the *ejidos* enjoyed economic success, serious troubles began for the collectives as soon as the Cárdenas administration came to an end. In the regions where the agrarian reform was implemented, the Mexican countryside was dotted with agricultural collectives scattered among *haciendas*. The collective *ejidos* with their communal labor, profit sharing, cooperative credit, and marketing system were economically and socially isolated from the surrounding environment in which large-scale commercial farms predominated.

Other problems grew from deficiencies in the agrarian code that provided the legislative basis for the program. The code permitted the large landowners to retain a substantial part of their old estates, and with these estates, much of the political and economic power they had monopolized in the pre-reform era. For example, landowners could choose the 150 hectares (370 acres) they would retain as a "small private property" (*pequeño propiedad*). Naturally, they chose the part of the *hacienda* that included the house, stables, barns, warehouses, wells, irrigation canals, and the network of roads and communication lines connecting the estate with the outside world.[4] In addition to retaining this choice land, landowners were permitted to subdivide and sell any land not required for distribution to neighboring peasant communities. As a result, the *hacienda* was often "broken up" into 150-hectare parcels and "sold" to various members of the same family or to a *prestanombre* ("name-lender"), a lawyer or some other trusted person who, for a fee, would lend his or her name to be used for a land title. This system of subdividing a huge estate that is nevertheless worked as a single unit came to be known as "neolatifundism," the creation of new, illegal *latifundia,* or large landholdings.

Moreover, as the *ejido* leaders sought to increase the self-sufficiency of their collectives by developing cooperative credit societies, marketing co-ops, mutual crop insurance companies, collective agricultural machine stations, and a variety of other cooperative enterprises, they came into conflict with powerful new agribusiness interests. To the extent that *ejido* cooperative institutions were successful, they directly threatened the interests of the old landowners who had converted themselves into agricultural entrepreneurs dealing in equipment, supplying credit, and marketing crops. Under pressure from these agribusinessmen, almost all the peasant-run projects aimed at increased economic independence for the collective *ejidos* were eventually quashed by the withdrawal of government approval or state funds.

The Move away from Land Reform

The collective *ejido* system, for all its technical problems and for all the contradictions in the development of an isolated collectivist experiment, might still have survived as a viable system were it not for the conservative swing in agrarian policy. After 1940 state policy actively encouraged the break-up of the collective *ejidos*. Militant peasant organizations, which under Cárdenas had received official sanction and been encouraged to organize peasants to agitate for land distribution, were discouraged or even brutally repressed. As a consequence, the amount of land distributed to peasants was drastically reduced. Equally important, the quality of the land distributed was markedly inferior to that dealt out during the Cárdenas years.[5] Furthermore, the size of landholdings redefined by law as *inafectable,* that is, unavailable for expropriation, steadily increased while authorities at national and state level turned a blind eye to neolatifundism, the illegal ownership of land in excess of the established maximum limits. All of these changes increased the tendency toward concentration of land in the hands of a new landholding elite comprised of domestic agribusinessmen and foreign corporations acting in collaboration with Mexican *prestanombres.*

Perhaps the most significant policy shift could be seen in the area of government expenditure. From 1940 onward, the bulk of government spending was channeled to the support of private commercial agriculture at the expense of the *ejidos* and *minifundios,* the tiny subsistence farms. Massive state investment in dams and irrigation networks was directed to assist large private owners, while the proportion of government credit earmarked for support to the *ejidos* declined steadily. Lacking credit, *ejidatarios* were forced to borrow money at usurious rates from private banks and moneylenders, often giving up half or three quarters of the crop to repay their loans.[6]

Government spending on agricultural research also reflected the same bias in favor of the large, commercial landholdings. From 1940 to 1970 state-sponsored experiments concentrated on raising the productivity of grain and cotton cultivated on large commercial estates. Techniques developed in the "green revolution" dramatically raised the productivity of wheat and cotton crops. But such increases were produced only with the heavy use of chemical inputs, mechanized equipment, and well-irrigated land—precisely the things that peasants lacked.

The Food Crisis

This systematic shortchanging of *ejido* and smallholding peasant agriculture continued unchecked until production had declined to levels below subsistence on the plots of *ejidatarios* and *minifundistas.*

Deprived of credit and technical inputs, these small producers reached the point where their plots no longer provided food to sustain their families, let alone a surplus for sale to urban Mexicans. Meanwhile, commercial producers who enjoyed the flexibility that ready credit provides, sought higher profits by giving over ever-greater proportions of their land to cash crops: coffee, tomatoes, strawberries, and other fruits and vegetables destined for the U.S. market. Commercial holdings that had been planted in edible grains and legumes were increasingly converted to sorghum to fatten beef cattle for export. By 1970 only 22 percent of the land in the irrigation districts was devoted to corn and bean production. As a consequence of this shift away from basic food crops, Mexico was now obliged to import 15 to 20 percent of all foodstuffs.[7]

By 1980 the annual bill for food purchased in the United States had reached $2 billion. While one third of the work force was employed in agriculture, productivity was now so low that agricultural production contributed less than 10 percent to the gross national product. In short, by the 1970s the "logical limits" of the policy favoring the private sector had been reached.[8]

A New Program

The decline in agricultural production that prompted a crisis in the balance of payments in the late 1970s also provided the stimulus for a new emphasis in research and state spending on smallholding agriculture. Financed by the World Bank and channeled through the Mexican Program for Public Investment for Rural Development (PIDER), a series of development plans were designed to increase crop yields on "rain-fed," that is, nonirrigated smallholdings. In a swing back toward the *campesinistas,* who had always argued that, given proper support, peasant agriculture could be viable and productive, this program attempted to apply modern technology, new credit resources, and government-sponsored "commercialization opportunities" to smallholding peasants. In the central Mexican state of Puebla, the pilot program was posed as an effort to extend the "miracle of the green revolution" to subsistence peasants. Thus, in the late 1970s, in the full flush of exuberance produced by the oil boom, agricultural development officials began to formulate a new role for the smallholding sector, insisting that, with the right ecological and institutional conditions, large increases in the production of basic foodstuffs could be achieved by peasants.

The results of the Puebla project were mixed. Agricultural production rose, but the program also accelerated the impoverishment and marginalization of the poorest peasants. The better-off peasants managed to accumulate a modest amount of capital, for the program gave them access to relatively inexpensive government credit. Furthermore, they were able to operate on a scale that allowed them to circumvent exploitative intermediaries and sell directly to the state commodities agency. But the poorer peasants were actually driven off the land by rising rents for land, increased reliance on moneylenders, and higher risks of crop failure.[9]

Despite these early indications that the new "peasant-oriented" development projects had some serious contradictions, in March 1980 President López Portillo announced the establishment of the Mexican Food System (SAM), a comprehensive plan to raise productivity among smallholding subsistence producers—the same rain-fed agriculture targeted by the Puebla plan. Cast as an effort to raise the nutritional level of the population by stimulating the production of basic foods within the peasant economy, SAM provided incentives to encourage the production of staples for the national market by guaranteeing price support, generous credit terms, and discounts on all agricultural inputs to anyone producing beans, corn, rice, or wheat. With the introduction of a "shared-risk" concept—that is, compensation to smallholders in the event of crop failure—the government created a system of subsidies to production as well as supports for processing and consumption. Announced with great fanfare and optimism, SAM was projected to bring about self-sufficiency in corn and beans by 1982 and in all other staples by 1985.[10]

In the end, SAM produced results tragically similar to those of the Puebla pilot project on which it was modeled. Favorable weather conditions and massive government spending brought about some immediate rises in productivity. But over the long run, the project benefited commercial farmers, middlemen, and the better-off peasants rather than the rural poor who constituted the supposed "target group."[11] When Miguel de la Madrid succeeded López Portillo, SAM was officially terminated and the entire bureaucratic structure dismantled when cutbacks in state spending began in line with the austerity measures imposed in 1983.

An End to Agrarian Reform

Until the 1980s, most Mexicans believed that the agrarian reform made by Cárdenas was "irreversible and final."[12] And indeed, the land distributed to the peasants was never snatched away by the government and restored to the old *hacienda* owners. However, the post-1940 official attitude and legislation reversed the progress of the *ejidos* and undercut their productive potential. The lack of government support for the *ejidos* and particularly the shortage of low-interest credit for *ejidatarios* made their survival as farmers so difficult that many sought a solution amounting to a total throwback to prerevolutionary days: they secretly and illegally arranged to rent their *ejido* parcels to a large commercial farmer. Then the *ejidatarios* would work for the commercial entrepreneur as peons on the parcel that was, on paper at least, their own land. By the mid-1970s, unable to afford the agricultural inputs, some 80 percent of all land reform beneficiaries had lost effective control of their parcels in just this manner.[13]

Recognition, confirmation, and consolidation of this trend came with the rural development program implemented by López Portillo. Until he came to office, none of the post-1940 leaders had ever taken any measure against the *ejido* as an institution. Even if the real effect of their policies was to undermine the land reform sector, all modern Mexican presidents had defended the *ejido* as a primary symbol of the revolution and its achievements. Indeed, virtually all speeches and presentation of statistics on the subject were composed so as to suggest that the reform process, which in fact had peaked under Cárdenas, was still in progress and was being carried forward with ever-greater enthusiasm and dedication.

López Portillo, in contrast, promoted a policy that represented an undisguised move away from land distribution as the means to bring social justice to the peasantry. In the name of efficiency, he reorganized the land reform bureaucracy. Under the new structure, government agencies explicitly designed to defend the peasants in the face of competing claims from private agricultural enterprise were either dismantled or their powers subsumed by other ministries with no special responsibility to the *ejido* sector.

López Portillo then announced that he would resolve all outstanding land claims during his term in office. However, the procedure through which land distribution was to be "concluded" was that the state governors (political appointees all) were empowered to settle all disputes within their domains. Thus, enormous discretionary powers came to rest in the hands of the state governors, the vast majority of whom were major *latifundistas*.

The rationale offered for a policy that ended land distribution was that it would inspire confidence in private commercial landowners, calming their fears of expropriation, and stimulating them to reinvest their profits in agriculture. Establishing a trend that would become the key to agricultural development policy over the next two administrations, López Portillo focused on incentives to private investors, particularly foreign capital. To this end, transnational corporations already active in Mexico (Anderson-Clayton, Birds Eye, Campbells, Carnation, Del Monte, Nestlé, Ralston-Purina, and United Brands) were urged to expand their operations, so that eventually every stage of food production from cultivation to processing, distribution, and marketing came increasingly under the control of these giants.

The most definitive blow to the hopes of the landless peasantry was dealt by the López Portillo administration with the Law for Agricultural and Livestock Production—a *latifundista*'s dream—which removed virtually all remaining restrictions on the concentration of productive land in the hands of the few. Previous agrarian reform law had limited the amount of land which could be legally held by an individual according to a precise formula geared to the quality of the land and its potential use. Thus, *latifundistas* were forced to pretend to graze cattle on prime land or to employ the services of *prestanombres* as the owners of record for various portions of what was actually one individual's giant estate. With the new legislation, the need for such subterfuge was removed, as the limitations previously imposed on the size of holding were effectively lifted.

In retrospect, it is possible to discern an almost perfect continuity between the policies instituted by López Portillo and implemented by his successor, de la Madrid, and the changes in Article 27 of the constitution sought by Salinas. When Salinas came to power in 1988, he was determined to "liberalize" the Mexican economy by cutting government spending, selling off all state-owned enterprises, and pushing rural Mexico further into the market economy. With the withdrawal of government funding, the primary source of investment funds for the countryside had to come from private capital, domestic or foreign.[14] The question was how to attract this investment. To do this, the new regime made clear that dramatic changes in the agrarian reform legislation would be carried out, and the remaining restrictions on *ejido* property, indeed the very concept of commonly held property, would be radically revised.

In November 1991 Salinas announced his proposal to amend Article 27 to permit the privatization of *ejido* land. The constitutional obligation to distribute land to qualified peasant petitioners was thereby ended. What had been inalienable communally held property would now be available for sale or rent to either Mexican or foreign companies. *Ejidatarios* would now have the right to sell, rent, sharecrop, or mortgage their land parcels as collateral for loans, and they would no longer be required to work their parcel themselves in order to retain control of the land or their right to live in an *ejido* community. Finally, the amended version of Article 27 eliminated the legal prohibition against production associations formed between foreign private investors and *ejidatarios,* thus opening the *ejido* sector to direct foreign investment.[15]

Overall, the changes to Article 27 largely confirm patterns that were widespread before the amendment became law. Clearly, it has been a very long time since the *ejido* sector flourished under Cárdenas. A successful agrarian reform program always requires a great deal of initial and continued input from the state in the form of investment in infrastructure (dams, irrigation canals, roads, rural electrification), the provision of credit, and the development of supporting institutions such as agricultural extension services and marketing facilities. When these expenditures were forthcoming during the Cárdenas administration, *ejido* agriculture showed great promise. However, when after 1940 this crucial state input was in large part withdrawn and redirected toward the private commercial sector, the entire land reform faltered and sank into a morass from which it never emerged.

As a consequence, with the exception of sporadic efforts to reverse the pattern of neglect and underfunding of peasant agriculture—that is, programs like PIDER and SAM—it has been half a century since the *ejidos* enjoyed the support of the regime or since the *ejido* system offered the peasantry any real hope of prospering through dint of hard work. Thus, for five decades Mexican and foreign corporations have been amassing land by gaining control over the *ejido* plots of peasants who could not make a go of it on the resources they possessed. Over the same period *ejidatarios* have been migrating to the cities or the United States to seek work while illegally renting their plots or employing the labor of a landless peasant to work the land in their absence. The amendment to Article 27 simply legalizes what have become entrenched practices. And it paves the way for NAFTA by removing the last legal impediments to foreign involvement in Mexican agriculture.

Before Eduardo and I conclude our meeting at Sanborn's I press him for his predictions on the future of rural Mexico. Does he think the reform will accelerate the rate of land concentration in the hands of corporate owners? He reminds me that it imposes some limitations on size of holdings but adds that these prohibitions seem fairly easy to evade. Will *ejidatarios* sell out in large numbers and move to the cities? He points out that many of the 3.1 million *ejidatarios* are already in the cities or the United States trying to earn enough to send home to keep the *ejido* plot going and support those members of the family left behind in the village. Moreover, he says that in the absence of any reliable figures on how many *ejidatarios* already follow this survival strategy, it is difficult to project with precision the rate of increase in their numbers. What is absolutely clear, however, is that the overall trend of outmigration from the countryside to the cities, the border region, and the United States will inevitably accelerate with the change in the legal status of the *ejido*.

I ask whether the anticipated foreign investment is beginning to flow into the Mexican countryside, raising the productivity of agriculture. Eduardo says that this is surely the regime's hope, but that according to all available information, the results thus far have been modest. Will private investors extend the network of processing plants and other agro-industries in the rural zones, giving employment to some of the displaced subsistence producers? Eduardo thinks it is likely they will, but it is also certain that these jobs will never be numerous enough to offset the loss of employment on the land.

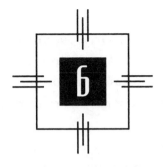

6

The Countryside

3 P.M.: *Ramón Ortega*

When Ramón Ortega tries to describe the size, symmetry, and color of the cauliflower he is able to produce, he is at a loss for words. To render the idea the closest he can come is to remove the tightly woven straw *sombrero* that he wears—indoors and out—and to place it on the chair in front of me. "As big and perfectly round and creamy white as this hat," he tells me. "When someone can grow a cauliflower that beautiful," he says by way of explanation, "the idea that this person could contract directly with Campbells doesn't seem so extravagant."

And, indeed, it did not seem outrageous to Ramón when he set out ten years ago on his famous journey to the Campbell's processing plant outside the central Mexican city of Celaya, an event that enjoys the status of a legend among the other *ejidatarios* in his community. "Don Ramón's Journey"—the tale that was solemnly recounted to me by many of the people I would meet in the Ejido Santa Marta—was, in fact, a trip of only forty-five minutes on the second-class bus that plies the highway that runs through the Bajio region between the town of Salvatierra in the southeastern corner of Guanajuato State and the agro-industrial center of Celaya. But for the twelve *ejidatarios* who have succeeded in becoming contract suppliers of cauliflower and broccoli to major international food processing companies, it was a trip from marginalization to modernity and a degree of modest material comfort, if not real wealth or security.

By the time Ramón set out on his journey to Celaya he had been thinking a long time about making the switch to vegetables from *maíz* and *frijol,* the corn and beans that are the staple food of poor Mexicans both urban and rural. "There's no question," he told me, "that *maíz* and *frijol* have their advantages. The truth is that anybody can make these plants grow."

It is now three in the afternoon, and Don Ramón, as his neighbors refer to him respectfully, has finished his work in the fields. The smell of fresh tortillas is drifting from the kitchen as he rests on the cinderblock veranda he added to his house ten years ago. Dozens of coffee cans filled with soil and nailed to the wall of the house are sprouting geraniums in reds, pinks, and orange. Several dogs, cats, and chickens are coming and going as Don Ramón explains to me the advantages and disadvantages of various crops.

Corn and beans, he points out, are relatively easy to cultivate because they are improved by, but do not absolutely require, fertilizer or any of the expensive chemical inputs that commercial vegetables need. "They can be killed by drought, same as any living thing," but they are not so delicate and susceptible to blight as the cash crops. "The best thing about corn and beans," Ramón explains, "is that if things go badly, you store them and eat them yourself. Your children will never starve as long as you are planting *maíz* and *frijol.*"

Whatever their advantages, Ramón believes that corn and beans are a dead end, "a recipe for poverty," as he puts it. At best these crops can be harvested only twice a year. And because corn and beans are staples, their prices are effected by government food policies. Of course, part of that policy is supposed to be a program of subsidies to stimulate and assist basic grain producers. But very often the price for corn and beans is set so low that it makes no sense to cultivate more than the peasant family needs for its own consumption. Complicating the issue still further is the fact that while CONASUPO,* the state marketing board, set up programs to purchase corn and beans directly from the peasant producer, a peasant who wants to sell his corn directly to CONASUPO still has the problem of transporting the crop from his land to the CONASUPO collection center.

Thus, in the Bajio region "intermediaries" like Don Gustavo Vargas still hold sway, as they have from the time of the revolution. These moneylenders and speculators extend credit to the impoverished peasant and buy back his crop at the prices they establish, using their own "specially calibrated" scales to measure the weight of the grain. The more distant the peasant from market, the more isolated the village, the more complete is the control of the moneylender who is the only one equipped to move the crop of a poor peasant from the field to the marketplace.

To be sure, the Ejidal Bank, originally established by Lázaro Cárdenas, was supposed to undercut the power of the exploitative intermediaries by providing low-interest loans to the *ejidatarios* and assisting them in transporting their harvest to market. However, once Cárdenas left office, the Ejidal Bank, like so many state institutions, became riddled with corruption and inefficiency, and it failed to perform even its most basic obligations to the *ejido* communities it was established to serve.

In a very small number of places in Mexico, the bank works properly. In most regions it does not and the Bajio is one of those areas where it never worked well. "The *ingenieros* from the bank are supposed to give us technical advice," Ramón explains. "But these guys don't know a mule from a horse. They don't know the first thing about farming. All they know about is stuffing their pockets. They make it so difficult for a peasant to repay his loan from the bank

* Compañía Nacional para Subsistencia Popular (National Company for Popular Subsistence).

that he is always in debt." Ironically, after applying policies that inevitably drove the *ejidatarios* into debt, the Ejidal Bank—and, later, the Rural Bank that replaced it—would periodically declare that it was no longer possible to lend to the chronically indebted *ejidatarios,* since they were bad credit risks. Whenever this would occur, the abusive speculators and moneylenders would move into the vacuum created by the lack of state funding to peasant agriculture.

Ramón always gave a lot of thought to how he could escape the hold of Don Gustavo, the local moneylender. He thought about it every year through the 1950s when he signed on as a *bracero* to pick tomatoes in California or cotton in Texas. He thought about it the whole time his children were small and he was trapped in corn and bean production because he couldn't afford the expensive chemicals he would need to grow anything more profitable. And he thought about it whenever he ran into one of the agents from the Ejidal Bank, an event—he assured me—that always filled him with anger. Ramón had no illusions that the Ejidal Bank, however many times it was purified, renovated, and even renamed at the start of a new presidential administration, was going to rescue him from his cycle of indebtedness.

Finally, when his children grew old enough to go out to work and to migrate to the United States, Ramón could count on the money they sent home to finance his planting, and this opened new possibilities. With his children's help, Ramón's first real chance to break out of debt came in the 1970s, and it came in the shape of an orange flower, the *flor de zempoaxochitl*—the marigold.

Once cultivated only for ceremonial use on November 1, All Saints' Day, marigolds are now grown as an industrial crop in central Mexico. The blossoms are ground to a paste and added to chicken feed to turn the yolks of eggs bright orange and the flesh of a cooked chicken an appetizing golden color. Here was a crop for which Ramón's eight irrigated acres were perfect. During the two-month harvest period, he cut his marigolds once a week and managed to produce almost three and one half tons each time he harvested. Ramón did well with his marigolds—so well, in fact that he was able to add two spacious rooms to his one-room dwelling, and to replace his straw roof with asbestos shingles. Most important, the profits he cleared in marigolds permitted him to take the leap that would make all the difference in his prospects in the years to come. He bought himself a small tractor and a second-hand pickup truck.

By the early 1980s Ramón was keenly aware that however profitable his marigolds had been, with the arrival of multinational agribusiness in the Bajio, there was even bigger money to be made in vegetables. Basic American Foods, Birds Eye, Campbells, Del Monte, and Green Giant had all set up processing plants on these rich plains to take advantage of the twelve-month growing season, which permits the production of vegetables and fruit for the North American market straight through the winter. Ramón started to experiment with "luxury" vegetables of his own: carrots, cucumber, broccoli, and cauliflower—fast-growing plants that can be harvested three or four times per year, plants that no traditional peasant farmer had ever even thought to grow for sale beyond the local market until the demand was created by the agribusiness giants.

But the agribusiness concerns were not interested in contracting with individual peasants like Ramón. These multinational corporations operated entirely within a logic of economies of scale, and they looked to large Mexican growers, the private landowners who had managed to concentrate hundreds of acres of land, as suppliers for their export operations and processing plants.

Still, with all he had learned from his experimentation with different crops, Ramón felt that he was ready to grow vegetables under contract to one of the big companies. The problem was to get a foot in the door. Thus it was, in 1982, that Ramón set out to see what kind of deal he could strike with Campbells.

Ramón boarded the bus for Celaya where the highway passes the *ejido* lands, about a mile from the village center. His most immediate problem was that he was unsure where to get off. As it turned out, his seatmate, a middle-aged man, well dressed in rural style—with tooled leather cowboy boots, a crisp white shirt, a bolo tie, and, most impressive, a felt ten-gallon hat—assured him that he himself would be getting off at the Campbells plant and would show Ramón the way. Ramón's new friend, Arnoldo, turned out to be an agronomist at the plant. Ramón thought he would never have a better chance to try out his audacious idea than with this agronomist, trapped as the man was in the window seat at the back of the bus. And so, as they rode through the green Bajio valley, where the sun shines almost every day of the year and a good farmer brings in four crops annually, Ramón described to Arnoldo the wondrous fertility of his eight irrigated acres and his own skill at growing vegetables—cauliflower, broccoli, and squash—as large and round and perfectly colored as his hat.

Less than a week later Arnoldo and another engineer from Campbells arrived at the Ejido Santa Marta to survey the land that Ramón and two of his neighbors proposed to cultivate under contract with the company. Here they were fêted and—an important detail that is never left out of any account of Don Ramón's journey—plied with legendary quantities of beer, which, it seems, they held very well. What the *agrónomos* found was an *ejido* that may have been shortchanged by the Ejidal Bank in terms of credit and technical advice but was the beneficiary of the careful attention of another government agency, the Ministry of Hydraulic Resources.

The *ejido* dates from 1933, when thirty-two villagers in Santa Marta were each given parcels of slightly more than twelve acres in response to years of agitation and formal petitioning by a militant group of landless peasants—among them Ramón's father. This land distribution was typical of the agrarian reform in the period before

Cárdenas came to power; the plots dealt out to the peasant petitioners were high in the *cerro* and comprised of the arid, rocky soil that formed the outlying, uncultivated area of an old *hacienda*. Some years later, another chunk of land was added to the *ejido*, roughly five miles from the original site. The new piece sat in a broad valley, but it was swampland. Finally in the 1960s, in response to the *ejidatarios*' pressure, Ministry of Hydraulic Resources engineers arrived on the scene to drain the swamp, dig wells, and irrigate the drylands. After thirty years of the most precarious existence, the *ejidatarios* of Santa Marta found themselves working some of the most fertile and potentially productive land in Mexico—eight to ten good acres apiece.

The contractual relationship with Campbells lasted only three years when Ramón and eleven of the other *ejidatarios* successfully negotiated what they regarded as a better arrangement with another U.S.-based multinational food processing company (which I will refer to here as "Fresh Veg"). Fresh Veg supplies on credit the fertilizer and insecticide that a grower will need, along with tiny broccoli seedlings from its gigantic football field–sized greenhouse in Celaya, each batch of plants carefully numbered and quality controlled. Fresh Veg also provides the requisite technical advice in the form of a field agent who travels from one farm to the next, advising growers on the exact timing for planting, irrigation, applications of chemical inputs, and harvest. When Ramón harvests his broccoli, he loads the produce onto his *camioneta* and drives to the Fresh Veg plant, where he waits for his broccoli to be inspected, graded, and unloaded. Only then does he know what price he will receive for his crop.

When I asked Ramón why he made the switch from Campbells to Fresh Veg, he said the answer was simple. In the third year of his relationship with Campbells, the company had refused to pay him for a truckload of what he described as perfectly good cucumbers which he had delivered to the plant. Some of the other *ejidatarios* contracting with Campbells had similar experiences. As Ramón says,

> *We all know from the outset that the vegetables have to meet a high standard. But we have a right to expect that good-quality produce will be accepted and credited to our accounts at full price. If the weighers and checkers start playing games with us at the point when we are sitting at the factory gates with a load of produce ripening in the back of our truck, then we might as well go back to Don Gustavo and his crooked grain scales.*

By the time that Ramón grew disillusioned with Campbells, he felt confident that he could manage not only the production of quality vegetables but also the relationship with any of the new agro-industries on the scene. The key to success, he said to me, was that once the seedlings are in the ground, you cannot relax for even a day. The application of fertilizer and insecticide, the weeding, and the irrigation all have to be carried out with precision. Even the smallest lapse in attention can result in a crop infested with some form of blight, or stunted or irregular in form and color—a crop that will be rejected at the processing plant or graded so low that the payment received will not cover the costs of production.

And the costs of production are high, Ramón explains. The biggest expense is labor. Although the original conception of the *ejido* envisioned a "family farm" in which the *ejidatario* would work his land with the occasional assistance of family members, the reality is that corn and beans fit the model but commercial crop production requires the employment of *jornaleros,* day laborers—landless peasants who work for a daily wage. Since every task to be carried out—weeding, spraying, watering, and so on—must be done "all at once" to an entire field, Ramón has to hire *jornaleros* to help him execute the job quickly. While his tractor saves him a bundle of money at some points in the growing cycle, for the other operations he needs human labor. And, ironically, the rural economy is so depressed that the cost of agricultural labor is *high*. This is because the vast majority of landless peasants have long since migrated to the cities, the border region, or the United States. The few agricultural workers who remain behind are in great demand, and although the minimum wage for agricultural labor in this region at this time was eight pesos per day, Ramón explained that he had a hard time getting anyone to come to work for him for less than eighteen to twenty pesos per day.

Then there is the matter of fungicides and insecticides. Fresh Veg will spray Ramón's crop for him or supply him with the chemicals to do the job on his own. Ramón feels he can't afford the extra expense of having the sprayers come from Fresh Veg. Thus, alone or with the help of one of his sons, Ramón mixes the chemicals and, with a tank and hose strapped to his back, he works his way upwind through his fields, pumping the poisonous spray over his broccoli plants.

It was on such an occasion a few years earlier that Ramón confused a can of concentrated insecticide with a diluted mixture, poured the wrong batch into his tank, and poisoned himself in the very first steps he took through the broccoli field. Luckily, a neighbor saw him fall in his tracks and rushed him to a nearby clinic, where the doctors—given the region in which they practice medicine—had a great deal of experience in the treatment of insecticide poisoning. Under the circumstances, Ramón spent only four days in the hospital, unable to hear, feel his fingers, or speak clearly. He was far luckier in this respect than Don Artemio, another *ejidatario* in Santa Marta, who slipped while spraying his crop and fell into a coma for eight days.

When I ask Ramón how he managed to persist at his efforts after he was poisoned, he explained that he sees the whole venture as a kind of crapshoot. Every time he brings in a high-quality harvest and is paid top peso for the truckload he delivers to Fresh Veg, he considers himself to have beaten the odds:

> *When you think about it, so many things can go wrong. Between bad weather, plant disease, or just plain bad luck, I never count too far ahead, and I always keep a small portion of my land in corn and beans, enough, at least, to feed my family.*
>
> *What's more, any day of the week Fresh Veg and the other companies may decide to go elsewhere. Or they may decide they don't want to contract with someone like me who is working a small* ejido *plot. But one thing they can't do to me now is to take away from me what I know about growing cash crops, because I've got it all up here, in my head.*

Ramón's concern that Fresh Veg might deny him a contract regardless of the quality of his crop is not unfounded. In fact, Ramón and the other eleven from Santa Marta are the only *ejidatarios* with whom Fresh Veg does business, and this arrangement is due largely to the desire and commitment of one man: Pablo Villegas, the Fresh Veg field agent for the southeastern zone of Guanajuato state.

When I ask Pablo Villegas why the arrangement he has with the *ejidatarios* of Santa Marta is anomalous, he sketches the full picture. At the Ejido Santa Marta he supervises twelve individuals whose total holdings come to less than 125 acres. All the other growers he deals with are private owners of large estates, none smaller than 150 acres and most much bigger. Working with the *ejidatarios* means establishing and maintaining good relationships with twelve people, an achievement that, on a per-acre basis requires a lot more time and effort than dealing with the other growers.

This, he said, he is willing to do, for several reasons. First of all, he grew up in the town of Salvatierra, a few kilometers from the Ejido Santa Marta, and he looks upon the *ejidatarios* as neighbors. Some, in fact, he has known since he was a boy. Second, these people are genuinely capable farmers and managers and, on an individual basis, do not require more supervision than the large landowners to whom he is supposed to supply technical assistance. Finally, he enjoys the support of his boss, the agricultural manager at the Fresh Veg plant, who shares his sense that, whatever the extra time involved, it is a decent thing to give these *ejidatarios* a chance to get in on the action of export agriculture.

Ramón is well aware that Pablo's commitment to contracting with him and the other *ejidatarios* is a personal choice on Pablo's part. "Pablo's a good guy," he tells me, "and he knows that we know what we're doing." But Ramón appreciates that the relationship that Pablo established with the *ejidatarios* does not fit comfortably within the profit-maximizing logic of a multinational enterprise. And, for this reason, Ramón feels uncertain about how long the arrangement could be sustained if either Pablo or his boss were to change jobs. Overall, Ramón thinks that there are so many uncertainties, so many things that can go wrong, that he cannot say for sure what he would be planting the next time I come to visit.

Indeed, for some of Ramón's neighbors, everything that could go wrong has gone wrong, and many have returned to corn and beans from the high-risk, high-profit crops they once tried to grow. One of them, Don Rodolfo, the village schoolmaster, was among the original three *ejidatarios* to contract with Campbells. Don Rodolfo told me that he had finally abandoned his effort to make a go of broccoli and cauliflower. He explained that his costs were too high because he had no tractor or truck.

> *Without a tractor, you have to pay* jornaleros *to harvest by hand. And with no* camioneta, *you have to hire* fletes, *commercial haulers, to carry your crop to the processing plant where you are*

> *forking out money the whole time they're waiting in line for quality inspection and unloading.*

Perhaps because he has gone into debt in his effort to grow cash crops, the schoolteacher was the person in Ejido Santa Marta who seemed to have the clearest take on the relationship between the growers and the agribusiness companies.

> *It's important to remember that we're the ones who take all the risks. Whether I contract with Campbells or Fresh Veg or any of the other companies, I am the one who loses out when things go badly. They don't lose at all. If something goes wrong and I can't deliver vegetables, they just buy from someone else.*

When Don Rodolfo had access to a brother-in-law's pickup truck, he just about broke even. But when this relative sold his *camioneta* to pay his own debts, Don Rodolfo had to add to his other expenses the cost of transport to the plant at two hundred pesos per trip. At this point, he calculated that he had no chance to turn a profit, even with a top-quality harvest.

This, Don Rodolfo says, is the difference between the haves and the have-nots in the Ejido Santa Marta. Those who have done well enough in the past to purchase a truck and tractor can latch onto the new opportunities that opened in the Mexican countryside when agribusiness corporations appeared on the scene. But Don Rodolfo says that the people who never managed to save enough to equip themselves with these things, those who have to pay others to harvest and haul, do better to plant low-risk, low-tech *maíz* and *frijol* on their land and find something else to do with themselves—like migrate to the border, the cities, or the United States, as most of the adult population of the countryside already has.

Don Rodolfo thinks that, in a way, Santa Marta is a microcosm of all of Mexico, or at least of all of rural Mexico. Those who are already better off, he says, are the ones who will profit from the arrival of the big, foreign companies. Everyone else will be lucky if they can just keep themselves in corn and beans.

4 P.M.: *Martín Calderón*

At four in the afternoon, the light has just begun to soften over Martín Calderón's green and golden fields, which stretch in every direction as far as the eye can see. Riding the five miles of road that runs from the entry gate to the heart of what was once the Hacienda Linda Vista, I am amazed at both the scale and the extraordinary variety of crops under cultivation. As we move from field to field the heady fragrance of herbs and spices fills the air: basil, coriander, and thyme to our right; parsley, marjoram, and shallots to our left; sage and chiles before us; and acres and acres of garlic and onion behind. Beyond the rows of cottonwood trees and prickly pear plants that serve as windbreaks, I see swatches of green, which, I am told, are fields of lettuce, broccoli, cauliflower, squash, celery, carrots, peas, beans, and sweet corn. In all, Martín has hundreds and hundreds of acres planted in export vegetables, and the rest in wheat, sorghum, barley, and alfalfa.

Of course, these are not really all Martín's fields. The fertile bottomland he manages in the Bajio region belongs, technically speaking, to ten different landowners, men and women Martín refers to as his "associates." While the fifteen-hundred-acre spread is administered as a single unit, "we are not able to say this openly," Martín cautions me, because the agrarian law does not permit the concentration of irrigated landholdings above 100 hectares (247 acres). Very soon, Martín assures me, the new president will change the agrarian law, bring land distribution to an official end, and any need for secrecy will be over.

These changes will mark a new dawn for Martín and the other large landholders of the rich Bajio region. Never again, Martín says, will they need to worry that landless peasants will invade their estates and demand the distribution of land in excess of the official limits. Never again will Martín and his associates have to debate the wisdom of improving their holdings with the addition of roads, irrigation canals, and wells for fear that the infrastructural improvements in themselves will affect the classification of the land as "available" or "unavailable" for distribution to landless petitioners. No longer will they have to go through the costly charade of erecting fences between contiguous properties that are, in fact, worked as a single unit. The land reform will be over, Martín explains, and the very concept of the neolatifundism will be replaced by the positive image of a productive, modern estate on which progressive, risk-taking capitalists are performing a service to the Mexican economy.

Martín explains that most of the large estates in the region are held by families that owned huge *haciendas* before the Mexican Revolution and the agrarian reform reduced them to a fraction of their former landed wealth. At the same time, however, the land distribution had what Martín characterizes as positive consequences, in that it forced these families to diversify into a variety of economic activities. Generally, the largest landowners dealt out their *haciendas* among different family members. Then, in accordance with the agrarian code, the new owner of each *hacienda* designated the most productive 150-hectare (370-acre) area of the estate as the section he or she would retain. The agrarian law allowed these people to sell other land that was not immediately required for distribution to petitioning peasant communities. The capital they raised in these land deals was thus available to underwrite new ventures in agricultural machinery, production of fertilizer and insecticide, and, eventually, even high-tech food processing—ventures that have made the biggest landowners in the Bajio among the richest and most powerful agribusiness people in Mexico.

In the case of his own family, Martín says that their land acquisitions date to the period in which large chunks of the old *haciendas* were sold off. Today their agribusiness interests are organized into a holding company that controls what he describes as three totally integrated sectors. The holding company is a family enterprise, but minority shares have been sold to investors outside the family. Martín says that, theoretically, they would have no objection to investment of foreign capital. Thus far, however, they have had no takers from abroad.

The base of the operation rests on agricultural production, where Martín, himself, takes charge. "The wonder of the Bajio region," he says, "is that just about anything will grow here. There are easily forty different crops that we have grown successfully. It's just a matter of knowing when to plant." Once the breadbasket of Mexico, the Bajio continues to be a center of wheat production, but all kinds of basic grains and vegetables grow equally well or even better, and wheat is gradually being displaced by export crops.

Before I set out for the estate that Martín refers to as the *rancho,* he explained his strategy for production. Part of the land is planted in "speculative crops," that is, the vegetables for which the market price varies. The rest he keeps in wheat, corn, and sorghum—crops for which the price is fixed and guaranteed by the Mexican state.

Of course, Martín knows that state price supports are bound to be reduced or disappear completely if the Salinas regime succeeds in implementing its full plan for a free market economy. But even then, he says, the price of basic grain crops will not vary in the way that the market for speculative vegetables rises and falls. His plan, for the present, is to continue to plant wheat, corn, and sorghum. Martín figures he will eventually phase out the wheat once Canadian and U.S. imports begin to flow into Mexico under the free trade agreement. There is no way, he says, that he can compete with the productivity of U.S. and Canadian wheat farmers. But sorghum can be planted in the rainy season which saves him the expense of irrigation and it grows so well in the Bajio, that the thirty-four tons per acre yield that he and others attain, Martín insists, is a world record. Corn, he tells me, is a tricky issue, because the bulk of corn consumed now in Mexico is imported from the United States and Canada, where the average yield is four times higher than that achieved by the most efficient Mexican growers. Nonetheless, Martín thinks he will continue planting corn.

> *The trick is that the Mexican government imports the yellow corn that is cultivated in your country as cattle feed. To make a decent-tasting tortilla, you need white corn. I believe that the Mexicans who can afford it will pay a premium to eat white corn tortillas. So I want to keep some of my land in white* maíz, *because I think white corn is going to become a kind of luxury crop.*

In addition to grain, Martín cultivates broccoli, cauliflower, cucumber, and spinach under contract with Fresh Veg and other large food processing companies that buy his vegetables for their fresh-frozen production. But for two key details, the arrangement that Martín has with the food processors is fundamentally the same as the one that Don Ramón and the *ejidatarios* of Santa Marta have with Fresh Veg. One important difference is that Martín does not require any advanced credit from Fresh Veg, and therefore the multinational guarantees him a higher price than the one they offer to farmers they have to finance. The other critical difference is that Martín's contract with these companies represents for him only a small fraction of his complex of financial dealings, one that is in no way crucial to his personal or corporate survival.

Nevertheless, like Don Ramón, Martín receives his seeds or his numbered, quality-controlled seedlings from the contracting company, the company's field agent visits Martín's estate (although Martín has his own agronomists on staff to coordinate the agricultural operations involved in growing the vegetables), and at harvest time Martín hires freelance truckers who deliver the produce to the processing plant, where his account is credited in accordance with the generally high quality of the crop he is able to produce.

In addition to the vegetables Martín grows under contract with processing companies, he is expanding his fields of onion, garlic, celery, parsley, and coriander. He grows these crops for direct export to Europe and the United States or for sale in Mexico. The best-looking onions and herbs, he explains, are marketed fresh. The rest are taken to the dehydration plant to be dried, pulverized, and packaged as spices. Martín points out that while people normally think of the Bajio as dominated by the U.S. agribusiness giants, his family's dehydration and packaging plant is one of twelve Mexican-owned operations now processing agricultural produce in the region.

When I ask him how the Mexican frozen vegetable outfits manage to compete with companies like Green Giant and Birds Eye, Martín explains that they do not compete directly but work with and through the U.S.-based multinationals. They can simply freeze and package the vegetables under the Green Giant or the Birds Eye labels, and then turn these bags of frozen vegetables over to the American companies to market in the United States. Alternatively, they hire their own brokers to market their frozen produce in the United States, or they package vegetables for sale under the store-brand labels of American supermarkets. Martín says that between the multinationals and the Mexican processors who collaborate with the multinationals, Mexican frozen broccoli holds a 70 percent share of the U.S. market.

The third part of the Calderón's integrated operation is the family's agricultural supply and machinery business. This operation, managed by Martín's brother, Rodrigo, involves the assembly of machinery from parts manufactured in Europe and imported into Mexico. The tractors and farm implements they turn out, including ploughs, reapers, tillers, harrows, sprayers, fumigators, and levelers, are all scaled down for the Mexican market, because the U.S.-made equipment is generally too large for Mexican agriculture. This sector of the family enterprise also includes distributorship of equipment, insecticides, and fungicides previously sold in Mexico by a large multinational company that pulled out of the country, turning its business over to the Calderóns, who act as the Mexican agents for these goods. The family also holds the distribution rights to a number of products made in Mexico and foreign equipment they import into Mexico. In addition, Rodrigo oversees a factory producing chemical fertilizer, a new venture that is meant to replace the fertilizer from the state-owned company, Fertimex, that the Calderóns distributed in the past.

Martín explains that these operations are not only integrated with one another but also are closely tied to transnational capital, despite the lack of foreign investment in the holding company. I ask Martín whether it bothers him to be linked to multinational corporations in this way. Does he feel nationalist stirrings when he looks at the dominance of U.S.-based transnationals in his home region? Martín says:

> *The truth is that the only people who carry on about the invasion of Mexico by foreign companies are the Mexicans who are incompetent, who are unable to succeed without exaggerated protection by the government. These are the same people who oppose the free trade agreement because they will never be able to compete, since they're not efficient at what they do.*

Personally, I couldn't care less where capital comes from. If foreign companies are respectful of our laws, if they share their technology with us as the agro-industries have, I have no problem with them. Of course, there are examples of companies that have one set of decent standards for their home country and apply lax standards here. But in general the foreign companies that have come to the Bajio have been leaders and have pointed the way for Mexican entrepreneurs to follow.

If there is anyone in Mexico who looks forward to NAFTA with good cheer, high hopes, and confidence, that person is Martín Calderón. Martín tells me that he is optimistic by nature. But while his feelings about NAFTA may be a matter of his personal disposition, they also spring from the fact that he is perfectly positioned to take advantage of the new situation.

When Martín talks about the free trade agreement, the views he expresses are virtually identical to those of the most enthusiastic government promoters. He begins, as they do, by acknowledging that the Mexican economy was "overprotected," and that this policy lulled domestic entrepreneurs into the belief that they would prosper indefinitely, even without updating their technology or striving for efficiency. He sees the captive market produced by the high tariff protection as a great disincentive to experimentation and innovation. He notes that the most inefficient Mexican businesses will inevitably disappear. And he speaks of the policy changes instituted by President Salinas as a kind of "wake-up call" received by entrepreneurs like himself.

Productivity was never an important issue for us in agriculture, because the government set all the prices and heavily subsidized the inputs. Then, two years ago, we suddenly found ourselves facing an altogether new reality that has forced us to awaken from the dream world in which we lived, where everything was simple and easy.

Having been abruptly forced out of dreamland into the real world of international competition, Martín remains cheerfully optimistic because the complex nature of his integrated operation gives him a variety of strategies to pursue; and even when he looks beyond his personal situation to the broader picture, he sees Mexican agribusiness as well placed to profit from free trade:

NAFTA gives us fantastic opportunities because Mexico is blessed with so many advantages in climate, primary materials, and the cheap manpower needed for labor-intensive agricultural processes. Our agriculture complements that of the United States and Canada. In the Bajio we bring in two harvests during the same winter months when North American fields are dormant. To be sure, many growers are going to have to shift from grains, which are cultivated much more efficiently in the U.S. and Canada, to winter fruits and vegetables. But the opportunities to expand in horticultural products is almost limitless.

While the other entrepreneurs with whom I spoke in the textile and electronics industries said they could not predict what changes would come about in their sector before the final NAFTA document was signed and sealed, Martín foresaw a series of transformations that he was certain would immeasurably improve his access to the U.S. food market. For a small, independent food processing firm like his, he says, NAFTA is a breakthrough that will free him from a series of nontariff barriers that previously restricted his ability to sell in the United States.

For example, when exporting our garlic into the U.S., we were always in trouble with the Food and Drug Administration because of what they describe as our "excessive use" of insecticide in growing our vegetables. For political reasons they held Mexican growers to standards that they would never dare to impose on

California farmers. Other problems arose because we use European-made insecticides and fungicides that do not have FDA approval since they are not marketed in the United States. These are the kind of barriers we've faced in the past, but all of this will be cleared away in the free trade talks.

Martín thinks that it will eventually be as easy for him to sell his produce in the United States as it is for the Bajio-based Green Giant or Birds Eye plants to ship their frozen vegetables northward for distribution by their parent companies.

And Martín is just as cheerful about the prospects for further diversification into other luxury crops. On my way to Martín's headquarters in Celaya, I passed through the strawberry zone of the Bajio, centered around the Birds Eye and General Foods freezing plants in Irapuato. I ask Martín about the boom that has made frozen strawberries one of Mexico's three leading agricultural exports.

Martín sees no limits in the future expansion of Mexican berries in Europe and Japan. He also has high hopes for the development of "fancy-pack" fruits and vegetables that, given the availability of cheap labor, can be grown, trimmed, and packaged by hand in Mexico to be marketed in vegetable "boutiques" in the United States. Korean immigrant grocers, he explains, have been the pioneers in this area. They have demonstrated that there is virtually no upper limit to the price that North American consumers will pay to enjoy a "perfect" piece of fruit or a vegetable that appears "out of season." Already Bajio growers are experimenting with cantaloupes that are rotated by hand every day so that they will ripen in perfect symmetry. Martín says that these fruits currently sell in Japan at five dollars each.

I ask Martín if avocados would not be a good export crop for him. He explains that a farmer needs the right kind of soil to grow avocados—soil that is "fluffy" rather than hard clay, which packs the roots and makes the plant susceptible to disease. Martín says he has the wrong kind of soil. But other Mexican growers, he claims, could make a fortune in avocados, except for the protection won by the California growers who have successfully excluded Mexican avocados from the U.S. market.

As it now stands, the only avocado exporter who has survived in Mexico has done so by marketing the crop in Europe. But Martín cautions that this is a very risky business. The avocados have to be kept at exactly 41°F (5°C) during the entire four-week period from the time they are picked, packed, and shipped to the time they reach the European grocer. The cost is about five thousand dollars for each container shipment, which works out to only twelve cents per pound. But the frightening part is that the one Mexican grower who has been successful at exporting to Europe—a woman who grows and packages avocados in Michoacán—ships 120 containers a month. Were there to be a some kind of "scare" involving avocados, as there was a few years back with Chilean grapes, about three million dollars would be lost on the avocados in the pipeline, even though they might not be tainted in any way. Martín says that, under the circumstances, the risk is too high. But with free trade, Mexican growers would be able to market avocados in the United States, and the transportation costs and risks would be vastly reduced.

On the return journey from Martín's estate to Celaya, I see an area where the land is parched and the only thing under cultivation appears to be a few stalks of sad-looking corn. I know without asking that these must be *ejido* lands.

Up to this point we have talked about the peasantry in terms of the history of agrarian struggle in the region. Martín has discussed the peasants only as the people he must worry may invade his land and cost him a whole planting cycle before he can get the state governor to have them removed. Even in this context, however, he refers to the peasants sympathetically. He sees them chiefly as the victims of political demagogues who manipulate the landless. For Martín, the peasants are tools of these self-appointed *jefes* who grow rich by collecting money from the landless with the promise of enrolling them on a list of land applicants. He insists that land invasions run in cycles precisely because it has traditionally been part of the demagogic appeal of each outgoing president to stimulate land invasions with vague promises of further land distributions. In the past, Martín says, every six years, at the end of each presidential term, the landowners had to hold their breath to see who would become the target of invasions by the landless. Today, however, he is breathing easier because he finds it inconceivable that the incumbent president, Carlos Salinas, will leave office without securing the property rights of landowners.

When I question Martín about the one-room huts, the straw roofs, the arid soil, the ox-drawn plows that are visible to anyone passing along the road where the *ejido* lands abut the state highway, he responds with discussion about productivity. For him the tragedy of the *ejido* system is that it has never been and cannot be a productive enterprise. The *ejido* plots were never large enough to enjoy economies of scale, and the *ejidatarios* themselves never received the training they needed to work their land efficiently.

In words that remind me of Don Ramón's description of the demands of his own work routine, Martín says,

> *The problem is that agriculture requires real management planning and scientific knowledge and all the modern concepts that industrial enterprises use. Nature is very demanding and sets all the conditions to which you have to respond. Everything has to be done with precise timing.*

Evidently Martín is unfamiliar with the history of the Cárdenas land distribution, in which every *ejido* community was endowed not only with a primary school but also with agricultural training courses that were meant to turn the teenage sons of *ejidatarios* into a corps of agronomists capable of managing the community's resources. Martín says,

> *Unfortunately, our* ejidatarios *lack the skills and training to be productive. If only there had been a program of education for the* ejidatarios *when the land reform was carried out, little by little they would have developed the skill and knowledge to make the* ejido *a productive enterprise. But, sadly, the* ejidatarios *have remained in a state of backwardness.*

Martín recognizes that some *ejidatarios* do not fit this description. There are cases, he says, of *ejidatarios* who work up to 250 acres of land because, though untrained, "they are naturally intelligent and they develop the skill to manage large areas of land. Soon they end up working the parcels of everyone around them who has given up on making a go of *ejido* agriculture."

For Martín, the solution lies in a change in the agrarian law which would permit the association of small and large growers with the *ejidatarios,* who would then enjoy the benefits of using the equipment and managerial skill that someone like him can offer.

> *With a hundred hectares or less you cannot invest in a tractor, let alone a spray or drip irrigation system. This has always been a fundamental problem of the agrarian law, which never allowed anyone to benefit openly from economies of scale by forming associations. But in this kind of association the income of the* ejidatarios *will rise and productivity will increase. The* ejidatarios *will have the advantage of receiving a weekly salary rather than waiting three or six months to cash in on the harvest.*

Martín argues that under the present system the *ejidatarios* end up falling into the hands of usurious moneylenders because they can't make it from one harvest to the next. But with the new type of association they will have a fixed income and at least *some* of the profits from the harvests. Under the circumstances, he believes their standard of living is bound to rise.

> *With the technology and the equipment that the large growers have and a bit more investment in machinery, a lot more land may be productively cultivated. Even with the existing machinery another 30 percent of land could be worked easily. You don't even need much additional investment, especially for the grower who already knows the zone, industry, and markets.*

I ask Martín if the confidence he feels in the present administration and its program for agriculture is likely to carry over into the future. "In my view," he says,

> *Salinas is the best president we have ever had. In two years he has brought about changes that I would have thought impossible. Under Salinas, the PRI is the party that has solutions to our problems. If Salinas can keep doing what he's doing, Mexico will be an entirely different place when he leaves office. That's because he's not only thinking in terms of his six-year term but is solidifying changes for the future. Take, for example, the free trade agreement. It will put a straightjacket on any future leader who might want to return the country to socialism. It simply won't be possible to return to the past. We have long needed a president like Salinas. I'd like to see the constitution rewritten to allow him to succeed himself in office.*

7

The Border

6 P.M.: *Rosario Valdez*

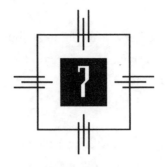

At 6 P.M., María del Rosario Valdez is one of millions of Mexicans stopped dead in traffic. The Transportes Frontera bus in which she set out half an hour earlier had barely pushed its way out of the Central del Norte, the main station for northbound departures, when it was caught up in the river of cars, trucks, and buses inching northward toward the toll road to Querétaro. When traffic is this blocked, Rosario knows that it can take an hour and a half just to get clear of the city. The worst of it is that the first stretch of highway runs uphill. Here the diesel fumes of the vehicles creeping along in low gear make the gray-brown smog that always hangs over the city even darker with the carbon particles that belch from hundreds of exhaust pipes. Rosario sits back in her seat and tries to relax. Soon it will be dark; at least then she will no longer have to look at the exhaust fumes.

Rosario has learned how to relax on the trip to the border because it is a journey she makes every week. She sets out each Thursday evening at 5:30 on the same second-class bus to Nuevo Laredo, Tamaulipas. Roughly five hours later the bus will pull into a restaurant along the highway in San Luis Potosí. There everyone will disembark and eat an overpriced supper. Once on board again, with a fresh driver, the bus will not stop until it reaches the border at eight the next morning. The ticket costs 117 pesos and the trip always takes fifteen to sixteen hours. Rosario sometimes dozes on and off through the night. But she never sleeps.

Arriving at Nuevo Laredo, Rosario eats breakfast at the bus station and takes a taxi from the terminal to the border crossing. Making her way past the beggars, the windshield washers, the sword swallowers, the children selling Chiclets, and the others whose attention is fixed on the cars waiting in line to cross, Rosario joins the mass of people who flow northward to the other side on foot, most going as day workers and the rest as shoppers. Here she passes over to Laredo, Texas—generally with no difficulty. This is possible, she tells me, because she has all the proper papers needed for temporary entry into the United States. Rosario was able to obtain the visa and other credentials because she applied when she was still employed as an elevator operator in the Ministry of the Interior. As she explains, "If you have a fixed job in Mexico with an identity card and a letter from your workplace, you can get all the legal papers you need because you don't look like someone who is crossing the border to stay."

In all, Rosario calculates that it takes her only an hour to go from the bus station in Mexico to the U.S. side of the border. By 9 A.M. she is ready to set about her business in Laredo. A twenty-dollar cab ride brings her to the object of her long journey, Los Tres Hermanos, a huge wholesaler of used clothing.

Rosario can't tell me exactly where the used clothing sold at Los Tres Hermanos comes from. What she knows is that it arrives in container shipments from Los Angeles, New York, and other large U.S. cities. Each week ten to twenty tractor trailers deliver between two hundred and three hundred bales of used clothing, each bale weighing somewhere between one half and three quarters of a ton. The clothing is unloaded at Los Tres Hermanos and spread out on tables where it is picked over and selected by hundreds of used-clothing vendors like Rosario, who converge on the store from all parts of northern and central Mexico.

Rosario has been buying and selling used clothing since the early 1980s. That is when she lost her government job in the austerity program that forced the Ministry of the Interior to cut thousands of workers from its budget. Rosario isn't sure who runs the ministry's elevators now, or if those who want to travel to the upper floors just push the buttons for themselves. But with the severance pay she received when her job was eliminated, she had the stake she needed to launch her business in used clothing.

Rosario had always liked the idea of selling. Even as a little girl she used to help out in an uncle's grocery in the peasant village where she grew up in Oaxaca, the village where her parents still cultivate their *maíz* and *frijol*. But she came to the capital, as did most of the girls from her pueblo, to work as a domestic servant, and when she met and married her husband, Alejandro, he found her a job in the ministry offices where he was already employed as a janitor.

Rosario explains to me that it is very difficult to leave a government job because of the access it gives to the state workers' hospital, the government housing projects, and the state employees' stores where food prices are lower. "If you're running an elevator in a government office, you can't say to yourself, 'Maybe I would be happier selling clothing in a market.' You have to think of your children and their security."

But when Rosario was laid off, the way was open for her to try her luck at market sales. To get started, she could count on the support and guidance of her mother-in-law, a woman with twenty-five years of experience in used clothing. With her severance pay pinned into their pockets, the two women traveled to the border, where Rosario was to learn how to purchase the stock and, most important, how to get it back to Mexico City. The routine Rosario established under her mother-in-law's tutelage differs little from the one she now follows every week.

Once she arrives at the immense *bodega,* or warehouse, Rosario sets about choosing the clothing that will become the inventory for her next week of sales in the *tianguis* circuit where she has her stall. The key, she explains, is to know what will move and how much to spend. There are other *bodegas* in Laredo where the clothing is cheaper, but very worn, and still others that specialize in clothing that is almost new but costs a good deal more. Rosario always buys at Los Tres Hermanos because that is where she finds the quality of used clothing that she feels is most likely to appeal to the customers who wait for her weekly appearance in their neighborhood *tianguis.* Normally it takes her a good five or six hours to find exactly what she wants in the massive piles of pants, dresses, slacks, shirts, shoes, belts, and accessories. But by midafternoon, for $150, Rosario generally buys five hundred pounds of used garments, a thousand pieces in all, packed and ready for transport to Mexico.

When I comment that this much clothing for $150 seems like a good deal, Rosario smiles and reminds me that purchasing the clothing is the cheapest, most straightforward part of her transactions. The real uncertainty and expense comes with bringing the goods back to Mexico. Rosario cannot tell me why commerce in used clothing should be prohibited, since the tariff barriers established to protect Mexican manufacturers were dropped in 1986. What she can say for certain is that she must pay bribes that range as high as $300 on her $150 worth of used clothing—payments that are referred to as "duties" by the customs officials, but are not recorded, stamped, or registered in any way.

> *When we cross to the Mexican side in the* camioneta *that we hire to go from the* bodega *to the bus station, they stop us at the* aduana *and ask, "What are you bringing in?" When we say*

what we've got in the bundles, they tell us how much money we have to pay them to be allowed to cross with our clothing. It's very simple. They just cite us a figure.

When I ask if she couldn't bargain with them as one does in Mexico City when being shaken down by the *policía de tránsito* after having made—or perhaps not made—an illegal turn, Rosario explains that it is difficult.

Sometimes we say, "Oh, I don't have the money, I spent it all in Laredo," but this generally doesn't work. They just tell us, "Good, then go back to Texas with your stuff." At that point we begin to bargain a little saying, "Oh, you're asking so much, you didn't charge us so much last time," or "the other customs guy, the nice one, he doesn't charge us so much." But in the end they don't come down more than a few pesos from their original price.

At the bridge from Laredo, Rosario normally pays 200–250 pesos to the customs agents and border police. At the bus station another set of officials and police charge again as much, as do a third set who are posted at a customs station about twelve miles from the border. Failure to pay the *mordidas* at any of these points would mean that her entire cargo of clothing would be confiscated. So Rosario pays what she is charged, as do the thousands of others who pass the *frontera* every day, whether carrying legal or contraband goods. "Can you imagine," she says, "how many people cross the border in the space of an hour? Every one of them pays *mordidas* many times the price of the goods they are carrying. No one escapes."

Even paying the bribes provides no absolute guarantee of relief from extortion. As Rosario explains:

On four different occasions they impounded my merchandise. When they do this they give you a little piece of paper that's sup-

posed to be some kind of receipt to retrieve the goods when you have paid your duties. Then they send you running back and forth to this office and to that office to report to this comandante and that comandante. They send you chasing all over the place while all the time it's costing you money to stay over at the border. In the end, you don't get your stuff back anyway. I've never known anyone who actually managed to retrieve the goods.

I ask Rosario if the free trade agreement won't change all this, if it won't cut her costs by more than half, once her activities are no longer defined as illegal. She stares at me for a moment and then replies patiently,

You have to understand, thousands of people at the border live from collecting bribes. The entire economy of cities like Nuevo Laredo rests on the money people extort from others. It's a way of life. One thing you can be sure of is that these guys are not going to stand around with their arms folded while their main source of income disappears. If free trade comes, they'll find another way to shake us down, or maybe they won't let us cross at all. The NAFTA treaty isn't meant to rescue people like us, it's meant to help the rich.

Having worked her way through the obstacles presented at three different customs posts, by 6:30 or 7 P.M. on Friday, Rosario has passed the twelve-mile checkpoint and can reboard the bus for the trip back to Mexico City. The bus is generally filled with other used-clothing merchants from the capital, people who have become like family to Rosario. "We all know one another. We look out for each other," she explains.

Once in her seat, with the bundles of clothing secured to the top of the bus or stored in the luggage compartments underneath, Rosario dozes until the bus pulls into the Central del Norte between nine and ten on Saturday morning. Here she disembarks, takes a cab directly to the market, grabs a bite to eat at a neighboring stall, and begins to sell the merchandise she has brought back from the border. Whatever remains of the previous week's stock of a thousand pieces, she bundles into a separate pile for sale to another peddler, Don Serafín, who specializes in ultracheap used clothing, selling door-to-door whatever the regular used-clothing vendors have been unable to unload.

With the old merchandise out of the way, Rosario organizes the newly arrived articles and sets into the rhythm of market sales that will take her to a different neighborhood each day. Saturday the entire *tianguis* moves to a plaza where business is generally brisk. On Sunday the market is held in a quieter neighborhood, but the merchandise moves relatively well. Rosario's Monday location is in a good spot, but the neighborhood is very poor. Tuesday's market is entirely unpredictable, especially in the rainy season. Wednesday and Thursday are very slow, in part because the best merchandise is gone. Thursday afternoon Rosario is off again to Laredo. When she leaves for the border to replenish her stock, her mother-in-law fills in at the market and at home until Rosario's return on Saturday morning.

When I ask Rosario if it wouldn't be easier to sell something she could buy from the wholesalers in Tepito, she responds in a manner very similar to Miguel when he explained why he did not want to switch from *fayuca* to another product. She feels there is too much competition in other areas, and she thinks the Tepiteño wholesalers charge too much, that they wouldn't give her a break, no matter how steady a customer she might become. Above all, she says, "anyone who is willing to make the sacrifices that we make traveling all the way to Laredo to buy goods can do all right with used clothing. You can't get rich, but you can get by."

Doña Anita, however, has another theory. Doña Anita runs the taco stand adjacent to Rosario's stall. She has sold tacos on the street since coming to Mexico City as a child from her native

Puebla more than sixty years ago. She knows all the merchants and has her own theories about their preferences.

The weekly trip to the border, she says, grinds people down. But for the women, she observes, it offers a break from the drudgery of their lives at home. Market people work every day of the week, but the market women work every day *and* every night, because they leave their stalls only to go home to face the cooking, cleaning, and child care. For the women, the trip to Laredo is grueling, she says, but in a certain sense, it gives them two days of relief from housework, husbands, children, and in-laws. And in that respect, it is appealing. Doña Anita says,

> *I tell my old man, "*viejo, *watch your step or I'm going to switch from tacos to used clothing and leave you every week to go to the border." The truth is that life on the border moves faster than here. People feel different, more alive when they go to the border, even if they go every week, and have to sit up sixteen hours on a second-class bus to get there.*

6 P.M.: *Adelita Sandoval*

At 6 P.M., Adelita Sandoval has returned to Tijuana from San Diego and is preparing dinner for herself, her husband Héctor, and the three children who still remain at home. She has a pot of *frijoles* boiling on the stove and is making *tortillas de harina*, the flour tortillas that are to northern Mexicans what corn tortillas are to those in the south. Adelita grew up in the state of Michoacán, west of Mexico City, so she came to flour tortillas relatively late in life. It is a source of pride for her that she now makes them so well.

> *It's not easy to mix the right proportion of flour, water, salt, and lard that gives you the very thin, delicate* tortilla de harina. *If*

you're not careful, they come out as thick and tough as huaraches, *or gummy and tasteless like the ones you get on the other side. Handling corn meal, shaping and patting it into a satisfactory* tortilla de maíz *is a whole different story from what you see me doing here. I was already a mother with five children before I came north and had to learn to make wheat tortillas. But now I really get them just right: thin—so thin you can almost see through them—but strong enough so they don't break and leave you sitting with beans in your lap.*

The flour, salt, and lard that Adelita is using in her cooking, the sugar, coffee, rice, beans, and all the staples with which she stocks her kitchen, are goods she buys on the "other side," in supermarkets or little groceries in Chula Vista or San Ysidro, California. When Adelita feels she can afford meat or dairy products or fresh produce she also purchases these goods across the border. Adelita says she finds it strange that the fruit and vegetables she buys in San Ysidro come from Mexico, but are available in California at prices lower than what she would pay for them in Tijuana. Moreover, the local Mexican markets offer only the sad-looking produce that has been left behind because it fails to meet export standards.

Reflecting on the many strange things she sees every day as she moves back and forth between the two worlds, Adelita tells me, "I don't notice it now as much as I once did, because I've lived here for twelve years and I guess I've gotten used to it. But, believe me, life at the border is really crazy."

First, we're all running to the other side to buy manufactured things we can't get here, or that cost too much here. If you want a hair dryer, or a radio, or clothing for your kids, or somebody steals your gas cap or breaks off your windshield wiper, you've got to find a way to get to the other side, or you give money to a friend who can cross to buy you these things in Chula Vista.

And then the americanos *come over here to buy huge sacks of rice and beans and flour. Or at least they* used to, *when prices on these goods were still set by the government. Now that the politicians have taken away all the price controls, we're running over there to buy even the most basic things. That's because, strange as it seems, it's cheaper to buy a bag of rice in the U.S., which is a rich country, than in Mexico, which is poor. And this is true even when something* comes *from Mexico, like oranges or tomatoes, or gasoline.*

Adelita reminds me that all these patterns shift radically with any change in the relationship between the peso and the dollar. Whenever the peso is devalued, *tijuanenses* find they can no longer afford to buy even the best bargains offered for sale in dollars. Then border cities like San Ysidro turn into ghost towns, with commerce falling to about 20 percent of what merchants there think of as normal. The border remains open to that half of the population of Tijuana who have the requisite papers—the passports or the border-crossing passes—that admit them into the United States under carefully defined, temporary conditions. But they don't have money to spend on the other side. And so, mostly, they stay home.

When U.S. citizens cross in the other direction, going from San Diego County into Baja California, the border may well seem the most open in the world, and the welcome they receive on the Mexican side is eager, to say the least. Motorists with California plates are waved through by the Mexican border police without inspection of any kind. Other visitors from the United States opt to ride the trolley that runs from downtown San Diego to the borderline, or they park their cars on the San Ysidro side and walk a few hundred feet into Mexico. Here they are channeled directly into Avenida Revolución, lined with bars, T-shirt stores, a Woolworth, a Jack in the Box, a jai alai complex, and dozens of curio shops filled with "handicrafts" that are, in fact, mass-produced in Mexican or Asian factories. On Avenida Revolución day-trippers can pose for a photo with a donkey painted to look like a zebra, they can stock up on tequila, *ronpope* (spiked eggnog), or Kahlúa, or they can view one of the strip shows that open at eight in the morning.

There is, however, something odd about all this tourist traffic. The population of Tijuana is more than one million and it "plays host" to fifty million visitors each year, but the city boasts only twenty-five hotels. Rarely do the American visitors stay the night. They troop through the markets by day and to the bars at night. They spend their dollars, they pass under a sign that exclaims in English, COME BACK SOON, AMIGOS! THANK YOU FOR YOUR VISIT, and they go home to sleep in California.

Crossing the border in the other direction is a different story, as Adelita knows very well.

> *It seems like half my life has been spent trying to get to the other side. The funny thing is that I didn't come here thinking I would work in the United States. I came to Tijuana to find a job in the assembly plants. I came because I had a cousin who was already working here in a factory. But after I'd lived and worked in Tijuana a few years I got the picture: you can work hard and get paid in pesos, or you can work hard and get paid in dollars. You can work here and get paid by the day, or work there and get paid by the hour. And even someone like me who comes straight from a little village in Michoacán can figure out which is better.*

Adelita came to Tijuana in 1980 to escape a violent alcoholic husband. She arrived with her widowed mother and five children, who ranged in age from eight months to ten years. The seven of them moved into a one-room dwelling rented by Adelita's cousin, Dolores, who had two small children of her own.

Adelita says that, at the time, she didn't worry much about crowding ten people into one room. She was one of eleven children and was used to the idea that children can sleep four or five to a bed, if, indeed, there is a bed for them to sleep in. What *did* worry her was the stench of garbage, raw sewage, and what she later learned was industrial waste that came from the "stream" that ran through the center of the settlement. In the countryside the air was often filled with the odor of fresh manure. But this smell was something completely different. Cañon Inez, the *colonia* where Dolores rented her cinderblock room, was, like most new housing on the border, perched precariously on a hillside and lacked the most rudimentary services: water, electricity, paved roads, and sewer pipes. In the rainy season the stream swelled to the size of a small river, overflowed, and spilled human waste and unidentified chemical substances into the muddy streets of the *colonia*.

When Adelita settled there, Cañon Inez was occupied almost entirely by new migrants and comprised overwhelmingly of households headed by women. Many of the women in Cañon Inez had been abandoned by the fathers of their children or, like Adelita, had chosen to leave abusive husbands. They counted on the new border plants to provide a way out of an untenable situation—a way out that previously had not existed for many women in Mexico.

Virtually everyone in Cañon Inez worked in the *maquila* plants. Mostly foreign-owned, these factories were constructed under the special tariff arrangements of the Border Industrialization Program, which began in 1965. By the time Adelita arrived in 1980, hundreds of *maquilas* were operating in Tijuana, and more than a thousand in the border region as a whole. These plants imported their raw materials or components duty-free from the United States. They then manufactured, assembled, or processed goods and exported the finished product directly to the United States, paying duties only on the value added to the products in Mexico. With almost the entire adult population of Cañon Inez employed in this sector, Adelita quickly learned all she would need to know to find work in a plant.

While Adelita's mother looked after the children, Dolores accompanied Adelita to the *maquila* where, together with two hundred other seamstresses, she produced ladies' apparel.

> *It wasn't difficult to find that first job. Dolores recommended me and all I needed to show was a birth certificate. They didn't even ask to see my primary school certificate. I started work that same morning.*
>
> *What was difficult was the work itself, or at least the conditions in which we had to work. I had always liked to sew, and we were very proud of the Singer we had in our home in the village—the kind you crank with your feet. But this work was nothing like the sewing I knew. In the* maquila, *you sewed the same piece over and over. For months I did nothing but zippers. Hundreds of thousands of zippers. Later I did nothing but pockets. At night when I lay down to sleep I would close my eyes and, I swear, I would see pockets.*

Adelita told me that the hardest thing was to adjust to the idea that she couldn't get up to stretch or walk around or clear her head.

> *We couldn't go to the bathroom when we needed to, and we could only eat lunch in the twenty minutes when the supervisor said we could take a lunch break. It was like being a little kid in school. In fact, we used to joke that this is why the* maquila *owners always want to know if you completed primary school. It's not because you need to know how to read or write in order to sew zippers. You just need to know how to sit still in your chair when, in reality, you have to leave the room to pee.*

Adelita explains that she worked only five months in this *maquila* when the plant closed down. Within three days, however, she was seated at a microscope in another factory soldering microcircuits at a rate of one thousand per day. Adelita worked at this job four months before quitting.

> *When I was sewing all day, my back ached, my kidneys ached, and my feet swelled up for lack of circulation. But with the microassembly what started to go was my eyesight. I had all the other aches and pains, but now my vision started to go blurry. At that point I just said no. I have to feed my kids and I've got to have a job that gives me the right to go to the Social Security hospital. But I was only twenty-seven years old and, I thought, I've got to hang onto my eyesight. I'm going to need it later in life!*

Leaving the electronics plant, Adelita went on to work in a Mexican-owned factory making rattan furniture. She says this was the only job she actually enjoyed. The pay was slightly lower than at the two foreign-owned firms where she was previously employed. "The air was bad—full of sawdust and fiber from the straw. And you don't want to think about the cuts you got on your hands." But in this factory, Adelita was able to weave a complete seat before passing the piece along to the department where they assembled the chairs. She could move around and she worked on different parts of tables and chairs.

Unfortunately, the furniture factory closed after two years of production. Over the next four years, Adelita went on to find employment making electrical switches, toys, picture frames, medical instruments, men's trousers, insulated wire, and plastic tubes. Only in the plastics factory did Adelita work until the end of her eight-month contract. The other jobs she left at the point that the noise, the chemical fumes, the airborne fibers, or the cramped position in which she labored became more than she wanted to bear. In each case, she would rest for a week, travel home to Michoacán to visit family, and return to Tijuana to take up work in another *maquila*.

I ask Adelita if it wasn't difficult to get rehired after leaving so many jobs in succession. She replies that when she started in the early 1980s, the personnel officers were, in fact, a lot more particular. They wanted details on all previous employment including the reasons for "termination." "But today," Adelita says, "with the turnover they have, the managers can't be too picky." She explains that, rather than fork over the *indemnización*, or severance pay, that employers are legally bound to pay to the workers they lay off, many of the plants contract workers for only six to nine months at a time. Then, during the slack season, the contracts run out, production is shut down, and all the workers are let go. When these *maquilas* want to resume production, they have to hire a whole factory full of people. "What's more," Adelita notes,

> *More than half the workers in any factory are likely to leave in the course of a year, and in some* maquilas, *the* rotación *is a lot higher. Each time I left a job, I'd just find a friend or neighbor who was working in a* maquila *and I'd get her to recommend me at that plant. Mostly the people who hire you just want to examine you to make sure you're not pregnant, and they want to see your birth certificate to make sure that you're not underage or overage. If you're too young to work, they may have to pay a fine or they may have to pay a bribe in order to avoid paying the fine. If you're too old, they don't want you either, because they figure you're not going to put up with bad conditions. They think you'll quit before long or, worse yet, that you'll turn out to be a troublemaker.*

Adelita tells me that she was never one of the women identified as a troublemaker because, much as she grumbled to the others, she never became involved with the union or anyone trying to organize a union.

> *I didn't stay long enough in one place to get involved. That's the way it is in this industry: the* maquilas *come and go, and we also come and go. I can't even tell you if the unions in the plants where I worked—the ones that were unionized—were good or bad. I wasn't around long enough to find out.*

I ask Adelita if she didn't seek the help of the union when she lost her job. "Oh, no," she explains,

> *you have to remember that I was never fired from any of these jobs. I just left, or they shut down the line and had no more work for me. I wasn't fired. No one's going to fire someone like me. I just sat there quietly stitching, soldering, wiring, sticking eyes in dolls' heads—whatever they asked of me. I'm not the kind of person who gets fired.*

Adelita explains that after the first years in the plants, she gave up her search for a "really good" *maquila* job. "In the end," she says,

> *it's basically the same work no matter which* maquila *hires you. You're going to arrive at the factory, punch in, put on your apron—on top of your overcoat, if it's winter—clean your machine and start cranking away. Unless you get* "promoted" *where you work for the same base pay, but in the quality control or packing department, you're going to sit all day at an assembly line or a module doing the same thing over and over again. You're going to work ten hours a day, Monday through Thursday, and eight on Friday, and get paid by the piece or by an hourly rate based on piecework standards. The plant is going to be cold in winter and hot in summer. The supervisors can be men or women, they can be* norteamericanos *or Mexicans. But, whoever the supervisors may be, it's always the* güeritos, *the* "blondies," *who have the last word.*

I ask Adelita if she found no significant differences among the plants. She explains that the *maquilas* on the Otay Mesa are newer and pay a little better than the others. But it costs more to get to the mesa, so there's no real advantage to those jobs, unless you are a very recent arrival in Tijuana and you live out on that side of the city. "Sure, there are a few differences," Adelita concedes:

> *Some of the plants have cafeterias. Some take you on excursions to the beach in Ensenada. Some give you a little present on Mother's Day. Some have beauty contests and prizes for the fastest workers. Some give you masks to wear, but it's often too hot to put them on. Others give you gloves to protect your hands, but then they give you assembly tasks that you can't do or that take too long if you're wearing gloves. Some of the supervisors let you talk to the other girls. But usually there's too much noise in any case, and when the machines aren't deafening, they play loud music to speed you up.*

But the basic limitations of the job, Adelita stresses, are the same in all cases: the work is monotonous, the daily pay is pegged to the hourly wage of a worker performing the same job north of the border, and the opportunities for advancement are almost nil. This is why, after six years, Adelita determined to leave the *maquilas* to find work on the other side.

The main reason that Adelita was able to contemplate such a move was that, by 1986, Héctor had come into her life. Héctor, whom Adelita met at a fiesta, was employed in a seafood restaurant in Rosarito on the coast south of Tijuana. He too had come to the border straight from the countryside of Colima, and had worked his way up from dishwasher to busboy to his present position as waiter.

Héctor's base pay was negligible. But he was *simpático* and courteous, and he could manage a little English for those requiring suggestions from the menu. As a consequence of his skill and charm,

Héctor did very well in tips. Most important, although he received only minimum wage, his benefits included social security. When Héctor proposed that Adelita, her mother, and the children come to live with him in a two-room house he had constructed on a *cerro* close to the center of Tijuana, they became, for official purposes, his common-law family. This meant they were covered by his social security benefits.

Inclusion under Héctor's coverage freed Adelita to look for a better-paying job, even one that did not provide social security. Thus, when Héctor's cousin, Graciela, proposed that she could get work for Adelita cleaning houses in San Diego, Adelita jumped at the opportunity.

Adelita held a border-crossing card that she had been granted during her two-year stint of steady employment in the furniture factory. This credential would now become her passport to economic betterment. Although the card is issued to those who wish to cross the border to shop or visit, not to work, Graciela had long known how to get around this restriction, and she now shared her expertise with Adelita. As Adelita explained it to me,

> *The pass allows you to cross to the other side in order to spend money, but they don't want you to come over to earn money. So you have to convince them that you're doing one when you're really doing the other. Fortunately, Graciela figured out how to do this.*

On the earnings from her house cleaning, Graciela bought herself a used car. Crossing the border in a private car, even a second-hand Chevrolet, gave Graciela an air of substance that is lacking for those who arrive in public transport and walk across to connect with the trolley in San Ysidro. To complete the picture, Graciela dressed attractively—even elegantly—for what would be, in fact, a workday of scrubbing floors and toilets. She polished her nails, carefully made up her face, and put on large dangling earrings. Adelita told me,

Graciela guided me through every step. First she found me two jobs with friends of her señoras, and then she lent me the clothing I would need to cross. I worked my hands with lotion for a week until all the redness was gone. I polished my nails and I bought a ring for each hand: one looked like a ruby and the other looked like a sapphire.

At first I felt nervous, but now the border crossing is routine for me. On the mornings we go to work, the migra *almost never even ask to see our papers. They look at our hands, the way we're dressed, and they figure us for the kind of middle-class ladies who have maids in their homes in Tijuana, and plenty of time to spend in the shopping malls on Avenue H in Chula Vista.*

Cleaning houses in San Diego, Adelita found she could make thirty-five dollars for four hours of labor. With recommendations from her first two employers, Adelita managed to patch together three full workdays of eight hours each. After splitting travel expenses with Graciela, she was left with just under $200 for three days work, or three and a half times the take-home pay she earned working a forty-eight-hour week in the *maquilas*.

There's no question that I am much better off now. Cleaning is hard work, but at least you can go at your own pace. The people I work for are all older people who have retired. They've all come from a place called Nebraska. I find them very polite, very gracious and trusting. They leave me alone in the house to do my cleaning. They put money for me on the windowsill or in a jar, and that's it. Nobody stands over me telling me what to do.

Adelita says that she is content for the present with the work she has found. But she and Héctor have a long-term plan. Their dream is to open a little restaurant where Adelita would cook and Héctor would serve and handle the rest of the operation.

Their problem, however, is that with the rise in the cost of living and the expense of the children's secondary schooling, they have not been able to save for their project. Adelita says that she imagines it will be many years before they will have accumulated enough to seriously think about leaving their present jobs to set up the restaurant. The one thing they know for certain is the location they want, on a busy street in downtown Tijuana, and the menu they will offer: soups and stews, and tacos, enchiladas, and burritos—all made with Adelita's famous flour tortillas.

6 P.M.: *Pedro P.*

At six in the afternoon the crowd assembled on the Mexican side of the border fence begins to grow larger and turn jittery. Within an hour, darkness will fall and the most eager and restless of the would-be migrants will make their move. Some will climb the twelve-foot corrugated metal fence. Others will pass under the barrier through one of the dozen or so holes that perforate its fourteen-mile length as it stretches from the Pacific Ocean at Playas de Tijuana, past the official border station, around the airport, up onto the Otay Mesa where the assembly plants cluster, and out into the desert. Here the fence ends—far from the cities and connecting roads, in canyons and badlands that no sensible person even thinks about crossing on foot.

At sunset the crowd swells. But almost any time of the day, scores of migrants can be found at "El Bordo," as this section of the fence is known. They nervously pace back and forth. They negotiate with the "coyotes," or "*polleros*," who offer to guide them across. They peek through or over the fence to study the moves of the *migra*—the agents of the U.S. Immigration and Naturalization Service (INS). They gaze up at the hill that rises steeply behind the U.S. border station where the border patrol's infrared scopes are mounted, ready to pick out migrants scattered—running and hiding—in the bushes below.

In the narrow strip between the border fence and the highway that runs along the edge of Tijuana, a half-dozen men and women march back and forth hawking tacos, tortas, candy, and soft drinks—food that sustains those migrants who sit by the fence all day, watching, waiting, and looking across into San Ysidro on the U.S. side. In the evening more vendors appear. These people sell the large plastic bags that migrants use to cover their shoes and legs as they wade, shin- or knee-deep, across the Tijuana River. Only some of the clandestine routes to San Ysidro involve crossing the river, an open sewage ditch that rises in the mountains south of Tijuana, runs through the city in a concrete channel, and then makes its way northwest across U.S. territory to empty into the ocean near Imperial Beach. But the vigilance of the border patrol in the other sectors along the fence is so intense that increasing numbers of migrants and their coyotes are choosing to cross at the western end of the line, the path that involves fording the river and plodding through wetlands.

The movement of Mexican migrants has not always taken this form. During World War II, Mexicans were encouraged to come to the United States to meet the labor shortages produced by the war. In the 1950s, U.S. agribusiness successfully lobbied for the creation of a *bracero* program that brought hundreds of thousands of seasonal farm workers to harvest crops throughout the Southwest. But even as the *braceros* were arriving in the United States under government contract, the first large waves of illegal immigrants began to flow across the border. And when the *bracero* program was terminated in 1965 under pressure from organized labor in the United States, illegal migration from Mexico continued because the demand for cheap labor never slackened.

The illegal migrants of the 1960s and 1970s were mostly peasants who sought work in the fields of California and Texas. Generally, they did not come on their own. Rather, they were recruited by agents who traveled through the poorest rural areas of central Mexico collecting farm laborers and loading them into open trucks. The labor contractors transported the peasants to the border, packed like chickens in a poultry truck. This is how the migrants came to be called chickens, or *pollos,* and the agents, *polleros.*

Once at the border, the methods used to bring the undocumented workers across were crude because vigilance was light: they were loaded into the back of trucks, concealed with cargo, or marched across the desert backlands. Some died on the way.

Today increased surveillance at the official border crossings and the effort to interdict drugs makes it impossible to bring people across concealed in the trunks of cars or vans. The work of the *pollero* has changed drastically and become differentiated and specialized. A team of coyotes generally works together to complete the transfer from Tijuana to Los Angeles. Moreover, the *pollero* no longer recruits his clients in rural Mexico and hauls them to the border. The would-be migrants are now mostly urban people who reach the border cities under their own steam, traveling by bus, train, or even airplane. Once they arrive at the *frontera,* they cross on their own or engage the services of a coyote to get them into the United States.

While migrants cross at all the major border cities, half of all undocumented Mexicans who make their way into the United States do so at Tijuana. This westernmost border town is almost twice as far from the densely populated regions of central Mexico as Nuevo Laredo, and can be reached only by a journey twice as long and expensive as that made by Rosario in her weekly run to the Texas border. Moreover, the Tijuana crossing is more difficult and dangerous than some of the others. In Ciudad Juarez, for example, the streets run right up to the river that separates the Mexican city from El Paso, Texas. Here people just take off their shoes, wade across, put their shoes back on, and stride into a neighborhood on the other side. But the migrant who crosses in Texas is still more than a thousand miles from Chicago, not to speak of New York. In contrast, crossing at Tijuana puts the migrant within three hours of Los Angeles and the greater Los Angeles metropolitan area of fifteen million. For this reason the majority of migrants come to Tijuana and find a *pollero* to help them evade capture by the eight hundred INS agents assigned to guard the U.S. border at this point.

I am at the fence with a *pollero* named Pedro P. He has been recommended to me as a "coyote's coyote"—a man with a nearly perfect record of success at his trade. Once, in 1988, in what still stands as the crowning achievement of his career, Pedro single-handedly guided twenty-three *pollos,* including seven children, over the border and across the river, delivering them safely to the K-Mart in San Ysidro, where a truck was waiting to take them to Los Angeles.

This evening Pedro has five paying customers at the fence. He plans to move them in a group sometime after 8 P.M. It is a slow night for Pedro, who sometimes makes as many as three separate trips in an evening. When he is running at full throttle, he takes the first group of *pollos* under the fence just after sunset, escorts them as far as San Ysidro, passes them along to his contacts on the other side, returns to Tijuana to pick up the next group, and repeats this routine twice more before the sky begins to lighten at dawn.

Pedro had just such an evening the previous night, working three shifts before returning at 5 A.M. to the house in a working-class neighborhood in the center of Tijuana which he shares with his wife, Patti, and his four children. Under the circumstances, I had trouble making contact with Pedro, although, as instructed, I left messages at a café, a pinball parlor, a billiard hall, an autobody shop, and a bar, all on the street where I had been told I would find him. As it turned out, Pedro had slept in after his night's labors and did not stop by to check his messages until noon. But even though he got off to a late start, Pedro managed to line up some business for the evening: five men from Durango who hoped to reach East L.A. by the following afternoon.

Pedro is thirty-two, tall, and dressed not in the leather jacket, designer sunglasses, and gold jewelry he can afford but in a windbreaker, cotton shirt, worn jeans, and a baseball cap. There's nothing slick about Pedro; he looks like the people he guides to the other side. His appearance, he says, inspires confidence in the migrants who come to him on the recommendation of friends and family. Pedro looks like someone they can trust. He looks like someone from their hometown.

More important, Pedro explains to me, his choice of clothes is critical in the event he and his *pollos* are picked up by the *migra* as they make their run for San Ysidro. If they are apprehended, Pedro's goal is to remain undetected as a *pollero* among the *pollos*. As long as the *migra* does not take him for the coyote in the group, and assuming none of his customers "finger him," as he puts it, the consequences of his capture by the border patrol are minimal. Along with his clients he signs the form waiving his right to a hearing, he is loaded into the bus that takes them back to the border station and is deposited on the Mexican side. Depending on the hour and emotional state of the group, Pedro and his charges are likely to try again that same evening.

If, on the other hand, Pedro is identified as the *pollero*, he is in big trouble:

> *The* migra *is going to catch you from time to time. It's inevitable. It happens to everyone—to me, perhaps, less than to others because I've been very lucky and I don't take too many chances.*
>
> *Once, however, I was caught with my* pollos *and the* gringos *decided—I don't know why—that I had to be the coyote for the whole group. I think one of the agents recognized me as someone*

he'd picked up before. My clients were sent back to Mexico, but I was put in the San Diego city jail.

The next day I was transferred to the Federal Penitentiary in Pecos, Texas. This is the place where they take coyotes, drug smugglers, and contrabandistas. *But I can tell you one kind of person you don't find serving time in Pecos. That's the Americans who employ the illegals. These guys are smart, and they pass along the risk to "labor contractors" who vouch for the workers, saying that their papers are all "in order." It's the contractors who end up in Pecos charged with falsification of documents and transport of illegal aliens.*

On this occasion, Pedro was charged with transport of illegal aliens and held for thirty days. He says he was not mistreated during his incarceration.

To tell you the truth, I would rather spend a month with the gringos *in Pecos than one day in a Mexican jail. Other coyotes have told me some bad stories about beatings and other stuff that went on when they were in custody in the U.S. But, in my case, the only thing I suffered was worry for my wife and my kids, who didn't know what had become of me and had nothing to live on while I was gone.*

Pedro is concerned he may be caught again. The penalties for a second offense are severe. For this reason he is meticulous about briefing his five clients before they begin their attempt to cross. If they are caught, it is imperative that everyone behave in a way that suggests that they are just six guys from Durango who have decided to make it across together.

In the ten years I've worked as a pollero, *I've brought thousands of people across—men, women, and children. And in all those*

> *years, no one has ever ratted on me. Mexicans are good people in this way. Besides, no one has any reason to finger a coyote who deals honestly with his customers.*

This question of integrity is one that Pedro returns to again and again in our conversation. Pedro explains that virtually all his business is based on recommendations and repeat customers. Some clients reappear every year in January after returning to Mexico from Los Angeles to spend Christmas with their families. Almost all his clients are referred by friends and relations he has "passed" before. Pedro says,

> *The stories you hear about coyotes who rob the* pollos, *who collude with* asaltapollos, *the bandits who assault the* pollos *while they're in no-man's-land—all these things really do happen. You hear about coyotes who rape the women they have promised to deliver safely to the other side, or who abandon people who have broken a leg or twisted an ankle jumping over the fence. These stories are true. But it is only a few* polleros *who do these things. This is a business like any other; you're going to find all kinds of people, good and bad, doing this work.*
>
> *My business is based on trust, on the recommendations of people I have passed to the other side. Folks come to me because I have a reputation for skill and reliability. I work with very competent people in San Ysidro—guys in whom the* pollos *can have confidence. People think of me as someone who is serious, who doesn't take stupid chances. I would never do anything that would put my name at risk.*

Pedro got his start as a coyote by assisting relatives and friends from his village who sought his help to get across. Sent to Tijuana as a boy to live with an aunt and uncle, by the time Pedro was a teenager, he had sneaked into the United States more times than he could count. By the age of seventeen, he had washed dishes in San Jose, picked cherries in Washington State, and scrubbed floors and washrooms in a large office building in downtown Los Angeles. Each time he crossed the border, Pedro says, he came to understand more about the movements and strategies of the *migra*. Once back in Tijuana, based on what he drew from these experiences, he was able to guide others—first his brothers and cousins, and then an ever-widening circle of acquaintances from his home region in Durango. Pedro says that when he realized he had a flair for getting people across, he turned professional.

Pedro's approach to business is shaped by the fact that he works on the basis of personal recommendations. While other coyotes make the rounds of the cheap hotels, stand around in bus and train stations, or patrol the area around the fence looking for clients, Pedro tells me he just hangs out in one of his usual spots downtown, and waits for people to come around asking for him. "This saves me a lot of sweat," he explains:

> *Apart from everything else, I don't have any hassles with other coyotes. Some of these guys can get real nasty if they think you're out looking for* pollos *in what they consider to be their corner of the bus station or their section of the fence.*

When a potential client makes contact with him, Pedro requests the phone number of the friends or relatives who are supposed to be underwriting the trip. He then phones Los Angeles to check that these people have the cash on hand to pay his associate when he delivers the *pollo* to Los Angeles. Pedro prefers to operate, as he puts it, "COD," because this arrangement reduces the risk in several ways. The migrants have less to lose if they are set upon by bandits at any point in the journey, and Pedro himself is not carrying large amounts of cash at the vulnerable moments he is conducting his group from the fence to San Ysidro.

Once the contact is made with the sponsors in Los Angeles, Pedro briefs his client, sets a time and a place to meet, and takes the individual or group to the fence by taxi. Here he is joined by Jaime, his partner. Jaime's job is simple: when night falls and Pedro is ready to move the group, Jaime goes under or over the fence to draw the attention of the *migra*, while Pedro passes his clients under the fence at another point. Pedro always moves his people *under* the barrier. Although it constrains his range of choice in selecting a spot to cross, he says it is much faster and safer for the *pollos*.

Once over the fence, Jaime either runs forward or ducks back under the fence—whatever it takes to give Pedro the chance to move his *pollos* out of the range of the *migra*'s surveillance. Pedro explains,

> *With the* migra, *it's always a game of cat and mouse. You study their moves, you figure out how many men and what kind of equipment they're using that night. And you rely on the fact that you know that they know that they can't stop everyone who decides to cross on a given day. The trick is not to be one of the people they catch that day.*

When Pedro reaches San Ysidro, he escorts his clients to a prearranged spot, where he is met by the coyotes who will take them on to Los Angeles. At this point, Pedro usually takes his cut of the total fee (one hundred dollars per head), which is an advance on the three hundred dollars his associates will collect on delivering the *pollos* to Los Angeles. When Pedro "sells" the *pollos* to other coyotes, he turns around and heads back to Tijuana, either to escort another group or to go home. Generally speaking, in an increasingly differentiated profession, Pedro specializes in "leaping the fence."

When business at the fence is slow, Pedro will take his clients all the way to Los Angeles, the San Fernando Valley, or points north. On these occasions Jaime is waiting in San Ysidro with a van, and the group proceeds north on Interstate 5 until just before the INS checkpoint at San Clemente, an hour up the highway from the border. The checkpoint is a serious obstacle because, when it is in operation, all traffic is slowed to a crawl. Then, anyone who looks likely to be transporting undocumented immigrants—anyone, in short, who looks like Jaime at the wheel of his van—is pulled over for inspection.

When the checkpoint is in operation, Jaime drops Pedro and the *pollos* at a point south of San Clemente. Pedro then proceeds overland with the group through the hills above the highway. Jaime collects the group at a prearranged spot north of the checkpoint.

> *The* migra *knows all the regular overland routes that we can use, and they patrol these with horses and helicopters. So we just have to invent new routes. To do this work, you have to believe that there's got to be one last way the* migra *hasn't thought of yet. The other thing to remember is that the people we guide are very needy. They're very desperate. So they'll put up with a lot to reach Los Angeles.*
>
> *Once past San Clemente, we can relax, especially as we get closer to East Los Angeles, where everyone speaks Spanish and looks like us. My job is to deliver the client safe and sound to an address in East L.A. Then I collect my $300 and leave. If, three minutes later, the guy I just dropped off sticks his head out the door to put out the garbage and is grabbed by the* migra, *that's not my problem. I just bring him there. Staying out of the way of the* migra *afterwards—that's his problem.*

Pedro explains that the rates charged the *pollos* vary from $250 to $350. The exact price depends on age (children travel for less) and distance. Three hundred dollars is standard for Los Angeles; $350 will take you to the San Fernando Valley. For a good deal more money, some coyotes—working through contacts at southern Californian airports—provide connections to destinations throughout the West. Pedro claims that he can get me to Chicago in two days if that's where I need to go. But, he adds, 99 percent of his work involves the standard Tijuana-L.A. run at the standard price.

Pedro says that it was once the case that women, like children, were charged less than men:

> *The* polleros *used to give a special rate to the women and the kids because they were crossing as part of a family. But now a lot more women are crossing. About a quarter or a third of the people I guide are women. And they're not traveling with their husbands or on their way to join husbands who are waiting in Los Angeles. These women are on their own, and they're headed to L.A. to look for jobs. And they get good jobs, too, because most of them have more schooling, more preparation than the men. So now, most coyotes charge them the same rate as men.*

While the fees paid by Mexican migrants are remarkably standardized, prices are much higher for Central Americans and other foreigners: at least six to eight hundred dollars per head. This price scale reflects the greater danger to the coyote who brings non-Mexicans across the border. Pedro explains that two separate issues make it a highly risky proposition to guide Central Americans. The first is that they are *indocumentados* in Mexico as well as in the United States. A *pollero* who contracts to take Guatemalans or Salvadorans across has to keep them hidden from the Mexican authorities the whole time they are in Tijuana waiting to cross. This is generally accomplished by stashing them away in a safe house near the borderline until minutes before they are ready to cross the fence. It also involves extra expense for the coyote in lodging costs and *mordidas* to the Mexican police.

"The second problem," Pedro emphasizes,

> *is that if I am guiding a bunch of Central Americans and we get caught on the way to San Ysidro, it's not going to take the* migra *more than two seconds to figure out which guy is the coyote. In general, it's not work I want to take on. The money is good, but the risk is just too high. The only way I even think about guiding Central Americans is if I have a big group of Mexicans to take over and I can mix the Guatemalans or the Salvadorans in with the others. It also depends on the Central Americans themselves. The sharper ones have already figured out how to pass for* chiapanecos.

Having learned what the *pollos* pay, I ask Pedro if he doesn't make bundles of money each week, even without the extra-high fees available for guiding Central Americans. Pedro replies,

> *It's true that I can take in thousands of dollars in a week—sometimes a thousand in a single night. But I also have my expenses. Apart from the calls to L.A., I pay a twenty-five-dollar finder's fee to anyone who sends me a customer. I pay twenty bucks for the taxi to the fence. Whatever is left of the hundred per* pollo *I collect in San Ysidro, I split fifty-fifty with Jaime.*
>
> *At the end of the day, I make a lot of money, but I have some very big hidden costs. The federal judicial police, the state judicial police, the municipal police—you name it—they come around as often as once a week to shake me down. They know more or less what I make, so they want as much as a thousand dollars a pop. And, believe me, they get a lot more than that from the drug runners.*

Pedro says that even members of the Grupo Beta are now "on the take." This elite corp of federal police was formed to coordinate with the INS to halt the worst abuses that occur on the border—the rapes, armed robbery, and murders. Pedro points out that the Grupo Beta has made the border zone safer for everyone. But, he says, some of the agents have been corrupted:

It's logical, isn't it? These guys are supposed to protect the pollos *from the* polleros*. Thus, they are in a perfect position to extort bribes from the coyotes because they have all kinds of information on us: where we live, where we cross, where we recruit our customers. The Grupo Beta is supposed to be especially honest and upright. But the temptation to shake us down is too great for some of these guys. They come around to your house and either you pay up or they expose you to their buddies, the* migra.

I ask Pedro if he is ever afraid. He says,

Of course, I'm often afraid. Everyone who does this kind of work is afraid. I'm scared of the police on this side and the migra *on the other, and the bandits who attack you in between. The worst thing is the bandits, because they carry knives and guns, and they go after you when you're on your way back from San Ysidro and you have all the money you earned that night in your shoe.*

Pedro says that his wife worries a lot and prays a lot. Patti attends an evangelical church and he often attends with her, although he still considers himself a Catholic and continues to go to Mass.

As for my children, they're too young to worry. The oldest boy is ten. They don't really understand what I do for a living. But Jaime's kids are older, and his wife tells them that their father works in a saloon and that's why he comes home so late and why they can't visit daddy at work.

I mention to Pedro that I have noticed that most of the coyotes are men in their twenties or early thirties, and I ask him how long he sees himself doing this work. Pedro shakes his head and replies by describing to me the jobs he has held in Mexico and what he earned at each: ten pesos per day working *ejido* lands as a *jornalero;* fifteen per day in construction; forty pesos as a cab driver. In the United States he has worked as a dishwasher, busboy, waiter, janitor, checkout cashier, custodian, bricklayer, plasterer, and bar bouncer. He has also picked cherries, apples, grapes, peaches, strawberries, oranges, grapefruits, tomatoes, lettuce, and squash. He says,

> *I continue to work as a* pollero *because it is the only job I can get in Mexico where I can make really good money. My problem is that I don't want to live on the other side. I don't want to bring up my kids in the United States. I want them to live here, in their own country, where they can feel proud of who they are.*
>
> *But, I'll tell you what my dream is. My dream is to get papers: to get a real green card, not a fake. Then I could work in construction on the other side, and live here in Tijuana with my family. I'd like to operate the heavy equipment. I know how, and you make great money doing that in the U.S. I'd just go across every day to work, and then I'd come home to Tijuana at night. I could be really happy with that kind of life. Not just economically OK, but really happy, really content.*

8

Lives of Struggle

8 P.M.: Roberto Martínez and Alicia Pérez

It is eight in the evening under an inky sky as I approach the headquarters of the teachers' union, where I have come to speak with Roberto Martínez. Located near the Zócalo, in the oldest part of downtown Mexico City, the headquarters of the local should be a comfortable environment for me: I am a teacher and a member of a unionized faculty, so I would expect to feel at home in this building. Or, at least I should feel more familiar with the surroundings than I do when standing with Pedro at the border fence or sitting on Don Ramón's veranda in the Ejido Santa Marta.

But the atmosphere in this place is grim and uneasy. The three-story structure is a kind of Lebanon of a building with different sections, floors, and offices occupied by opposing factions locked in irreconcilable conflict over power, territory, and resources. The undercurrent of tension grows from the concrete experience of the people who work here. Over the last two decades, the headquarters has been the site of raids, beatings, shootings, kidnapings, and attempted assassinations, as the entrenched leadership of the union has called on the police and its own corps of hired thugs to hold off the challenge of the "democratic tendency" that has organized within the union to contest the authority of those who have perpetuated themselves in office since 1972.

The National Union of Workers in Education (SNTE), with almost a million dues-paying members, is the largest union in Mexico and one of the most important in the system of "official" labor unions that are formally tied to the ruling party through affiliation in the PRI's labor sector. Formed in 1943, the SNTE was organized from the top down, as were the other official unions. This union was created in an effort to bring schoolteachers—long a progressive force in national life, above all in the countryside and in poor urban neighborhoods—under the control of the ruling party. Although in its earliest years the SNTE was led by teachers who enjoyed the support of the rank and file, in 1949 it was taken over by a political boss named Jesús Robles Martínez. From that point on, like workers organized in other *priísta* unions, the teachers were manipulated through patronage appointments dealt out to their leaders in return for the leadership's political conformity, loyalty to the ruling party, and efforts to get out the vote for the PRI at election time.

This classic pattern of political control seemed about to shift in 1972 when a faction of activists seized union headquarters and expelled Robles and the other *oficialistas* who had run the union for two dozen years with no goal more lofty than personal aggrandizement and enrichment. At first the new leaders presented a reform agenda, and they enjoyed widespread support from the rank and file. But their program for change quickly degenerated into the standard patterns of political corruption, clientelism, and thuggery, with "reforms" engineered only to perpetuate officeholders' tenure and to enable them to secure positions for their henchmen in national, state, and local government.

Given the Mexican teachers' tradition of leadership in community and agrarian struggles, the mass base of the union was not passive in the face of the takeover of the organization by yet another corrupt clique. But the teachers were impeded in their efforts to construct a competing independent union by the legislation that governs labor relations in Mexico: the section of the Mexican labor code covering public sector employees recognizes only one union for each sector. Thus, dissident public employees had no choice but to organize "currents" within existing *oficialista* unions, challenging the control of corrupt bosses by presenting alternative slates of candidates in union elections at all levels.

Throughout the 1970s, in every sector of government service, those organized workers who were reluctant to accept the PRI's imposition of corrupt and politically quiescent leadership formed "democratic tendencies," "currents," and other dissident factions within the official unions. The development of these factions became the principal means by which public sector employees could contest the power of dishonest leaders—who, in Mexico, are called *charros*, or cowboys. In the teachers' union the dissident group, which called itself the National Coordinating Committee of Workers in Education (CNTE), was comprised chiefly of militant regional teachers' movements, particularly those representing the teachers of Oaxaca and Chiapas, the two very poor states in southernmost Mexico.

From its formation in the 1970s, the CNTE was tolerated and, to some degree, even encouraged by the Ministry of Education because the corrupt practices of SNTE leaders had gotten completely out of hand. At this point the government welcomed the democratic tendency's pressure to clean up the union from within. But the early 1980s marked a reversal of the ministry's attitude of tacit support for the CNTE. By this time the austerity program imposed by President de la Madrid was in place, and that program required what the economic planners refer to as "control of wage demands." In practice, such a policy meant the suppression—by violent means, if necessary—of labor militancy of any kind.

Thus, through the 1980s the CNTE activists within the SNTE passed through difficult times. Yet support for the democratic movement grew steadily and, with patience, these dissidents found they could gain key positions in the union through a painstaking process of grass-roots mobilization around union elections. By the 1990s, the dissidents had their foothold in the union, had elected many of their most prominent activists to union office, and were clinging—both figuratively and literally—to the territory they had gained. In the SNTE local that I am visiting, a section of the union that represents sixty thousand middle- and secondary-school teachers, the democratic unionists hold half the places on the executive committee.

I have arrived at this local headquarters at a moment of uneasy truce, and I carefully follow the instructions that will bring me straight to the office where I can expect to find Roberto and other members of the democratic faction. I walk quickly up the central staircase, taking note of the bullet holes and other damage, and into the offices where I hope to see Roberto.

Roberto himself takes the bullet hole–studded corridors and all the rest in stride. His entire adult life has been lived amid the assorted dangers that confront those Mexicans who, against all odds, insist on opposing the monolithic control of the official party and its supporting institutions: the official unions, the neighborhood *caciquillos,* the police, and the army.

Roberto was born in Jalisco in western Mexico, but was brought to the capital in the first months of his life. Roberto's father was a carpenter and his mother a market vendor and factory worker who managed, by middle age, to qualify as a nurse. Roberto explains that it is hard for him to say how much his parents' social and political attitudes shaped his own commitment, or how much his activism encouraged them. But his mother, at age sixty-one, is active in the democratic tendency within the health workers' union. And his father, who is now retired, works full-time in urban popular movements mobilizing rural migrants to demand squatters' rights and organizing and coordinating the cooperative construction of popular housing.

Roberto grew up in the center of Mexico City, in an old three-story colonial house built around a central courtyard. He explains that some of these structures crumbled in the 1985 earthquakes, but when he was a boy in the 1950s, this was a common form of popular housing, with an entire family occupying each of the individual rooms opening onto the courtyard. Roberto says it was a crowded and noisy place, but he has very good memories of a childhood spent playing with other boys and girls in the patio of this colonial house.

When we speak of his childhood, I ask Roberto what was his first "political memory." Unlike the vast majority of people to whom I have put this question in interviews, Roberto hesitates only briefly before responding.

> *When I was a boy, my mother was a factory worker, so I heard plenty of discussion at home concerning the conditions of the workers in the factory, the efforts to build an independent union, the complicity of the* oficialista *union leaders with the bosses. This is the kind of thing we discussed around the dinner table.*
>
> *The other political talk I remember from childhood was the chat in the courtyard among the neighbors concerning the PRI: that the PRI only came around at election time to hand out gifts; that the PRI bought votes; that the PRI never kept its promises; that the politicians were corrupt. That was the sort of thing I heard as a boy: not much talk about what to do about any of these problems, but the people certainly were not taken in by the* priísta *rhetoric. Later these expressions of discontent were clarified for me by the political analyses of some of the teachers I met in secondary school.*

Roberto cannot remember exactly when he knew he would become a teacher, but he explains that this ambition was a very common one among those from poor families like his own.

At first my parents were totally focused on the idea that, at least, I must complete primary school. Then they began to hope that they would find the resources to permit me to go on for the three years of secondary. If everything were to go really well, they dreamed that I would have a "career." And for people of our modest social class, the notion of a "career" most often translated into the hope that a son or daughter would become a maestro *or* maestra.

Roberto says that it also helped that he was lucky with the teachers he encountered in the course of his schooling.

I did well in my studies, and I never ran into the kind of teacher who abuses students. Of course, it's also the case that the teachers in that epoch were a lot happier than they are today. In that period the profession was a lot better paid and offered some dignity, especially for a person of humble origin.

For most working-class people like himself, Roberto explains, a determining factor in the choice of a teaching career was the fact that the preparation to qualify was cheap; a student in "normal school" could easily obtain a government scholarship to cover the cost of books and transportation. It was also fast: a teaching certificate could be obtained in three years of study following the three years of secondary school. "At age eighteen, you had your papers in hand and you were ready to earn a salary." Moreover, the graduates of the National Teachers' School were all guaranteed classroom placements upon completing their studies. The monthly salary at the time Roberto received his teaching credentials in 1966 was a thousand pesos—then worth eighty dollars. In the mid-1960s, this represented a reasonable sum for an eighteen-year-old, who was likely to live at home with parents. And new graduates like Roberto could teach primary school during the morning and continue with advanced studies in the afternoon and evening. The typical pattern was for the *maestros* to attend a couple of years of *preparatoria*, preparatory school, leading eventually to admission to the National University.

It was during Roberto's years at Prepa Numero 7 that the student movement of 1968 broke out. The movement marked the point in Mexican history when the standard techniques of political and social control proved incapable of containing the discontent and suppressed violence endemic in Mexican society. The movement began in late July, when students from two rival secondary schools clashed in a street fight, and it escalated steadily as riot police and paramilitary shock troops were used to suppress any hint of public unrest.

It was no accident that the summer of 1968 proved the moment in Mexico when the system of control broke down. The movement was, to some degree, a product of the times, inspired in part by the activities of radical students around the world. But a more immediate cause of unrest was the celebration of the Olympics, an event that mocked the reality of mass misery in Mexico in both symbolic and concrete terms. The student movement expressed the anger and frustration of young Mexicans at the distorted priorities that had been set for Mexico by those in power. The expenditure of millions of pesos on the Olympics was only symptomatic of what the students regarded as the criminal mismanagement of the country's resources and the social injustice produced by the policies of the ruling elite.

Faced with this explosive situation at the very moment that "official" Mexico was preparing to play host to the world as the site of the games, the government of Gustavo Díaz Ordaz (1964–1970) applied a level of force unprecedented in postrevolutionary Mexico. And the students, in turn, responded with increasingly radical demands. Soon, secondary-school students were joined by thousands of university students in daily demonstrations called to protest police brutality and, in particular, the army and police occupation of academic facilities.

As the repressive measures grew, many students who were initially indifferent to the events left their classrooms to prepare for the battles to come: they commandeered buses and built barricades, occupied school buildings, and laid in supplies of food, medical equipment, rags, bottles, and gasoline. A National Strike Council was formed, comprised of representatives from 128 secondary and postsecondary institutions. The council was charged with the task of coordinating the activities of hundreds of student brigades that roamed the city distributing leaflets, collecting donations of support, and bringing medical care and legal services into peripheral slum communities.

Roberto was elected by his fellow students to represent them at the sessions of the National Strike Council. He became active, as well, in the movement of elementary-school teachers who wanted to fuse their own trade unionist demands for better pay and working conditions with the broader struggle that was emerging in the National University and the National Polytechnic Institute.

By October 1968 the sentiments that had propelled students out of their classrooms and into the streets had begun to move other sectors of the population. Over the course of four months, the movement evolved into the most articulate and threatening challenge that the Mexican political system had faced since the end of the revolution. At this point the students' courage had begun to inspire support from organized labor and peasants.

With the Olympics scheduled to begin on October 12, the Díaz Ordaz regime moved to contain the situation. During a rally called by the National Strike Council in the Plaza of the Three Cultures in the Tlatelolco neighborhood in downtown Mexico City, soldiers poured into the area and, surrounding the plaza, took up combat positions. Firing into the crowd from behind the Aztec ruins and from the rooftops of the buildings facing the square, the troops mowed down hundreds of unarmed demonstrators even as they fled for cover, and then moved in to seize and imprison hundreds more.

Roberto was arrested on October 2 in the plaza and held with other political leaders in the infamous Lecumberri Prison. Three months later Roberto was among the prisoners freed when the president declared a general amnesty for the New Year. Upon his release, at the insistence of the parents of his pupils, Roberto was reinstated in the teaching post he had lost during his imprisonment. Roberto had become a greatly liked and much respected figure in the poor *barrio* where he had been assigned to teach, and now the people of that community organized to demand his return to their children's classroom.

But Roberto's problems were not over. As he attempted to continue his studies at the university level, enrolling in the faculty of law, he found that the entire public university and preparatory system was now infiltrated by *porras,* bands of paramilitary gunmen whose role was to present themselves as students and disrupt every meeting and public event that might lead to new mobilizations on the campuses. It appears that some of these gangs were in the pay of the Department of the Federal District, because their arms and vehicles could be traced directly to that unit of government. Other *porras* seem to have been sponsored by political groups on the extreme right, and the violence perpetrated by these bands was geared as much toward embarrassing the president, Luis Echeverría (1970–1976) and portraying him as "soft on socialism," as it was toward directly assaulting student activists. Whoever may have been their sponsors, when they were not shooting up student demonstrations, the *porras* were acting as *agents provocateurs,* instigating violence that the press then dutifully reported as "fighting between rival student factions." Moreover, the same conservative forces that were prepared to bankroll gangsters disguised as students also sponsored pseudo-guerrilla groups to carry out rural terrorist activities meant to discredit the leftist guerrillas who were active in the countryside in this period.

It was a difficult and dangerous time to be on a university campus or in the preparatory schools. Roberto explains,

> *One day I was at my old preparatory school with a group of other university students who had graduated in the same class with me and we were distributing leaflets to the students exhorting them to organize against the infiltration of the* porras *in the school. Suddenly a shock troop of seventy* porras *appeared and set upon us. One of our* compañeros *was armed with a pistol which he fired into the air. When two of the* porras *were wounded in the fight, my friend, afraid he'd be implicated, fled with the pistol. But he was caught, and thrown into jail—as it turned out, for seven years.*

After this incident Roberto felt his best chance of survival depended on getting away from the scene of the continual violent confrontations that characterized student life in this period. Thus Roberto interrupted his law studies and, through contacts among teachers from Oaxaca, he escaped to an indigenous community of Zapotec Indians in southern Mexico. There he worked as a volunteer teacher in the secondary school and quickly became involved in the struggles underway to build an agricultural cooperative and to secure the natural resources of the community for common use.

> *The move to Oaxaca was a natural thing for someone like me who had studied in the National Normal School in the 1960s. Among our fellow students at the normal school there were always a lot of* compañeros *from Oaxaca, Guerrero, and Chiapas. These are the most wretchedly poor parts of Mexico, and the people who came up to the capital from these places were usually folks from poor families who had seen it all. They were bright and highly conscious and determined to go back to their indigenous communities*

> *and use their role as* maestros *to work with the people to change their condition. You couldn't help but be impressed with the* compañeros *from the south. We all respected and looked up to them. And in the democratic teachers' movement, we still do.*

As it turned out, Roberto did not find the personal safety he had sought in the countryside. In the fall of 1970, only months after his arrival in the village, he was seized by the police, who claimed that he was fomenting armed revolution and guerrilla struggle in the zone. He was imprisoned in the capital of Oaxaca, where he was accused of penning a subversive publication called *La Escoba*, "The Broom."

> La Escoba *was a little newsletter put out by the boys and girls in the secondary school where I was teaching. It called on the people of the village to "sweep away all the trash," and it protested the arbitrary rule of the municipal authorities. It was pretty basic stuff. I believe that someone in the local offices of the Ministry of Education, and perhaps the village priest saw this little newspaper as a big threat. My arrest was probably meant to intimidate the students who worked on the paper.*

Roberto sees the timing of the incident as a stroke of personal good fortune.

> *I was taken into custody and moved from Oaxaca to Mexico City, where I was detained for several months and then released, without ever having been formally charged. All this occurred just a little while before the development of a serious guerrilla movement in the countryside, including in the rural zone where I had taken refuge. Had I been in Oaxaca when the guerrilla struggle and the counterinsurgency drive were in full swing, I doubt I would have survived.*

> *As it was, a good number of my fellow students from normal school, frustrated after the repression of the student movement of 1968, went off in the 1970s to join the* guerrilleros *who were attempting to make the revolution through armed struggle among the peasants. Of course, a lot of these people died in that effort. Others ended up as political refugees in Cuba.*

Released from prison, Roberto barely broke stride. He resumed his political activities in the capital, and he switched from law school to the Superior Normal School, where secondary-school teachers receive their training. In this same year, he married Alicia, a teacher he met in 1968 in the National Strike Council where she was representing students from the Superior Normal School.

The school was a hotbed of radicalism, above all during the summer sessions when teachers came to the capital from all corners of Mexico for refresher courses—an atmosphere that Roberto describes as made-to-order for the development of nationwide ties among politicized teachers. This was also the period when the veterans of the 1968 movement continued to be released from prison or to return from exile. Together with other *compañeros* from the student movement, Roberto and Alicia participated in new mobilizations around the same old issues: the repressive nature of the Mexican political system, corruption of public life, and the glaring social injustice that had accompanied economic growth in Mexico.

By early summer of 1971, hope had begun to grow among the thousands who had participated in the 1968 movement that the period of repression was over, and that the new president, Echeverría, was serious about his attempts to reform and open the political system. On Corpus Christi Day, June 10, 1971, more than ten thousand students left the National Polytechnic Institute in a well-organized march to the Monument of the Revolution in downtown Mexico City. The stated goal of the demonstration was the release of the remaining political prisoners held since 1968.

However, the underlying motive was the desire to reorganize and revitalize the student movement, which had remained in disarray since the slaughter in the Plaza of the Three Cultures.

As the march made its way toward the center of the city, roughly a thousand *porras* assembled and waited to intercept the students. Outfitted with knives, pistols, machine guns, and cattle prods, the *porras* passed freely through the lines of uniformed police stationed along the parade route. While nine hundred special service police sealed off the area and the riot police heightened the confusion by launching tear gas into the crowd, the *porras* attacked the unarmed demonstrators, killing about thirty students and bystanders outright and pursuing the others as they fled through the streets. The *porras* then rooted students out of the shops, cinemas, and churches where they had sought refuge, and proceeded to invade the hospitals where the wounded had been taken, attacking injured students as they lay on the operating tables and in the wards. The toll was high: an estimated fifty students were killed, another fifty "disappeared," and hundreds more were wounded. Roberto tells me that his younger brother, Emilio, was one of the victims.

> *Emilio was hit by bullets fired by one of the sharpshooters stationed on the rooftops above the parade route. He was marching along with the others at the intersection of Avenida Tacuba and the Avenida de los Maestros, near the Normal School when suddenly he was hit. A friend of mine saw him fall. It was an expanding bullet that ripped through his chest. My friend was with Emilio, and tried to drag him to safety in the courtyard of a* vecindad. *But there was nothing to be done. He died in the space of a few minutes. He is buried in Iztapalapa with other people who were killed in the Corpus Christi Massacre.*

I ask Roberto how his parents responded. Did they ask him to give up his own political activities?

For my parents, of course, this was a tragedy that will always mark their lives. Remember, this was the second time they went through the experience, because I had disappeared on October 2 in the massacre at the Plaza of the Three Cultures, and they spent days going from one morgue to another looking for me among the cadavers—discovering, only later, that I was in detention. But even after that experience they never asked me or my other brother to desist, to curtail our political participation. On the contrary, they dealt with it by becoming more politically involved themselves. On the twentieth anniversary of my brother's death, my mother was elected to serve as a representative in the nurses' union.

In 1972, following the tragedy of Corpus Christi, Roberto, Alicia, and their newborn daughter joined a brigade of "democratic *maestros*" working in a rural community in the state of Puebla in central Mexico. Invited by the new village administration, a group that had managed to wrest power from the local boss, the teachers came to run a literacy program. Their goal was to support the new mayor, a young woman, in her efforts to spread the spirit of democratic participation among peasants who had known only authoritarianism and the mutually reinforcing control of the PRI-linked *cacique* and the ultraconservative parish priest. Roberto explains,

It was an important experience. But we teachers had to withdraw when the conflict between the democratic group and the followers of the priest threatened to turn into a direct, violent confrontation. Ironically, this same priest was later forced out of the community when he was revealed to be a bribón, *that is, someone who steals alms from the collection plate. But that happened after we returned to Mexico City.*

Just as Roberto is describing the kinds of political activities that he and Alicia pursued in these years, Alicia arrives at the union office. She has come into the center of the city for a meeting and has stopped by to give Roberto a ride home. This gives me the chance to get her perspective on these same events.

Alicia explains that she and Roberto each pursue their own political activities, but "at all the decisive moments" they have acted together, as was the case with their efforts in Puebla. For her, Alicia says, the experience in Puebla was only one of a series of important initiatives they pursued in this period to overcome the sense of frustration and fear that set in after the repression of the student movement.

> *Those of us who had participated in the movement of 1968 responded to its suppression in many different ways. Some, as Roberto has told you, went off to join the armed guerrilla struggle in an attempt to reproduce the success that Fidel Castro and Che Guevara had in the revolutionary war in Cuba. Others, like Roberto and I, were determined to build links with the masses of poor Mexicans by living in these communities, both rural and urban, and working with people in the projects they initiated for themselves.*

Alicia says that they went into these efforts with an "almost religious" dedication: "we believed that everything depended on the links you could build with the people."

> *The experience in Puebla was very important because, in this village, the project that the people had undertaken was to force the local* cacique *out and replace him with some honestly elected municipal officials. But this turned out to be a very dangerous business and, as often happens in these cases, the* jefe *fought back with* pistoleros. *At that point we had to ask ourselves how far we were supposed to go in our support of the people, and at what moment it has to become their battle to fight. For us the time in*

Puebla was a political apprenticeship, and we are still in contact with people there.

Alicia's own political formation began, if possible, even earlier than Roberto's. Her mother, a teacher and single parent with three daughters, participated in the teachers' strike of 1958, a landmark moment in Mexican labor history. In a movement for better working conditions and union democracy, Alicia's mother was one of the few women to serve as a director of the strike council. Alicia recalls,

This was the famous strike in which the teachers seized and occupied the Ministry of Education. I was the littlest of the three daughters, but I went everywhere with my mother: to the marches, to the strike council and the occupation of the ministry offices. My sisters refused to come along and sleep on the floor of the Ministry of Education, and they had to be left with neighbors. But I was enchanted with this life and, obviously, at some point my mother's social conscience must have rubbed off on me.

Alicia explains that, even today, at age sixty-eight, her mother continues her union and political activities.

There's no question that my mother was a revolutionary woman for her times. She worked, supported three daughters on her salary, and managed to study as well. She was promoted from the classroom to the job of school inspector—one of the few teachers ever to reach this post through merit rather than connections. Unfortunately, when the people at the Ministry of Education realized how dangerous it was to have a militant person like my mother running around the school district in daily contact with young teachers, talking to them about things like union democracy, they grew frightened, and she was kicked upstairs to a desk job in the min-

> *istry. But even then and, indeed, even today she continues to have a lot of influence among the teachers in her zone.*

Given their background and their experience of activism, I find that Alicia and Roberto cannot separate their personal economic situation from their political commitments. We talk about their daughter and son, their extended family, and other details of their personal and family lives. But when I ask them how they have managed to get by in the decade of declining real wages and general economic crisis, they respond by describing the overall situation of the teachers and the broad mobilizations to improve the *maestros*' condition. For this couple the question of personal or family survival is intricately intertwined with their involvement in collective struggle.

Roberto emphasizes that teachers have never been paid well, and that primary-school teachers earn only half of the salaries paid to secondary-school teachers. However, in the 1970s the real income of all categories began to rise and, for the first time, teachers began to approach a middle-class standard of living.

> *Teachers had always traveled on public transport, but in this period the figure of the* maestro *arriving at school in a Volkswagen Beetle became commonplace. In the 1970s teachers could aspire to rent a two-bedroom apartment or to buy a tiny lot outside the city to build a little house.* Maestros *started to travel abroad during school vacations, to attend the theater, to buy books and records and even home appliances—a gas stove or a refrigerator—articles that had never before been within their means or aspirations.*

Moreover, during the Echeverría administration, the education sector expanded and more teaching posts were created. Alicia says that in order to fill these positions the practice of "double placements" developed. This permitted teachers to teach in one school in the morning and another in the afternoon, thus doubling their salaries. Teachers with a second placement could live comfortably, especially if, as was often the case, they were married to another teacher who may also have occupied two teaching slots.

However, from the end of the 1970s, with the collapse of the oil boom and the austerity cuts that followed, Alicia says the condition of teachers declined dramatically, especially at the border with the United States and in the oil-producing states along the Gulf of Mexico, both regions where the cost of living is considerably higher than in the rest of Mexico. In fact, teachers' salaries have declined to the point that *maestros* in primary schools earn only one and one half times the minimum wage, or roughly $12 per day, while those who teach in secondary schools earn three times the minimum wage. Alicia explains,

> *For anyone who is the principal wage earner in a family, male or female, it is impossible to think about getting by on one salary. Hardly anyone now relies solely on a teaching job. The answer for many teachers is to maneuver to obtain a second placement, and the whole business of assigning these extra jobs has become an area of patronage and corruption, with officers of the SNTE selling second jobs to needy teachers, and young teachers paying bribes to those who are about the retire to get the older teachers to recommend them for the post.*

Roberto says that teachers are now moonlighting at all kinds of second and third jobs—driving cabs, vending in the streets, whatever kind of work they can find in the informal economy. Many are among the illegal migrants to the United States, and in the border region, many teachers work in commerce, moving back and forth across the line with their border-crossing cards, buying goods on the American side for resale in Mexico.

Roberto and Alicia agree that it is not just the economic standard of the *maestros* that has declined but their prestige as well. Alicia explains,

> *The public school teacher used to be a poor but dignified figure, particularly in rural Mexico, but in poor urban communities as well. In middle-class neighborhoods the status of teachers was more precarious, because many of the children's parents were likely to have levels of education superior to that of the teachers, and they sometimes looked down on the* maestros*. But for the popular classes the* maestro *or* maestra *was an important person.*
>
> *Now poor children come out of school and they see their teachers selling ice cream in the town plaza or used clothing in the market square. Their teacher rides by at the wheel of a taxi. Obviously this undermines the authority and prestige of the teacher in the classroom. And you can imagine how the quality of the teaching has declined as the* maestros *rush—sometimes great distances—from one school in the morning to another in the afternoon. Understandably, a great many people are leaving the profession, especially those who have exhausted themselves trying to work two or three jobs.*

For Roberto and Alicia, the answer to the low social prestige and the economic difficulties of the teachers comes back to the struggle to democratize their union and turn it into a force that can work to win a better deal for the million or so school teachers in Mexico. They explain that with a *cacique* at the head of the organization, the union cannot serve as an instrument to fight the deteriorating economic condition of the teachers.

"When the oil boom turned to bust and the debt crisis hit," Roberto says, *the rich simply moved their money out of Mexico. But the salaried middle class, in particular government employees like the teachers, saw their real wage scale collapse and they fell from the middle class into poverty. The change is visible to the naked eye: now it's rare to see a teacher appear in a tie and jacket or a nice dress. At this stage the teachers are lucky to have a shirt on their backs.*

As long as we have a union run by charros *who enrich themselves while they're working to help the regime impose "austerity cuts" on the base, none of this will change. Only when genuinely representative, democratically elected leaders come to power in the union can we hope to reverse the pattern of impoverishment and decline in the teaching profession. This is why we continue to struggle.*

9 P.M.: *Mercedes Pacheco*

At 9 P.M. the vendors at the Mercado Argentina are packing up for the night. Mercedes Pacheco is loading her fruit back into the crates on which it was displayed all day in little piles: a pyramid of red apples here and a stack of yellow mangos there. Mercedes shows me that the mangos she bought this morning in the Merced market are still green and gold in color. The day-old mangos are pure gold. But the mangos from the day before, now spotted with brown, are selling at a reduced price. And then, there is a last pile that have grown quite dark and soft to the touch. These Mercedes will eat or leave behind for the people who sleep in the streets around the market—people more miserable than herself.

Mercedes explains that if she buys the mangos when they are green she has a week in which to sell them with at least some tiny margin of profit. The apples, on the other hand, will last up to a month, which gives Mercedes more leeway. But a crate of apples can cost almost twice as much as one of mangos, so the outlay is greater for Mercedes and oftentimes she just can't come up with the cash to cover it. Moreover, as she explains, with the mangos or the occasional papaya or watermelon that she picks up in the market, she can always cut up the fruit, sprinkle a little pulverized chili on it, and sell it by the slice rather than sit and watch it rot.

Mercedes also sells candy and gum: Milky Ways, Mars Bars, and Strawberry Bubble Yum. These items, she explains, last as long as you like. Some of her chocolates go back six months or more.

> *This is why I prefer candy to fruit. The sweets last forever. I buy it all from a merchant in Tepito. The candy comes from the other side. Anyway, that's what the storeowner says. I can't say, because I can't read, so I don't know what it says on the box. The problem with the candy is that sometimes kids come by on their way home from school and snatch a few pieces, and there go my profits.*

Mercedes has been in the streets of the capital selling some kind of food—first peanuts, and later avocados, fried pork rind and now, fruit and candy—since she arrived in the city at age eight from an indigenous community in the state of Mexico. Even today, some thirty-five years later, Mercedes still wears the brightly colored skirts and pleated blouse that mark her as a Nahuas Indian. Her hair, now streaked with gray, is plaited in two long braids with red, pink, and yellow ribbons wound through the plaits and tied together in a bow at the bottom. And she is more comfortable speaking Nahuatl than Spanish.

Mercedes calculates that working her seven-day week, she can earn somewhere between eighty and one hundred pesos selling fruit and candy. She would like to sell something more profitable and less risky than food, but she faces two obstacles. The first is that she lacks capital to invest in nonperishable goods. The second is the way in which market stalls are assigned in the Mercado Argentina, a large public market a few blocks from the Zócalo. Mercedes has been vending her wares in this *mercado* since she won the sponsorship of Doña Nacha, a political *jefe*—recently a *priísta* candidate for the chamber of deputies—whose following consists principally of indigenous women who have migrated to the capital.

> *I thank God for the help of Doña Nacha who got me a place in this market. When I was peddling my fruit in the streets, I would sit on the sidewalk and the police would come in their* camioneta, *seize my stock, and threaten to arrest me. One day they did arrest me, and I spent fifteen days in jail. Another time I was imprisoned for three days. The first time they threatened to cut off my braids—I don't know why, just to be mean, I guess. The second time was worse. They threatened to take away my baby.*
>
> *Doña Nacha got me out of jail and she found me this stall in the Mercado Argentina, where she has placed a lot of her people. I wish that Doña Nacha could get me permission to sell something else, like clothing or* fayuca. *But the board that governs the market won't sell any more places for people vending those things. Not even Doña Nacha can change that. Fruit is what people like me get to sell. Other people don't want to do it because you have to work every day of the week—otherwise your merchandise is rotting while you are resting at home.*

Mercedes's husband, Ángel, works alongside her. Mercedes explains that she and Ángel, who come from the same village, were *novios*, sweethearts, by age thirteen. When she became pregnant with Antonia, their eldest child, they married and he joined her in the city.

There was not much to keep him in the village. Ángel had only two and one half acres of unirrigated land, not nearly enough to support even a small family. Mercedes explains,

Once the children were born, there was no way for us to return to our pueblo, except once a year for the festival of Our Lady. What could we do there? Ángel could work as an agricultural laborer for a few centavos a day, and I could take in wash—but you can't support a family doing that kind of work. Only the people who have a decent parcel of land have remained in the village.

When Mercedes and Ángel first came to the city they lived with relatives in the heart of the capital, in a colonial building on Calle Paraguay, just behind the National Palace. Their living quarters were much like those described by Roberto—a single room opening onto a central patio. But while Roberto's family of four lived together in one room, Mercedes, Ángel, and their newborn child shared similar quarters with Ángel's sister, Lourdes, and her family of seven. Their circumstances improved when, after two years, Mercedes and Ángel managed to rent a single room in the same house for their growing family. Here they remained for twenty-five years, until the earthquakes of 1985 reduced the building to rubble. After eighteen months of living in a tent in the street in front of their former home, Mercedes and Ángel were given the opportunity to buy into a government housing project erected for earthquake victims on the far periphery of the capital.

We are supposed to pay seventy pesos a month in rent and then, when we have paid altogether fourteen thousand pesos the house will belong to us. The truth is that this house is in terrible condition. It's new, but the roof already leaks, the windows don't close and the rooms are so small that when you put a double bed in one, it fills the room so that you can't even close the door properly. But we can't complain to the authorities because we're way behind in the rent, and they'll just throw us out on the street. Right now, with all the interest figured in, we owe about three thousand pesos. What happened was that first I had problems with my liver. Then my littlest daughter was sick. Then a few months ago my merchandise was stolen from the storehouse where I rent space to leave it at night. So now we're way behind in our payments.

I ask Mercedes what she will do if they lose this house. She replies, "What choice have we got? We'll have to find some relatives who will take the six of us in. What else can we do?"

I am anxious to know what Mercedes sees as her prospects for the future. I ask if she knows that the Mexican government is negotiating a free trade agreement with the United States and Canada. Because she cannot read, Mercedes has not noticed the headlines about the free trade agreement which dominate the front page of newspapers in Mexico. However, she has heard some talk about the agreement, and I ask her if she thinks the changes underway may improve her situation in some respect. Much like Rosario, when responding to the same question, Mercedes explains that the agreement has absolutely nothing to do with people like her. "This agreement," she says, "is for rich people. It's not meant to help people like me."

As we speak, Mercedes and Ángel continue to pack their fruit on the two *diablitos* they will pay eight pesos to store for the night. They are anxious to get going because they still face a journey of two hours to reach their new home. In the rainy season the trip takes even longer. When the rains come in the spring, the bus they catch at the end of the subway line to connect with their housing project has to swing around the huge puddles that collect where there are no paved roads or storm sewers. Mercedes says,

At least when we lived in Calle Paraguay, we worked from eight in the morning to nine at night, but we only walked a few blocks to our house. Now we are lucky to eat our dinner by 11:30 at night, because it takes us so long to get home. Then we get a few

hours of sleep and rise again at five to be here in time to serve the first customers at eight.

The problem is, we have no choice. Today it costs too much to live in the center of Mexico City. As it is, we pay more to store our fruit overnight in a bodega *near the market than to rent our house on the edge of the city.*

Before Mercedes and Ángel have crated the last of the mangos, I try to buy a bag of the ripe ones, explaining that I plan to bake a mango pie. But Mercedes packs me a bagful of the better, semiripe mangos and then refuses to let me pay. The more I decline her generosity, the more insistent she becomes. Finally, I thank her, say my goodbyes and return to the guest house where I am staying.

When I arrive at the guest house, I go straight to the kitchen and turn over my bag of mangos to Rosita, the cook. She thinks it peculiar that I have come home with produce at this late hour. Indeed, it is strange, and I explain to her how it is that I received this gift. Rosita shakes her head and says to me, "You see, this is how it works in Mexico: the poor are always feeding the rich."

9

Conclusions

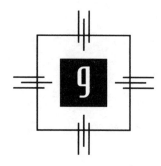

When Mercedes's fresh mangos appeared at breakfast the next morning, the assemblage of two students, four researchers, and three travelers seated at the large dining table at the center of the guest house began to debate the meaning of this gift. Some called Mercedes foolish, while others saw her as generous. A couple of those gathered thought it was an act of pride and dignity for an impoverished person like Mercedes to make a present of a salable commodity to someone who could well afford to pay for the goods. Others suggested that the event was less complicated: Mercedes may simply have liked me and drawn pleasure from our lengthy talks. Those most attuned to the Mexican political system thought that Mercedes's offering might constitute the opening gesture in what she hoped would become a patron-client relationship. They argued that Mercedes viewed me as an influential person and figured that her generosity would be reciprocated in the form of future favors and protection.

While I would have preferred to think that Mercedes was moved only by kindness, I could not reject the suggestion that her gesture was prompted by the instinct for survival that makes patron-client links so strong in Mexico. As the experiences of the people presented in this book indicate, in the face of poverty and overwhelming uncertainty, many Mexicans find themselves in constant search of a powerful person to intervene on their behalf. Whether it is Mercedes seeking the help of Doña Nacha or Miguel paying his protection money to Don Gerardo, one logical response to material deprivation and random victimization at the hands of the authorities and local strongmen is to establish some connection to a patron. Indeed, even an economically powerful person like the industrialist, Bernardo, feeling vulnerable when confronting rapid policy changes he cannot fully anticipate or control, may look to reinforce his links to boyhood friends who may be able to provide a personal connection to those in power.

The Political System

The Mexicans interviewed in these pages come from a wide range of backgrounds and conditions. Nonetheless, despite the geographical, gender, and class differences among them, they share some common experiences. All these people, rich or poor, lack a sense of political competence and effectiveness. Generally, they do not feel that they can intervene in national life to shape the course that their country will take. Tossed about by the shifting currents of the world market, unable to influence policy through the ballot box, at the receiving end of programs concocted by a narrow political elite that has shown itself unwilling to share power, these people do not enjoy even the quite limited sense of influence over events that participation in an imperfect democratic system affords. To be sure, the condition of a poor person like Lupe, whose nest egg is wiped out when her son becomes the target of police extortion, differs in dramatic degree from the fate of an economically powerful person like Sergio, the electronics manufacturer. But, ironically, Sergio also sees himself as the victim of policies over which he has no control. Indeed, none of the rich people I interviewed expressed the assurance that he could shape policy in any direct way, and only one, Martín, the landowner, was unambivalently satisfied with the course that the Salinas administration was taking. If wealthy industrialists like Sergio, Bernardo, or the textile manufacturer, Rubén, feel they lack the means to influence policy, if their associations and chambers are not consulted by policymakers, so much greater is the frustration and powerlessness of a peasant like Ramón or a domestic worker like Adelita. Strikingly, only those people who are politically active like Alicia and Roberto in the teachers' union or Conchita and Lupe in their urban popular movements, express anything other than resignation when talking about the iron control of those who rule the country.

Contributing to these feelings of powerlessness is the lack of information on current political and economic affairs available to Mexicans of any social class. As Josefina says, "The government only tells us what it wants us to know." Josefina observes that an accident in the Metro Etiopia never appears in the newspapers because the regime wants to maintain the appearance of a perfect safety record. For his part, Bernardo insists that the press is full of fanciful accounts in which industries on the verge of collapse are presented as thriving, and trade talks that failed are portrayed as successful. The negotiation of NAFTA, a central topic of public discussion and congressional and parliamentary debate in the United States and Canada, was treated as a national security secret by the Mexican regime. After months of announcements to the effect that their government had no intention of moving toward free trade, those few Mexicans able to lay hands on a copy of the *Wall Street Journal* were amazed to read on March 27, 1990, that arrangements for negotiations of such a treaty were, in fact, already in place.[1]

Clearly, Mexicans who are outside the narrow circle of government power—including rich, as well as poor and middle-class Mexicans—receive very little information. And the data they do receive, such as government statistics on inflation, employment, or balance of payments, are widely viewed as unreliable at best. As

Sergio notes with irony, "Even if elections were fair and honest, it would be hard for us to act as 'responsible citizens' because we don't know what the hell is going on!" Indeed, the shock with which most Mexicans received the news that armed struggle had erupted in San Cristóbal de las Casas on New Year's Day 1994 was due to the regime's success over the previous two years in suppressing word of the growing movement among indigenous people in the state of Chiapas.

Deprived of the information they would need to participate in a national debate, unable to weigh in with opinions on government policy, denied even the chance to cast votes that get properly counted, many Mexicans turn to other means to exert influence or, in the most defensive terms, to guard themselves from misfortune. They seek personal connections and protection.

As a result, the orientation of the political system is clientelistic rather than participatory. Political loyalty is exchanged for favors, and votes are traded for the satisfaction of immediate material demands. Although Conchita is disappointed that many of her neighbors seem ready to return to the PRI fold after having voted for the opposition candidate, Cuauhtémoc Cárdenas, in fact these people are only responding within the logic of a system built on patronage. The PRI hopes to regain the ground it lost in 1988 when people like Conchita, Josefina, Miguel, Lupe, Rosario, and virtually all their friends and relations supported Cárdenas and overwhelmingly carried the Federal District and the central Valle de Mexico for the opposition parties. People in San Miguel Teotongo understand that the PRI needs to build its formal electoral support to restore some measure of legitimacy to its rule. Although they are alienated from the PRI and identify it as an instrument of their oppression in its support for the local *cacique* who has terrorized them, they also see the PRI as a tool that can be used to gain urban services for their community. And so, when the president himself appears in the main square of San Miguel to offer sewers to the people of that community, some are ready to reward him with their vote.

Opposition Movements

Not only is political participation in the PRI oriented around the trade-off of votes for government goods and services, but this pattern also marks the behavior of many Mexicans mobilized by opposition parties and urban popular movements. When Josefina views the new social movements that have grown rapidly in poor neighborhoods, she sees them chiefly as alternative dispensers of patronage. For Josefina, the equation is simple: "You have to go every day to demonstrations and meetings and sit-ins, and after you do this for a year or so, they put your name on a list and you get a house." Lupe herself indicates that she originally understood her participation in the Asamblea de Barrios precisely in those terms: attendance at rallies and support for opposition candidates are exchanged for help in gaining material benefits.

This instrumental attitude grows not out of a lack of principled conviction but out of the desperation of people who live perilously close to the edge. They cannot afford the time to participate politically if they have no expectation of some material payback for the hours they invest. Among the 45 percent of the population that can be classified as "poor" and "very poor,"[2] few enjoy even one day of leisure per week. As we have seen, Miguel, Rosario, Ramón, and Mercedes work every day, and Josefina uses her Sundays to clean her own house and launder her clothing. These people have no spare time to dedicate to politics. Even Conchita has to measure the material benefits of her hours spent in the communal kitchen against the alternative economic activities she might pursue in the same block of time. To be sure, she is well aware of the emotional satisfaction that her involvement in the movement provides and, like Lupe, Conchita is conscious of the personal transformation she has undergone as a consequence of her commitment to a women's group. But Conchita must also calculate the costs and benefits of her political activism, because she is too close to the margin to afford the luxury of participation if her activism had no economic compensation. In short, Conchita and Lupe are political activists. They are not resigned to accepting PRI rule without protest, nor do they merely seek the help of powerful patrons. But they could not take the time away from the pursuit of basic survival needs if their activism had no material payoff.

The "Democratization" Process and Economic Modernization

At present both Mexican and foreign observers are anxiously surveying the political horizon, trying to detect any sign of "democratization" in Mexico. Theoretically, this could come in the form of a reduction in electoral fraud, the growth of opposition parties, the reinforcement of independent tendencies in the trade unions, the emergence of a public debate on national issues in the media, or some kind of institutional reform. Supporters of NAFTA have raised expectations that Salinas's efforts to restructure the economy will somehow lead to the development of more democratic patterns in all areas of Mexican society. In line with the most optimistic predictions of "modernization theory," the neoliberal boosters of structural adjustment like to suggest that these economic changes will inevitably produce a more participatory democratic system, free of corruption and personalistic politics.

The problem with this argument is that the control of the PRI is built on a system of fraud and clientelism. When he took office, Carlos Salinas might well have wished to rid Mexico of the most pernicious strongmen and political thugs. But the new president quickly found that he could not sweep away corruption with the stroke of a pen in the same way that he can sell off state property to private investors. In essence, Salinas cannot break the power of the *caciques*, because the PRI depends on them to secure the votes it needs to cloak its rule with a mantle of legitimacy. Too many ruthlessly powerful figures have too much at stake for Salinas to meddle with this system.

Several profiles illustrate the degree to which corruption is embedded in all areas of public and private life. The transit police who prey on people like Lupe's son, the political bosses who control the street markets, the border officials who extort kickbacks from Rosario, the police who demand payoffs from Pedro, the agents of the government bank who line their pockets rather than provide technical advice to peasants like Ramón, the *caciquillos* who control whole neighborhoods and *ciudades perdidas* like San Miguel Teotongo are all tolerated by the regime because they are loyal to the party and work to keep it in power.

Foreign observers sometimes imagine that the PRI's corruption centers on elections and consists only of fiddling with voter registration, physically intimidating opposition supporters, stealing ballot boxes, or miscounting votes. In fact, millions of Mexicans are touched by corruption every day of their lives. In general, poor people are more exposed to these abuses than those who are better off. But middle-class and wealthy Mexicans are also vulnerable every time they eat a piece of pork or beef that has not been inspected, because the meat inspector is on the take, or rent an apartment in a structure that has been certified as meeting safety standards only because the building inspector has received his *mordida*. Sergio observes that corruption is as pervasive as pollution, infecting the lives of all Mexicans. And, thus, in this sense too he notes that he may live in an exclusive neighborhood, but he still has to breathe the same poisoned air that poor people breathe.

The pervasiveness of corruption in the Mexican system is even more evident and troubling when we consider how hardworking people are forced into arrangements that are technically illegal. This goes for all the street vendors we have met: Miguel, Rosario, and Mercedes (before her patron installed her in a legal spot in the market). Moreover, Rosario and Miguel deal in imported goods—

electronics and used clothing—that are officially contraband and this makes them even more vulnerable to police extortion. Adelita must pose as a shopper to cross the border to work. Pedro, Rosario, and Miguel have to calculate payoffs to political bosses and police as part of their business overhead. Even Josefina, who tells me that her life is an "open book," has to be listed as an employee in a factory where she does not in fact work if she is to have access to health care. Rubén, on the other hand, is more fortunate than these others—and not only for the obvious reason that he has a lot more money. His economic position gives him the luxury of saying no to a set of business practices that would entangle him in the bribery and corrupt dealings involved in slipping contraband goods into the country.

Under the circumstances, a little tinkering with electoral or campaign laws is not going to change a system of political control based on corruption. Nor has the dramatic shift in economic policy improved Mexico's human rights record. On the contrary, economic programs that have substantially increased the suffering of the poor inevitably run the risk of stimulating social unrest. As a consequence, the neoliberal policies have been accompanied by some give-aways like the president's National Solidarity Fund, created to mollify the poor. But they have also been accompanied by a ferocious intensification of political repression. Thus, the expectation of many foreign observers that the regime of an English-speaking, Harvard-educated, pro-U.S. economic "modernizer" would usher in a new age of freedom from the brutal suppression of dissidents has not been borne out. Reports from Amnesty International, Americas Watch, and independent human rights organizations based in Mexico make plain what Mexican activists have known all along. Whether we focus on the fate of journalists, independent peasant and labor leaders, indigenous community activists, striking workers, or opposition party supporters, the systematic persecution of dissidents has reached unprecedented heights under Salinas and includes the harassment, kidnapping, torture, disappearance, and murder of hundreds of Mexicans.[3] With the outbreak of the rebellion in Chiapas in January 1994, the persecution of dissidents also came to include a savage and indiscriminate military retaliation against the entire civilian population of the indigenous communities around San Cristóbal de las Casas.

Given the ferocity with which the political elite has repressed protest in Mexico, the surprising thing is not that so many people swallow their anger—as Rosario does at the border—and accept the extortion, corruption, and fraud, nor that others (like Josefina) quietly accept the increasing impoverishment that results from the regime's economic policies. Rather, what is most striking is that people like Lupe and Conchita find the courage to join with others to make demands on the system, or that Roberto and Alicia brush off their encounters with prison and death, and go forward to regroup and reorganize to challenge the system. If we were to count all the Mexicans who participate in rural and urban popular movements, democratic tendencies within the unions, and other active forms of opposition to the regime, these people would number in the hundreds of thousands. And if we add in those who gave their vote to the opposition coalition headed by Cuauhtémoc Cárdenas or the right-wing opposition party, PAN, we are looking at millions of Mexicans. Nonetheless, even those who have the best reasons to want to change the political system face obstacles to mobilization. These range from outright repression to the structural barriers to participation that a person like Josefina encounters. Under such conditions, although a substantial minority of Mexicans do organize to fight back, the fact is that many have become resigned to PRI control.

This political quiescence does not mean that Mexicans support the PRI. On the contrary, nearly everyone encountered in these pages is deeply alienated from the official party. Indeed, the unanimity of disaffection from the ruling party among people of such disparate social conditions is noteworthy. In all of my interviews, I found no one who praised the PRI for anything, although I found some people, like Martín, who were happy with the policies of the individual whom the PRI had elevated to power, and others, like Conchita's neighbor, who thought that the president—not the party—had been good to the community in "giving" it sewers.

Survival Strategies

Although people may be alienated from the PRI, they do not necessarily react politically as Lupe, Conchita, Roberto, and Alicia have done. Even in regions of rural Mexico well known for their tradition of explosive peasant struggles, the economic crisis of the 1980s did not give rise to widespread collective protest. This is why the rebellion in Chiapas, a movement explicit in its denunciation of Salinas's economic policies, caught the regime off guard. Until the Zapatistas' armed uprising, as one expert noted, "the predominant pattern in the countryside was not community or regional organization and protest (although some such activities did occur), but rather a series of adaptations within rural households to ensure economic survival."[4] That is, rather than mobilize for collective action, both rural and urban Mexicans have more often responded to the crisis by formulating personal and family strategies meant to provide the security that the broader society denies. Since these people cannot rely on the state or the PRI, they rely on their relatives and they rely on themselves.

For starters, they work hard—harder than people do in many other cultures. The industriousness of poor Mexicans is so obvious that even economically privileged people acknowledge it readily. In the many interviews I conducted with Mexican businessmen and industrialists I heard bitter criticism of politicians, the unions, the federal labor law, the economic planners, and others—but not one of these informants said that the Mexican worker was lazy. These capitalists may not, in many cases, have expressed any sympathy, let alone empathy, for the people put out of work in the process of economic restructuring. But they never said that poor people stood around with their arms folded, not wanting to work. This, I believe, stands in contrast to the attitudes expressed by the economic elite in other countries toward the people they employ. The capacity for hard work of men and women like Ramón or Josefina is so evident that it is beyond dispute. As one acute observer of rural Mexico has noted ironically, "creating employment, inventing ways of working harder, is part of peasant leisure."[5]

Apart from engaging in the kind of self-exploitation of a person like Josefina who simply pushes herself harder and harder as prices rise, the people encountered in these pages share an ability for personal economic planning that involves meticulously accurate calculation of costs and benefits. This is no less true of the poor Mexicans we have met than the rich. This capacity for highly efficient management—sometimes of the most paltry resources—becomes evident when Adelita decides to leave the *maquilas* in favor of housework across the border, when Ramón weighs the profitability of a broccoli crop and the merit of selling to one or another multinational firm, or when Pedro chooses to take migrants only as far as San Ysidro rather than accompanying them all the way to Los Angeles. It is also obvious when Rosario selects her stock at the Tres Hermanos store, or when Mercedes apportions her scarce resources among apples, mangos, and candy bars, or when Lupe calculates how she can best spend the money from the *tanda*. Moreover, the seven women in this book elaborate detailed financial plans to maximize their earnings from work, and then they return home to micro-manage their household budgets.

Along with good management, the resourcefulness displayed by people in these pages is striking. Sergio's driver, Don Jesús, is a classic example of the inventive, practical Mexican who can fix anything out of a few bits and pieces that come to hand. This is a quality that anyone who has ever driven through Mexico in an old or unreliable car would know well—a characteristic admired not only by foreigners but by Mexicans themselves. Bernardo, for example, underscores the clever tricks that his employees have invented to make the work process go more smoothly, ingenious devices that leave his Japanese business partners gaping in admiration.

Indeed the entire informal economy in Mexico is a massive manifestation of the resourcefulness of poor Mexicans. Lacking the safety net of unemployment insurance, those who lose their factory jobs or find they cannot get by on the minimum wages paid in "formal sector" jobs, create a wide variety of occupations for themselves. These range from services (for example, guarding parked cars) and entertainment (sword swallowing) to street commerce and production in small family units. Perhaps the most common family strategy employed by poor Mexicans is the one pursued by Adelita and her partner, Héctor. One family member strives to secure work in the formal economy—a job that may pay poorly but carries social security benefits—while the rest of the family scrambles as best they can to earn a higher income in jobs they create for themselves in the informal or "submerged" economy.

In addition to their resourcefulness, the physical mobility of the people featured in these profiles is also remarkable and indicates their willingness to migrate great distances in search of work. Pedro, Adelita, and Héctor have moved to the border from Durango, Michoacán, and Colima. Ramón is settled on the land, but has a history of labor migration, and he is the father of children who have left their rural community to find work in the city or in the United States. The parents of Miguel, Conchita, Josefina, Rosario, and Roberto brought them to the capital from Guerrero, Morelos, Puebla, Oaxaca, and Jalisco, thus forming part of the great rural exodus that quintupled the population of the Federal District after 1940.

Through careful planning, resourcefulness, very hard work, and a willingness to uproot themselves, the poor people I interviewed manage to survive if not to prosper. But the rhetoric supporting the neoliberal economic model promises much more than that. It suggests that the "internationalization" of the economy will inevitably offer new, even better opportunities for these same working-class Mexicans.

In the course of the interviews I found that the internationalization of the Mexican economy had, indeed, already opened new possibilities to some Mexicans, although not always on very attractive or secure terms. Adelita's experience in international production was so negative that she prefers to cross the border, with all the personal risks that decision entails, than to work in the *maquilas* in Tijuana. While Martín is looking forward to producing winter vegetables for the U.S. and Canadian markets, and Ramón is attempting to break the cycle of rural poverty by cultivating export crops, several of Ramón's neighbors in the Ejido Santa Marta have sunk into greater indebtedness as a result of their efforts to produce luxury vegetables for the international market. As the rural schoolmaster, Don Rodolfo, observes when reflecting on his own failure in export agriculture, the peasants who are already well off, who already own tractors and pickup trucks, may be able to position themselves to produce for the U.S. market. They may derive some benefit from NAFTA. Everyone else, as he puts it, "will be lucky if they can just keep themselves in corn and beans." Indeed, Ramón is well aware that his success in selling his crop to multinational agribusiness firms is very tenuous and depends on the goodwill of a few individuals within large corporate structures who are prepared to overlook the "inefficiency" involved in contracting with a smallholding peasant like himself.

Nor does NAFTA correspond to the greatest needs and ambitions of several of the people we have met. Pedro's dream is to hold a green card and to gain legal access to the U.S. labor market, thus ending his risky career as a coyote. Adelita would like to see the borders open to Mexican workers. Lupe would like her sons to pass freely back and forth between the two countries. But none of this was broached in the free trade negotiations. On the contrary, the issue of opening the border to Mexican migrants was systematically excluded from the discussions. Indeed, the argument of NAFTA supporters is that the agreement will create well-paid jobs in Mexico, allowing the Mexican poor to prosper, so they will no longer wish to enter the United States as illegal immigrants.

Finally, both those supporting and opposing NAFTA generally predict that, under the agreement, low-wage manufacturing jobs will move to Mexico. In fact, this process has been underway since the Border Industrialization Program was initiated in 1965, and it has accelerated throughout the 1980s and into the 1990s. But who will supply the labor force for these new factories? Both Josefina and Miguel indicate that they would not mind factory work, but they cannot afford to leave the jobs they have created for themselves in the informal sector. Factory jobs simply do not pay enough. Adelita also prefers housecleaning in the "hidden economy" to the kind of poor wages and working conditions offered by the *maquilas*. Under such circumstances, the expectation that the new factories that move to Mexico will rapidly fill with qualified women and men willing to work at minimum wage may prove unrealistic. Indeed, not one of the people interviewed for this book, however precarious and difficult his or her condition, looked forward to the opportunity of working for minimum wages in a transplanted U.S. or Canadian factory.

Perhaps the only poor person in these pages who stands to benefit from the reduction of tariffs is Rosario. Despite the skepticism she expressed to me in our talks, Rosario later found that the period of negotiations leading up to the signing of NAFTA was marked by a new tolerance on the border for those, like herself, who were entering with goods purchased in the United States. This policy, instituted in 1993, was designed by the Salinas regime to encourage support for NAFTA among merchants in the U.S. border towns.

With this new policy in place Rosario found that the border police generally waved her through without inspection.

As for the border police, as Rosario predicted, they did not stand with their arms folded as their income from *mordidas* disappeared. According to Pedro, the border police made up the shortfall in their personal incomes by intensifying the frequency of their visits and the amounts of money they extorted from coyotes and drug smugglers. Some left the force to devote themselves full-time to the drug trade where, logically, they had already established a wide network of contacts.

Businessmen and Economic Restructuring

If the employment prospects for poor people like Adelita, Josefina, and Miguel are not any brighter under a regimen of free trade, does economic liberalization hold out any more promise for the four businessmen?

Martín, as we have noted, is enthused about NAFTA because the agreement is tailor-made for his enterprise. The change in agrarian law, the revision of Article 27 of the constitution, was carried out precisely to strengthen and enhance the opportunities of operations like his. Martín has excellent land and lots of it. Able to grow any of forty different crops, he enjoys virtually unlimited flexibility. If he cannot compete in basic grains, he can shift to winter vegetables, spices, luxury fruits, or dozens of other highly profitable crops. Moreover, Martín's is a huge, vertically and horizontally integrated enterprise that permits him to emphasize any one of a variety of economic activities: basic agricultural production, food processing, agricultural technology and equipment, or marketing. He has an ample supply of capital from his family's holding corporation and the financial contacts to attract more capital should he need it. He also possesses the technology and space he may need to expand operations and the international contacts to penetrate the U.S. market. Little wonder, then, that Martín looks forward to NAFTA with glee.

However, only a minority of the businessmen and women affected by restructuring actually have the capital, contacts, and flexibility to make the adjustments necessary to prosper under a policy of economic liberalization. It is not as if every Mexican capitalist who wakes up in the morning feeling energetic can restructure successfully.

Unquestionably, Rubén is one of the best-positioned people in his field. He has family capital, so he is not forced to borrow at the prohibitively high cost of capital that prevails in Mexico as a consequence of the anti-inflationary monetary policies of the Salinas regime. Rubén and his family are not leveraged in any way: they have no monetary debts and no political compromises, and they are not involved in corrupt practices. This gives them a great deal of flexibility.

Like Martín, Rubén is already internationalized with links both to producers and to markets outside Mexico. He has a full network of U.S. connections in place, not to mention the contacts he has built in Asia. He knows how and where to purchase high-tech equipment and personnel. In sum, Rubén's family has approached the process of restructuring the way they train for the New York Marathon; they are forward-looking, disciplined, and systematic in analyzing their options and planning for the future.

While Rubén is not particularly attuned to the ways in which his situation may differ from that of others in his industry, Bernardo's experience as a leader in his association makes him very sensitive to the difference between his relatively strong position and that of other electronics entrepreneurs. For this reason he is aware that his degree of specialization and his Japanese partners have rescued him from the fate suffered by most in his industry. While others have been wiped out, Bernardo has profited and expanded. But his circumstances cannot be reproduced by others. Bernardo's ability to survive this period of uncertainty rests above all on the fact that he, like Martín and Rubén, had plenty of capital and well-established international links when the economy opened and Mexican industrialists lost the protection and government subsidies they had enjoyed since the 1940s.

International connections have also saved Sergio from personal financial disaster. Importing from Asia what he previously produced in his factory has enabled Sergio to continue to live a life of privilege and comfort. But the opening of the economy and the promise of free trade have brought to an end Sergio's existence as a manufacturer. He has survived, but only by fundamentally altering his activities—a situation he deeply resents.

Effectively, both Bernardo and Rubén have prospered by becoming *maquila* owners in a process that observers increasingly refer to as the maquiladorization of Mexico.[6] Today the assembly plants no longer cluster only at the border, nor are they necessarily foreign-owned. Bernardo has a *maquila* arrangement in his Mexico City plant, where his work force assembles parts shipped to him by his Japanese partners from their Korean and Taiwanese subsidiaries. When he reaches full production, Rubén's new plant in Durango will be a classic enclave operation with the equipment, technology, and raw material (cotton fiber) imported from abroad, and virtually all of the production destined for the U.S. market. The enterprise will have more value added in Mexico than some *maquila* operations, but it will not be substantially linked to the rest of the Mexican economy.

Every one of these cases of restructuring was accompanied by a net loss of jobs. Sergio laid off the vast majority of his work force when he ceased production. Bernardo scaled down the number of workers in his Mexico City plant and is not hiring anyone new. Rubén will have nine hundred apparel workers when he reaches the third stage of his plan, but jobs will disappear at the textile end of his operation.

Rubén, Bernardo, and Sergio recognize that these jobs have been lost. And all three are enlightened enough to be worried about the destabilizing effect of the massive unemployment and growing inequality engendered by the imposition of Salinas's neoliberal policies. But none of them questions the model itself or the necessity of proceeding along these lines, and all three buy into the notion that eventually Mexico will become more productive and salaries will rise.

In short, the new economic model presupposes that poor Mexicans will earn more and raise their standard of living because it is assumed that wages are linked to productivity, and when productivity goes up, the standard of living rises for the working class. But it is difficult to see how this can happen to any significant degree as long as Mexico's competitive advantage continues to be based on cheap wages. Even a 20 percent rise in the minimum wage would bring Mexican workers only from four to five dollars per day.

Moreover, there is no guarantee that increases in productivity translate into higher wages. Bernardo's work force is a case in point. These women may be good workers and more productive than their Japanese counterparts, but you don't see Bernardo paying them more. He continues to pay them the wage specified in the collective contract.

Wage advances occur only when workers' organizations are strong enough to bargain for a greater share of increasing profits. In Mexico the more militant unions are under constant attack, the workers' right to strike is often denied by force of arms, and the most combative union leaders are harassed and persecuted. Under the circumstances, the capacity of Mexican workers to fight for their share of productivity gains is severely limited. Thus, higher productivity is not likely to lead to higher wages for Mexicans in the absence of a radical transformation of the organization of labor and of the political system itself.

Postscript

When I returned to Mexico early in 1993 I carried out follow-up interviews with each of the people who appear in this book. I found that some had experienced very little change in their lives, while the situation of others had not only altered but done so in directions that I could not have anticipated on the basis of what I had learned from them in 1991 and 1992.

Josefina and Mercedes continue to scrape by in precisely the same fashion as when I had last seen them. Josefina, however, now has the additional burden of providing for the care of her infant grandson, whose mother, Josefina's elder daughter, has gone to work on the other side. Josefina manages her new situation by paying a neighbor three pesos per day to look after the child, although she occasionally brings the baby with her to work.

Bernardo's and Sergio's lives are also relatively unchanged. They continue to weekend in Cuernavaca and to pursue roughly the same business strategies. Each reports that he is structuring his enterprise in such a way as to minimize the impact that NAFTA will have on his activities. Both expect that some form of agreement will be in place by 1994. Don Jesús is still in Sergio's employ, but Sergio has hired a new driver, and Jesús is mostly occupied with office errands. Meanwhile, Don Jesús continues to cook up his *tacos al carbon* on the braziers at the entrance to his *vecindad*.

Adelita is still cleaning houses in San Diego. Having received recommendations to two more friends of her present employers, she has managed to add a fourth day to her work schedule. In January 1993 savage rainstorms flooded Tijuana and washed out the roads that connect Adelita to the border. This was a period of hardship for Adelita and Héctor, as for most *tijuanenses,* because they had no income for the three weeks it took the floods to recede.

Pedro's income was not interrupted by the flooding. January is his busiest month, peaking when those who have returned home for Christmas in central Mexico must make their way back to California. When the Tijuana River swelled to the point that it could no longer be forded on foot, some coyotes rigged pontoon bridges of inner tubes and assorted flotation devices to bring their *pollos* across. Dozens of would-be migrants drowned when they lost their footing in the swift current and were carried out to sea. For this reason, Pedro says, the *migra* were anxious to discourage the use of the western river route across the border, so they lifted their surveillance on the eastern end of the line, and Pedro was able to bring his people across without incident at a section of the fence near the airport.

Conchita continues to serve breakfast each morning at the Women in Struggle Cooperative, and she remains active as ever in the Settlers Union. She says that she hears a lot of talk about organizing to attract more funds from President Salinas's National Solidarity fund. She also finds that some of the *compañeros* remain focused on fostering change by supporting Cuauhtémoc Cárdenas, and these people are looking forward to mobilizing under the Cárdenas banner in the 1994 presidential elections. However, others are dispirited because they believe another victory for Cuauhtémoc will be denied in 1994 as it was in 1988. In the end, she tells me she would not dare to predict how many of her friends and neighbors will actually come out to vote for Cárdenas in the next elections.

Lupe's new house is finally close to completion, and Jorge was able to send sufficient funds from California to provide for the down payment. He was able to do this with the help of his brothers, Ricardo and José Luis, who have joined him in East Los Angeles and found jobs washing dishes in a Chinese restaurant.

The two safely crossed the border at Tijuana on their third attempt, and did so, as they planned, without the help of a coyote. The sewing machine scheme has come to nothing, but now Lupe and Margarita are working on a plan to sell something (possibly shoes) door-to-door in the new housing project. Lupe's brother, Alfredo, had his surgery at the end of 1992, and Lupe says he looks "better."

Don Ramón described to me the ups and downs he has experienced with various crops in the time since my last visit. He has succeeded in forging a relationship with another multinational and no longer depends exclusively on Fresh Veg. However, he is facing increasing problems of plague and blight in his fields. As a result, he is planning a strategic retreat to the cultivation of marigolds for the local poultry market until he can figure out how to tackle the pests that have attacked his vegetables. When we spoke, Don Ramón did not mention that he had also suffered a personal tragedy. But Pablo Villegas, the Fresh Veg field agent, told me that Ramón's eldest son had been killed in an auto accident on his way home from California for Christmas.

When I went to the Ferroplaza to see how Miguel was getting on, I found that not only had he left the market, but—somewhat more surprising—he had given up commerce altogether and was now driving a cab. Rosario's life was also radically altered by the change in policy on the border. Easy, "bribe-free" access to used clothing has sent hundreds of peddlers scurrying for the *frontera,* and Rosario says the market in used clothing is glutted. As a consequence, she has given up her weekly journeys and now trades in *fayuca,* which she purchases in Tepito.

By the time I renewed contact with Martín, the new agrarian order that he had predicted in 1991 had become reality with the reform of Article 27 of the constitution. As he had hoped, it is now no longer necessary for him to disguise the fact that his fifteen hundred acres are organized and worked as a single agricultural unit. Moreover, the new legal situation not only opens the possibility but positively encourages Martín to form the kind of association with *ejidatarios* that he had assured me earlier was the "only way out" for the peasants. But, speaking in 1993, Martín confesses that neither he nor any other large landowners he knows have succeeded in developing links with smallholding peasants. The clandestine arrangements that were in place before the changes in Article 27 now have legal status. But Martín says that most smallholders remain too distrustful to conclude contracts with large producers like himself.

Rubén reports that the plans for the construction of the new factory in Durango continue apace. The land has been purchased and the new equipment is ready for shipment. However, in the meanwhile, a huge U.S.-based textile firm approached him, seeking a partnership arrangement. Together they have purchased a new factory in Chihuahua, where production of denim is to begin immediately, and the manufacture of jeans will quickly follow.

Perhaps the most dramatic change has come in the life of Roberto. He was asked by the opposition PRD to stand as a candidate for the chamber of deputies and, on the strength of his reputation as a militant democratic trade unionist, he was elected in a district with a heavy working-class population. Roberto seems neither impressed nor uncomfortable with the pomp surrounding his new status as *diputado*. Significantly, he chose to meet me at the union headquarters, where he continues to spend a good deal of time, rather than in his office in the chamber of deputies. Overall, Roberto says that he looks on this period of parliamentary service as simply another phase in a lifetime of political engagement, as a battle that must be fought on another front.

Alicia has continued to pursue her activities in the union and is working with a group in the National Normal School on the problem of teacher burn-out. In her view it is a good thing for Roberto to represent the PRD in the chamber, even though the party holds only a tiny minority of the seats. His presence provides the opportunity to raise issues that otherwise would never receive a hearing of any kind in the legislative debates. Alicia sees this term in office as "another important form of political work, a genuinely valuable contribution." But both Roberto and Alicia agree that after one term it will be time for Roberto to step down and pass the responsibility to another *compañera* or *compañero*.

Afterword

Up to the period covered in this book, the study of Mexico had always been a course in political certainties. Principal among these certainties was the absolute authority of the president during his term of office and the assurance that the PRI, whatever its obvious failings, would preserve its hold on power.

To be sure, political reforms implemented from the 1970s onward had altered the manner in which opposition parties were officially recognized as well as the ways they were permitted to participate in elections. New laws had changed the size of the legislative bodies and the system by which senators and deputies were elected. Changes of this kind opened the door to the growth of opposition parties such as the PRD and eventually made possible the election to the Chamber of Deputies of a greater number of leftist activists such as Roberto.

Yet notwithstanding the institutional changes proposed and implemented in the 1970s and 1980s, the PRI managed to maintain its overwhelming numerical superiority over all challengers. Over time, the most effective form of electoral fraud shifted from the use of *pistoleros* who rode into town, shot up the main plaza, and galloped off with ballot boxes, to a more modern dependence on the well-timed computer crash. However, both modern and traditional forms of fraud successfully coexisted, the use of state funding to buy votes continued unchecked, and the outcome was always the same: the PRI prevailed over the opposition at the national level and in all but four states.

Still, for all the continuity in the Mexican system, in the course of the administration of Carlos Salinas, a series of fundamental changes began to reshape Mexico. Some of these alterations were intentional and formed the core of Salinas's program of neoliberal reform. For example, Salinas was openly committed to dismantling the state sector and privatizing state holdings. As we have seen, he was determined to end state support and protection to the domestic industrial class; that is, to people like Sergio, Rubén and Bernardo. His economic policy called for the reduction of benefits for organized workers and the withdrawal of other social guarantees, such as controls on basic food prices or the subsidized public transport on which people like Mercedes, Josefina, Lupe and others depended. In line with his commitment to reducing the role of the state, Salinas abandoned a host of revolutionary principles, withdrawing virtually all historic limitations and legal curbs on foreign investment and influence within Mexico, and terminating the agrarian reform program that had once provided land grants to peasants like Don Ramón.

While pursuing these radical economic changes, Salinas also hoped to transform the political system. He actively sought to bypass the traditional networks of patronage distribution provided by the PRI, replacing these clientelistic links with handouts provided by PRONASOL, the "National Solidarity Program" loyal to himself. Of course Salinas's alteration of this aspect of the patronage system led to a crisis in the system of corporativist support for the PRI; the organized peasants, the official labor movement, and the officially sponsored middle-sector organizations that had formed the pillars of the ruling party now lacked a clear role. This in turn produced ferocious conflict within the official party between the so-called "dinosaurs" who had benefited from the old system of *caciquismo*, and the "reformers" who shared Salinas's vision of a streamlined, modernized PRI free from the control of labor and peasant bosses and local and regional strongmen—if not necessarily more open and democratic.

Sources of Instability

If Salinas's calculated intervention in the patronage system that sustained the PRI led to unprecedented instability in the political system, other radical changes during this period were totally unanticipated. At the top of the list of unintended consequences of Salinas's policies was the outbreak of a full scale armed rebellion in Chiapas in January 1994 and, more recently, in the impoverished rural regions of Guerrero, Oaxaca, Morelos, Veracruz, Tabasco, and Puebla. Neither Salinas nor his successor, President Ernesto Zedillo (1994-2000), have found a way to end or even contain these armed popular uprisings, and the low-intensity warfare that continues today in southern and central Mexico has burned out of control like the wildfires that swept much of the same region in 1998. Perhaps the only certain outcome of the armed conflict in rural Mexico is that it continues to expand the Mexican military's influence. This is a result that gravely worries many Mexicans, because through most of this century Mexico has been distinctive among nearly all Latin American states for the clear limits imposed on the size and role played by its army. It also concerns Mexicans because the inability of the military and civilian authorities to resolve the conflicts in Chiapas and elsewhere has opened the door to greater U.S. intervention in their country.

Both the breakdown of the political system and the loss of control by those at the top were dramatically highlighted by the wave of political assassinations at the highest levels which began with the murder in March 1994 of the official party's presidential candidate, Luís Donaldo Colosio, and culminated six months later with the point-blank shooting of the secretary general of the PRI, José Francisco Ruíz Massieu. These crimes, in which not only Salinas himself but his brother Raúl, his closest associates and others at the very top of the political elite have been implicated, remain unsolved and stand as clear indications of the decline of the rule of law in Mexico.

In a certain sense, however, the political assassinations are only the most dramatic and notorious evidence of the breakdown of public order in Mexico. By the late 1990s, the kind of extortion, exploitation, and arbitrary rule that poor Mexicans such as Miguel, Lupe, Conchita, Rosario and Mercedes had always suffered at the hands of those who held power had now become an everyday reality for upper- and middle-class Mexicans. Rule of law had declined to the point that middle-class Mexicans increasingly found themselves the targets of violent car thieves, muggers, and kidnappers, who were often in league with the "public authorities" when hey were not themselves uniformed police. Although the vast majority of crimes in Mexico go unreported, since few are investigated and only a small fraction of perpetrators are apprehended or punished, the official government statistics show that murders increased by 50 percent between 1990 and 1995, while robberies have increased six-fold in the last 15 years and those kidnappings that are actually *reported* come to at least 1,500 per year. With a justice system that is thoroughly discredited and has seen seven different men shuffling through the position of attorney general in nine years, it is increasingly evident that the police themselves are now "the main organizers of crime."

Under these circumstances, for the economic elite the employment of at least one personal bodyguard has become standard. Homes in neighborhoods where industrialists like Sergio, Bernardo and Rubén live are protected by private guards, armed with submachine guns and dressed in flak jackets, who stand in front of each house like a grotesque new form of lawn ornament. Meanwhile, the hijacking of whole container trucks of cloth on the main highway between the textile-producing cities of Puebla and Tlaxcala and the capital has become so common that insurance companies will no longer underwrite the risk. By the late 1990s, apparel factories operating exclusively with stolen fabric and thread were turning out garments for sale in the street markets. And among all the entrepreneurs I had interviewed in the early 1990s, every one had personal experience or knowledge of a close friend or relative who had been kidnapped and released in a 24-hour span after a ransom payment of at least one million dollars. Several were making plans to move their families and operations abroad until the "climate" in Mexico improved for people of their social class.

Another example of the decline in public order during this period has been the development of the Mexican drug cartels as the key link in the international division of labor in narcotics in the Americas. During the Salinas years, as the U.S. Department of Drug Enforcement tightened its surveillance of East Coast points of entry for drugs into the United States, smugglers' routes shifted westward to Mexico. No longer content with a fee of one to two thousand dollars for every kilo transported to the United States on behalf of their Colombian associates, Mexican drug traffickers began to demand a cut of as much as half the cocaine they smuggled for the Colombians. As a consequence drug cartels long based in northern Mexico grew vastly rich and powerful and were reinforced to the point that they came to equal and eventually surpass the infamous Cali and Medellín cartels in Colombia.

To be sure, the expanded role of the Mexican druglords was not entirely new. Salinas's predecessor, Miguel de la Madrid, was said to have established an understanding with the leaders of the Mexican *narcotraficantes* whereby his regime was prepared to ignore their activities in return for the druglords' commitment to repatriate and invest their profits in Mexico. However, in the Salinas years the relationship between the cartels and the Mexican state changed; De la Madrid's "gentlemen's agreement" gave way to a full interpenetration of the political and the drug elites. Investigations into drug laundering carried out after 1995 by both Swiss and U.S. government agents clearly established that in the Salinas years hundreds of millions of dollars were paid in bribes by drug traffickers s to officials at the highest levels of law enforcement, including the deputy attorney general, the supervisor of the federal police, the chief of antidrug operations, as well as the president's brother. With these links in place, the strongest Mexican druglords emerged as economic and political actors as powerful and, in some respects more powerful, than anyone else in the country.

The breakdown of the rule of law, the increased influence of the *narcotraficantes*, and theZedillo regime's loss of control over whole areas of the country contributed to *and* were reinforced by Carlos Salinas's fall from grace. Notwithstanding the shameful human rights record of his regime, Salinas had once been a hero of the international financial community and the U.S. administration's preferred candidate to become head of the new World Trade Organization. However after the murders of Colosio and Ruíz Massieu, wide suspicion about Salinas's involvement in the assassinations, revelations of his family's vast enrichment during his term in office, and the discovery of hundreds of millions of dollars squirrelled away by his associates in foreign bank accounts completed Salinas's humiliation and led to his self-imposed exile from Mexico.

Significantly, Salinas's fall meant loss of immunity from public scrutiny and culpability for acts of malfeasance, corruption, and gross human rights abuses that his predecessors in the presidency had traditionally enjoyed. This development represented a striking change in the Mexican political system. While the poor people interviewed for this book had never harbored illusions about the integrity or legitimacy of those who held power in Mexico, the overall impact of the revelations about rot at the top under Salinas, coupled with the personal fear experienced by Mexicans in their everyday lives, combined to delegitimize the political system for Mexicans across the social spectrum. And at the same time that

Mexicans came to feel less confidence than ever in their political leaders and less control over their political lives and personal security, the economic crisis produced by the collapse of the peso in 1994 engulfed all social classes-improving the condition of a few, while gravely damaging the interests of an astonishingly broad range of Mexicans.

The Economic Crisis and Its Impact

If the January 1994 outbreak of rebellion in Chiapas and the political assassinations that followed later the same year were not clear indicators of the breakdown of the Mexican system, the devaluation of the peso in December certainly put an end to any hopes that Mexicans may have cherished of an easy transition to economic prosperity and political stability under NAFTA. Eager to promote his chances to become Secretary General of the newly constituted World Trade Organization, Carlos Salinas refused to confront the problem of a significantly overvalued currency during his final year in office. When Salinas's successor, Ernesto Zedillo, faced the unwelcome task of adjusting the peso, his 15 percent devaluation set off a panic in Mexican and foreign financial markets. Under the circumstances, only a rescue package of U.S. $70 billion sponsored by the United States and IMF was sufficient to prevent the total collapse of the system and, importantly, great losses to U.S. investors.

In broad, macroeconomic terms, the bailout worked. By 1996, official figures began to indicate a recovery. As direct foreign investment grew, Mexican government bonds began to sell briskly in foreign markets, and the country registered a trade surplus. Indeed, Mexicans like Bernardo, Rubén or Martín who produce electronics, textiles and winter vegetables for the U.S. market, found that the devaluation of the peso gave their products a competitive edge in international trade.

However it quickly became clear that the peso devaluation, much like NAFTA itself, benefited only some Mexican companies, generally the largest. As the peso dropped and interest rates on loans skyrocketed, the cost of borrowing capital became exorbitant for middle-sized and small-scale Mexican entrepreneurs. At that point, anyone who could not draw on his or her own resources or family capital to expand into the globalizing economy had to shut down operations. Indeed, in the two years following the peso crisis, 60 % of all small industries and agricultural producers were forced to lay off workers, and an estimated 20,000 businesses shut down altogether, producing a total loss of 1.5 million jobs. Although new jobs were created along the border in maquila industries after the peso crisis, 90 % of the businesses listed on the Mexican Stock Exchange "were laying off workers as a consequence of economic stagnation, low profits, globalization and an inability to compete in the international market."

These job losses, combined with the inability of undercapitalized Mexican entrepreneurs to create new places for new entrants into the labor force, pushed unemployment to unprecedented levels. Thus in an economically active population of 34 million, 15 % were openly unemployed, another 40 % were underemployed, and even the government figures that measure joblessness showed unemployment up 106 % in the cities while the problem was, of course, far more pressing in rural zones.

Moreover, the drop in employment was accompanied by a sharp decline in real wages for those who still held jobs as the minimum wage grew only 136 % while the cost of living increased 371 %. Logically the fall in real wages and family income had devastating consequences for those Mexicans, like the poor people profiled in this book, who were already living in the margins. Education and literacy levels, which had been climbing steadily from the 1940s through the 1970s, now declined precipitously as parents who could no longer afford the price of school uniforms and books—

and even more dramatically, could not forego the labor power of their children—pulled their sons and daughters out of school to work in tiny family enterprises or to sell or beg in the streets. In an indication of the anguished decisions that now came to guide family survival strategies, the number of children living and working in the street doubled between 1993 and 1996. Moreover, along with the fall in educational and nutritional levels, came an increase in communicable diseases, especially tuberculosis and hepatitis as well as all illnesses associated with tainted ground water. Perhaps the most dramatic and poignant expression of the desperation of impoverished Mexicans came in 1996, when hungry peasants held up trains in Monterrey and Durango and attempted to carry off sacks of corn and wheat.

Although some of the richest Mexicans took their knocks in this same crisis, and the number of Mexican billionaires—which had grown from 2 to 24 during the Salinas years—dropped to ten, the gap between rich and poor continued to widen. Mexico's income disparity, among the worst in the world before the peso crisis, now grew even more extreme as the richest 10 % of the population came to hold 41 % of Mexico's wealth, while the bottom half of the population shared only 16 % of all national income. An illustration of this extreme concentration of income is the case of Carlos Slim, a close associate of Carlos Salinas, who became the new owner of Teléfonos de México (among other assets) thanks to Salinas's privatization program. According to *Forbes* Magazine, by the age of 54 Slim controlled companies that amounted to 22 % of the market capitalization on the Mexican Stock Exchange, and enjoyed an estimated net worth of 6.6 billion dollars. This accumulation of wealth meant that "the assets of the richest man in Mexico total[ed] more than the annual income of the poorest 17 million people combined."

As the gap between rich and poor continued to grow, middle-class Mexicans also reeled under the effects of a combination of forces. Like the poor they found the cost of living dramatically increased for all basic consumer items. Moreover, prices of the imported goods which they had grown accustomed to consuming rose steeply as the peso fell. Fuel, electricity and transport became vastly more expensive as the privatization of state holdings brought market-value price tags to what had previously been public service utilities. But perhaps the biggest blow to the middle classes was the rise in interest rates. By 1994, 6 million Mexicans had acquired credit cards as high-pressure sales campaigns sponsored by the newly privatized banks induced the middle classes to buy even their groceries on credit. As interest rates on consumer loans soared to 50 and eventually to 100 % in the wake of the peso crisis, 60 % of cardholders now found themselves deeply in debt, and the repossession of cars and houses became commonplace among those middle-class Mexicans who had bought into the notion of 'plastic' as the ultimate expression of modernization.

Some Signs of Change

Notwithstanding the many discouraging developments in both the political and economic lives of Mexicans, a more competitive political system nonetheless appears to be emerging. With the PRI and its leadership so thoroughly discredited, many Mexicans have turned to opposition parties in the hope that their dissenting votes may finally be counted. At the close of the millennium, processes of institutional reform which have been under way for decades are beginning to produce some space for significant change. For example, the creation of an elected position of mayor of the Federal District to replace the PRI-appointed 'Regent' opened the door for the 1997 election of the PRD's Cuauhtémoc Cárdenas as mayor of the 20 million inhabitants of the Federal District. The decentralization of power from the federal to the state and municipal level is another reform that promises to bring significant change, insofar as it is at the state level that the opposition parties have their base of electoral strength and the best chances of actually taking power. And of course, as the gains made by opposition parties since 1994 have cost the PRI its majority in the Chamber of Deputies, that legislative house has been transformed from a PRI-controlled rubber stamp for programs issuing from the Mexican executive to a genuinely deliberative body capable of initiating policy change.

Progress toward institutional reform of the Mexican political system, however halting, has also raised interest at all levels of civil society, both in Mexico and abroad. Domestic and foreign press coverage of Mexican politics has increased as the Chamber of Deputies and the Senate have been transformed from bodies filled with *priista* hacks, rewarded for their political loyalty with seats in the two chambers, to sites of serious contention and often raucous debate over key issues. Moreover, political awareness and activism of Mexicans living in the United States has grown as the promise of an emigré vote stimulates political participation, while the success of California's anti-immigrant legislation Proposition 187 has demonstrated to Mexican migrants the need to mobilize to protect themselves. The increasing possibility of multiparty competition for emigré votes among the PRI, PAN and PRD has heightened interest in the electoral process on both sides of the border.

Ernesto Zedillo, currently president, has produced his own civic surprises and presided over a key moment of political transformation. The willingness of Zedillo to recognize opposition victories in the congressional, gubernatorial, and mayoral elections of July 6, 1997, as well as his express readiness—or resignation—to work within a pluralistic political system have changed the terms of Mexican politics. Zedillo has committed himself to end what has been called *presidencialismo*, the absolute control of the Mexican president over all political decisions, including nominations of official party candidates at the state level, and decisions on whether to recognize opposition victories at the state and local level. However, this reform appears to be a somewhat mixed blessing as local and state politicians may now do as they please without fear of intervention from an all-powerful president, and some of the most savagely repressive moments of the last few years, such as the 1995 police ambush of 37 unarmed peasants on their way to a demonstration in Guerrero, were perpetrated by local politicians who assumed that they were free to operate without the oversight or control of the president.

In the balance, both official statistics and anecdotal evidence show most Mexicans to be substantially worse off economically at the end of the 1990s than a decade earlier. Politically, however, some have found an avenue for the expression of their discontent in electoral support for the two main opposition parties, PAN and PRD. And in some regions of Mexico—notably northern Mexico—those dissenting votes have produced victories at the state level for opposition candidates who have actually been permitted to assume office. However for impoverished, culturally marginalized Mexicans like the indigenous people who rose in rebellion in Chiapas and the poorest zones of the Republic, small reforms and state-level victories of opposition parties cannot begin to redress the gross inequalities and disadvantages that they currently suffer, nor can such incremental steps rescue them from a future of continued struggle and—in all likelihood—repression.

Endnotes

1. Sam Dillon, "Mexico Can't Fathom Its Rising Crime," *The New York Times*, Sunday 28 June 1998, section 4, p. 1.
2. Ibid.
3. Tim Golden, "In Breakthrough, Mexican Official Testifies in Texas," *The New York Times*, 15 July 1998, p. A-1, A-6.
4. Ibid.
5. Ibid.
6. Fernando García, "Mexico en la OCDE: mas desempleadas al club de los ricos," *El Financiero*, April 30 1994, cited in Carlos A. Heredia and Mary E. Purcell, *The Polarization of Mexican Society: A Grassroots View of World Bank Economic Adjustment Policies* (Mexico, D.F.: Equipo Pueblo, 1994), p. 7.
7. Carlos Ramírez, "Archivo Politico," *El Financiero*, 22 May 1994, p. 29, cited in Ibid, p. 8.
8. Anthony DePalma, "Income Gulf in Mexico Grows and So Do Protests," *The New York Times*, 20 July 1996, p. 6.
9. Ibid. DePalma notes that 22 million live in what official government statistics call "extreme poverty," which represents an increase since 1995 of 5 million people in this condition.
10. *Forbes*, 18 July 1994, p. 194.
11. Heredia and Purcell, Op. Cit., p. 10.
12. Wayne Cornelius, *Mexican Politics in Transition: The Breakdown of a One-Party-Dominant Regime*, (San Diego: Center for U.S.-Mexican Studies, 1996), pp. 29-33, 67-75.

Glossary

apertura opening
arroyo stream or brook
borracho a drunkard
bracero a day laborer; orginally the term applied to Mexican farm hands who worked under contract in the United States. Eventually the term was applied to all Mexican temporary laborers.
cacique a political boss; orginally, an Aztec village ruler
camioneta pickup truck or van
campesino peasant
canadiense Canadian
cerro hill
chiapanecos people from the southern Mexican state of Chiapas, which borders on Guatemala
ciudad perdida "lost city," a shantytown, generally on the outskirts of the city
colonia a neighborhood or settlement
comadre and *compadre* literally these terms refer to the people one chooses to be godmother and godfather of one's children, but the terms can be applied by extention to close friends
compañeros/compañeras comrades, companions, friends
diablito "little devil," a cart used by vendors to transport their wares
fayuca clandestine goods
güero and *güerito* blond or, in the diminutive form, "blondie." These terms may be affectionately or derisively applied by Mexicans to Americans and other foreigners who are fair in coloring if not necessarily blond.
huaraches leather sandles
ingeniero engineer
maquila an assembly plant
maestro/maestra teacher
mariquano a user of marijuana
mordida a bribe (literally a "bite")
músico musician
norteamericanos the word Mexicans use for people from the United States. Although Canadians often use the term North American to refer to themselves, for Mexicans they are not *norteamericanos*, but rather *canadienses*.

pistoleros gunmen
político politician
priísta someone affiliated with the PRI
pueblo village
rancheras Mexican country music, much of it dating from the revolution
ricos rich people
simpático/simpática pleasant, congenial
tianguis the Nahuatl word for "market"
tijuanense people from Tijuana
usted the formal term for "you," it signifies respect for the person addressed
vecindad a one-room, one- or two-story tenement built inward from the street around a narrow courtyard
viejo old man

All other Spanish terms are explained in the text.

Notes

Introduction

1. Banco Nacional de Comercio Exterior, *Informe* (Sept. 1980); Euromoney, *Mexico: A Survey* ([London] March 1981), p. 4.

2. George W. Grayson, "The Mexican Oil Boom," in Susan Kaufman Purcell, ed., *Mexico–United States Relations* (New York: Praeger, 1981), pp. 146–47.

3. Christopher Buckley, "Mexico's Oil Boom and What's in It for Us," *Esquire,* December 19, 1978, p. 44; and *The New Republic,* "Oil of ¡Olé!," August 19, 1978, p. 5.

4. *Financial Times,* April 27, 1982; Jaime Ros, "La Encrucijada del Corto Plazo," *Nexos* 59.5 (Nov. 1982), pp. 35–39.

5. Judith A. Teichman, *Policymaking in Mexico: From Boom to Crisis* (Boston: Allen and Unwin, 1988), pp. 34–35; and Roger D. Hansen, *The Politics of Mexican Development* (Baltimore: Johns Hopkins University Press, 1971), p. 49.

6. Secretaría de Hacienda y Crédito Público, *Mexico's Development Financing Strategy* (México, D.F.: SHCP, 1986), cited in Merilee S. Grindle, "The Response to Austerity: Political and Economic Strategies of Mexico's Rural Poor," in Mercedes Gonzáles de la Rocha and Agustín Escobar Latapí, eds., *Social Responses to Mexico's Economic Crisis of the 1980s* (La Jolla: Center for U.S.-Mexican Studies, 1991), pp. 132–33.

7. Instituto Nacional de Estadística, Geografía e Informática, *June 1986 Report* (México, D.F.: 1986), cited in Wayne Cornelius, *The Political Economy of Mexico Under de la Madrid: The Crisis Deepens, 1985–1986* (La Jolla: Center for U.S.-Mexican Studies, 1986), pp. 32–33.

8. International Labor Office, *Report of the Director General* (Geneva: ILO Publications, 1992), p. 11; and Plan nacional de desarrollo 1989–1992, *Informe de ejecución 1992*, México, D.F., p. 157.

9. World Bank, *Poverty in Latin America: The Impact of Depression* (Washington, D.C.: The World Bank, 1986), pp. 22–23.

Chapter 2: The Historical Background

1. A more detailed account of this history is provided in the first two chapters of my book, *Mexico in Crisis* (New York: Holmes and Meier, 1978, 1983, and 1988.)

2. Charles C. Cumberland, *Mexico: The Struggle for Modernity* (New York: Oxford University Press, 1968), p. 233.

3. Clark W. Reynolds, *The Mexican Economy* (New Haven: Yale University Press, 1970), p. 24; Walter Goldfrank, "World System, State Structure, and the Onset of the Mexican Revolution," *Politics and Society* 5.4 (1975), p. 431.

4. Richard Roman, "Ideology and Class in the Mexican Revolution: A Study of the Convention and the Constitutional Congress." Ph.D. diss., University of California, Berkeley, 1973, p. 151.

5. José E. Iturriaga, *La estructura social y cultural de México* (México, D.F.: Fondo de Cultura Económica, 1951), p. 33.

6. Daniel Cosio Villegas, "The Mexican Left," in Joseph Maier and Richard W. Weatherhead, eds., *The Politics of Change in Latin America* (New York: Praeger, 1964), p. 127.

7. Cumberland, *Mexico: The Struggle for Modernity*, pp. 250–53, 247–48.

8. Andre Gunder Frank, "Mexico: The Janus Faces of 20th Century Bourgeois Revolution," *Monthly Review* 14.7 (Nov. 1962), p. 374.

9. Cumberland, *Mexico: The Struggle for Modernity*, pp. 260–61, 263–68; for translated excerpts of the constitution, see Paul E. Sigmund, *Models of Political Change in Latin America* (New York: Praeger, 1970), pp. 11–12.

10. L. Vincent Padgett, *The Mexican Political System* (Boston: Houghton Mifflin, 1966), p. 48.

11. Robert E. Scott, *Mexican Government in Transition* (Urbana: University of Illinois Press, 1964), pp. 116–17.

12. William Cameron Townsend, *Lázaro Cárdenas, Mexican Democrat* (Ann Arbor, Mich.: George Wahr, 1952), pp. 56–58.

13. Joe C. Ashby, *Organized Labor and the Mexican Revolution* (Chapel Hill: University of North Carolina Press, 1967), pp. 26–27.

14. Raymond Vernon, *The Dilemma of Mexico's Development* (Cambridge, Mass.: Harvard University Press, 1963), p. 71; Nathaniel and Sylvia Weyl, *The Reconquest of Mexico: The Years of Lázaro Cárdenas* (New York: Oxford University Press, 1939), pp. 237–39.

15. Arnaldo Córdova, *La ideologia de la revolución mexicana: La formación del nuevo régimen*, (México, D.F.: Ediciones ERA, 1973), pp. 177–78.

16. Vernon, *Dilemma of Mexico's Development*, p. 70; Padgett, *Mexican Political System*, p. 111; Betty Kirk, *Covering the Mexican Front* (Norman: University of Oklahoma Press, 1957), pp. 48, 86.

17. Padgett, *Mexican Political System*, p. 93; Howard Handelman, "The Politics of Labor Protest in Mexico," *Journal of Interamerican Studies and World Affairs* 18.3 (Aug. 1976), pp. 269–70.

18. Padgett, *Mexican Political System*, p. 99.

Chapter 5: Agriculture and Rural Development

1. Indeed, one United Nations study showed that if agricultural productivity is measured in terms of all units of input *except* the owner's labor (that is, productivity per unit of capital invested, irrigation water, seed, fertilizer, etc.) the smallest peasant plots turn out to be the most efficient type of farming in Mexico (see Rodolfo Stavenhagen, "Social Aspects of Agrarian Structure in Mexico," in Rodolfo Stavenhagen, ed., *Agrarian Problems and Peasant Movements in Latin America* [Garden City, N.Y.: Doubleday and Co., 1970], p. 251). Contemporary studies also show that "*ejidos* are as productive as private farms when differences in land quality, access to water and credit and other inputs are taken into account." Wayne Cornelius, "The Politics and Economics of Reforming the *Ejido* Sector in Mexico," *LASA Forum* 23.3 (Fall 1992), p. 6; also see Jaime González Graf, "La reforma del campo mexicano," *Nexos* 167 (Oct. 1991), p. 48.

2. A more detailed treatment of this period in Mexican agrarian history can be found in chapter three of my book, *Mexico in Crisis* (New York: Holmes and Meier, 1978, 1983, and 1988).

3. Shlomo Eckstein, "Collective Farming in Mexico," in Stavenhagen, ed., *Agrarian Problems and Peasant Movements*, p. 276.

4. Nathan L. Whetten, *Rural Mexico* (New York: Century Co., 1948), pp. 221–22.

5. François Chevalier, "The Ejido and Political Stability in Mexico," in Claudio Veliz, ed., *The Politics of Conformity in Latin America* (New York: Oxford University Press, 1967), p. 175.

6. Ibid., p. 179.

7. Marc Edelman, "Agricultural Modernization in Smallholding Areas of Mexico: A Case Study in the Sierra Norte de Puebla," *Latin American Perspectives* 7.4 (Fall 1980), p. 32; Cynthia Hewitt de Alcántara, *Modernizing Mexican Agriculture: Socioeconomic Implications of Technological Change, 1940–1970* (Geneva: United Nations Research Institute for Social Development, 1976), p. 53; Edwin J. Wellhausen, "The Agriculture of Mexico," *Scientific American* 235.3 (Sept. 1976), p. 129.

8. James H. Street, "Mexico's Economic Development Plan," *Current History* 80.469 (Nov. 1980), p. 375; Banco Nacional de México, *Review of the Economic Situation in Mexico* 57.662 (Jan. 1981), p. 9; Cynthia Hewitt de Alcántara, "Land Reform, Livelihood, and Power in Rural Mexico," in D. A. Preston, ed., *Environment, Society and Rural Change in Latin America* (New York: John Wiley and Sons, 1980), p. 33.

9. Edelman, "Agricultural Modernization," pp. 30, 32.

10. John J. Bailey, "Agrarian Reform in Mexico: The Quest for Self-Sufficiency," *Current History* 80.469 (Nov. 1981), pp. 350–60.

11. Bolívar Hernández, "Las contras del SAM," *Unomásuno* (México, D.F.: 8 Diciembre 1980).

12. Chevalier, "The Ejido and Political Stability," p. 167.

13. Hewitt de Alcántara, *Modernizing Mexican Agriculture,* p. 314.

14. Sergio Zendejas, "Mexico's Agrarian Dilemma Revisited," *Enfoque* (Fall 1992), p. 8.

15. Zendejas, "Mexico's Agrarian Dilemma," p. 1; and Cornelius, "Politics and Economics," p. 4.

Conclusions

1. Adolfo Aguilar Zinzer, "Authoritarianism and North American Free Trade: The Debate in Mexico," in Ricardo Grinspun and Maxwell A. Cameron, eds., *The Political Economy of North American Free Trade* (New York: St. Martin's Press, 1993), p. 207.

2. Carlos Tello, "Combatting Poverty in Mexico," in Mercedes González de la Rocha and Agustín Escobar Latapí, eds., *Social Responses to Mexico's Economic Crisis of the 1980s* (La Jolla: Center for U.S.–Mexican Studies, University of California, San Diego, 1991), p. 58.

3. See Americas Watch, *Human Rights in Mexico: A Policy of Impunity* (New York: Americas Watch, June 1990); Amnesty International, *Torture with Impunity* (London: Amnesty International, 1991); Jorge Luis Sierra Guzmán et al., *Una visión no gobernamental* (México, D.F.: La Comisión Nacional de Derechos Humanos, 1992); and the Report of the Canadian Committee to Protect Journalists, summarized in Olivia Ward, "Terror Muzzles Mexican Media," *Toronto Star,* January 27, 1992, p. A-11.

4. Merilee S. Grindle, "The Response to Austerity: Political and Economic Strategies of Mexico's Rural Poor," in González de la Rocha and Escobar Latapí, eds., *Social Responses to Mexico's Economic Crisis,* p. 130.

5. Arturo Warman, *"We Come to Object": The Peasants of Morelos and the National State* (Baltimore: Johns Hopkins University Press, 1980), p. 238, quoted in Grindle, "The Response to Austerity," p. 136.

6. See Kathryn Kopinak, "The Maquiladorization of the Mexican Economy," in Grinspun and Cameron, *Political Economy of North American Free Trade,* pp. 141–62.

Selected Bibliography

Urban Issues

On life in the slums and shantytowns of Mexico City see Carlos G. Vélez-Ibañez, *Rituals of Marginality: Politics, Process, and Culture Change in Central Urban Mexico, 1969–1974* (Berkeley and Los Angeles: University of California Press, 1983); Henry A. Selby, Arthur D. Murphy, and Stephen A. Lorenzen, *The Mexican Urban Household: Organizing for Self-Defense* (Austin: University of Texas Press, 1990); Susan Eckstein, *The Poverty of Revolution: The State and the Urban Poor in Mexico* (Princeton: Princeton University Press, 1988); Larissa Lomnitz, *Networks and Marginality: Life in a Mexican Shantytown* (New York: Academic Press, 1977); and Oscar Lewis's two classics, *Five Families* (New York: Basic Books, 1959) and *The Children of Sánchez* (New York: Vintage, 1961). On the patterns that determine where the rich and poor live in Mexico City, see Peter Ward, *Mexico City: The Production and Reproduction of an Urban Environment* (Boston: G. K. Hall and Co., 1990).

Studies of the condition of people like Mercedes, that is, indigenous migrants to the capital, are Douglas Butterworth, "A Study of the Urbanization Process among Mixtec Migrants from Tilaltongo [*sic*] in Mexico City," *América Indígena* 22 (1962), pp. 257–74; and Lourdes Arizpe, *Indígenas en la ciudad de México: El caso de las "Marías"* (México, D.F.: SepSetentas, 1975).

On the informal economy, see Alejandro Portes, Manuel Castells, and Lauren A. Benton, eds., *The Informal Economy* (Baltimore: Johns Hopkins University Press, 1989); M. Estellie Smith, ed., *Perspectives on the Informal Economy* (New York: University Press of America, 1990); and Lourdes Arizpe, "Women in the Informal Labor Sector: The Case of Mexico City," in Wellesley Editorial Committee, eds., *Women and National Development: The Complexities of Change* (Chicago: University of Chicago Press, 1977), pp. 25–37. On informal "homework" or piecework production in the poor neighborhoods of Mexico City, see Lourdes Benería and Martha Roldán, *The Crossroads of Class and Gender: Industrial Homework, Subcontracting, and Household Dynamics in Mexico City* (Chicago: University of Chicago Press, 1987).

On family survival strategies, see Mercedes González de la Rocha and Agustín Escobar Latapí, eds., *Social Responses to Mexico's Economic Crisis of the 1980s* (La Jolla: Center for U.S.-Mexican Studies, University of California, San Diego, 1991); Merilee S. Grindle, "The Response to Austerity: Political and

Economic Strategies of Mexico's Rural Poor," in William L. Canak, ed., *Lost Promises: Debt, Austerity, and Development in Latin America* (Boulder, Colo.: Westview, 1989), pp. 190–215; and Sylvia Chant, *Women and Survival in Mexican Cities: Perspectives on Gender, Labour Markets and Low-Income Households* (Manchester, Eng.: Manchester University Press, 1991).

For a study of food provisioning, see Cynthia Hewitt de Alcántara and Gabriel Vera, *Inside Megalopolis: Exploring Social and Spacial Diversity of Provisioning Structures in Mexico City* (Geneva: United Nations Research Institute for Social Development, 1990).

Environmental Issues

The report on Mexico's environmental problems referred to by Sergio Espinoza is United Nations Environment Programme, *Environmental Data Report (1989)* (2d ed., Oxford: Basil Blackwell, 1989). For a summary discussion of the report, see the *New York Times*, May 11, 1991, p. 1. For a general discussion on Mexico's environmental problems, see Stephen P. Mumme, "System Maintenance and Environmental Reform in Mexico: Salinas's Preemptive Strategy," *Latin American Perspectives* 19. 1 (Winter 1992), pp. 123–43; Daniel Goldrich and David V. Carruthers, "Sustainable Development in Mexico? The International Politics of Crisis or Opportunity," *Latin American Perspectives* 19.1 (Winter 1992), pp. 97–122; Fernando Menéndez Garza, "Mexico City's Program to Reduce Air Pollution," and Richard A. Nuccio, "The Limits of Environmental Protection in Mexico," both in Joseph S. Tulchin and Andrew I. Rudman, eds., *Economic Development and Environmental Protection in Latin America* (Boulder, Colo.: Lynne Rienner Publishers, 1991); and Alfonso Vásquez Botello and Federico Páez, *El problema crucial: la contaminación* (México, D.F.: Centro de Ecodesarrollo, 1988). On the use of pesticides in Mexican agriculture, see Angus Wright, *The Death of Ramón González: The Modern Agricultural Dilemma* (Austin: University of Texas Press, 1990).

On environmental problems as binational issues, see Richard A. Nuncio and Angelina Ornelas, *Developing Disaster: Mexico's Environment and the United States* (New York: World Resources Institute, 1987); Roberto Sánchez R., *El medio ambiente como fuente de conflicto en la relación binacional México–Estados Unidos* (Tijuana: Colegio de la Frontera Norte, 1990); Jan Rich, "Bordering on Trouble," *Environmental Forum* 8 (May–June, 1991), pp. 26–33; and virtually any issue of the *Transboundary Resources Report*, published three times per year by the University of New Mexico School of Law, Albuquerque, New Mexico.

Development Policy and Economic Elites

For readings on industrial development policy and the relationship between businessmen, industrialists, and the Mexican state, see Stephen H. Haber, *Industry and Underdevelopment: The Industrialization of Mexico, 1890–1940* (Stanford: Stanford University Press, 1989); Nora Hamilton, *The Limits of State Autonomy,* (Princeton: Princeton University Press, 1982); Roderic A. Camp, *Entrepreneurs and Politics in Twentieth-Century Mexico* (New York: Oxford University Press, 1989); Sylvia Maxfield and Ricardo Anzaldua Montoya, eds., *Government and Private Sector in Contemporary Mexico* (La Jolla: Center for U.S.-Mexican Studies, 1987); Cristina Puga and Ricardo Tirado, eds., *Los empresarios mexicanos, ayer y hoy* (México, D.F.: Ediciones el Caballito, 1992); and Judith A. Teichman, *Policy Making in Mexico* (Boston: Allen and Unwin, 1988).

On the private sphere of the Mexican economic elite, see Larissa Adler Lomnitz and Marisol Pérez-Lizaur, *A Mexican Elite Family 1820–1980: Kinship, Class and Culture* (Princeton: Princeton University Press, 1987); and Carlos Fuentes's novel, *The Death of Artemio Cruz* (New York: Noonday Press, 1971).

For agricultural development policies and their consequences, see David Barkin, *Distorted Development: Mexico and the World Economy* (Boulder, Colo.: Westview, 1990); Steven Sanderson, *The Transformation of Mexican Agriculture: International Structure and the Politics of Rural Change* (Princeton: Princeton University Press, 1986); Merilee S. Grindle, *Searching for Rural Development: Labor Migration and Employment in Mexico* (Ithaca: Cornell University Press, 1988); Cynthia Hewitt de Alcántara, *Modernizing Mexican Agriculture: Socioeconomic Implications of Technological Change, 1940–1970* (Geneva, United Nations Research Institute for Social Development, 1976); James E. Austin and Gustavo Esteva, eds., *Food Policy in Mexico: The Search for Self-Sufficiency* (Ithaca: Cornell University Press, 1987); Cynthia Hewitt de Alcántara, *Economic Restructuring and Rural Subsistence in Mexico: Maize and the Crisis of the 1980s* (Geneva: United Nations Research Institute for Social Development, 1992); and Kirsten Appendini, *De la milpa a los tortibonos: La restructuración de la política alimentaria en México* (México, D.F.: El Colegio de México, 1992).

The Border Region

Josia McC. Heyman, *Life and Labor on the Border: Working People of Northeastern Sonora, Mexico, 1886–1986* (Tucson: University of Arizona Press, 1991); Lawrence A. Herzog, *Where North Meets South: Cities, Space and Politics on the U.S.-Mexico Border* (Austin: Center for Mexican American Studies, University of Texas at Austin, 1990); Vicki L. Ruiz and Susan Tiano, eds., *Women on the U.S.-Mexico Border: Responses to Change* (Boulder, Colo.: Westview, 1991); Oscar J. Martínez, *Troublesome Border* (Tucson: University of Arizona Press, 1988); John R. Weeks and Roberto Ham-Chande, *Demographic Interrelatedness of the U.S.-Mexico Border Region* (San Diego: San Diego State University International Population Center, 1989); and Rodolfo Cruz Pineiro, *La fuerza de trabajo en los mercados urbanos de la frontera norte* (Tijuana: Colegio de la Frontera Norte, 1992).

For background reading on Tijuana, its history, and economy, see John A. Price, *Tijuana: Urbanization in a Border Culture* (London and Notre Dame: Notre Dame University Press, 1973); and on the phenomenon of cross-border commuters like Adelita, see Tito Alegría, "Ciudad y transmigración en la frontera de México con Estados Unidos," *Frontera Norte* 2 (July–Dec. 1990), pp. 7–38.

For studies of the *maquila* industry, see Leslie Sklair, *Assembling for Development: The Maquila Industry in Mexico and the United States* (Boston: Unwin Hyman, 1989); Harley Shaiken, *Mexico in the Global Economy: High Technology and Work Organization in Export Industries* (La Jolla: Center for U.S.-Mexican Studies, University of California, San Diego, 1990); Khosrow Fatemi, ed., *The Maquiladora Industry: Economic Solution or Problem?* (New York: Praeger, 1990); and Roberto Sánchez, "Condiciones de la vida de los trabajadores de la maquiladora en Tijuana y Nogales," *Frontera Norte* 2 (July–Dec. 1990), pp. 153–81.

Specifically on women in the *maquilas* see, Norma Iglesias, *La flor más bella de la maquiladora* (México: Secretaría de Educación Pública and Centro de Estudios Fronterizos del Norte de México, 1985); Maria Patricia Fernández-Kelly, *For We Are Sold, I and My People: Women and Industry on Mexico's Northern Frontier* (Albany: State University of New York Press, 1983); and Rosío Barajas Escamilla and Carmen Rodríguez Carrillo, *Mujer y trabajo en la industria maquiladora de exportación en Tijuana, Baja California* (Tijuana: Colegio de la Frontera Norte, 1990).

Migration

On patterns of migration, see Ina R. Dinerman, *Migrants and Stay-at-Homes: A Comparative Study of Rural Migration from Michoacán, Mexico* (La Jolla: Center for U.S.-Mexican Studies, University of California, San Diego, 1982); Merilee S. Grindle, *Searching for Rural Development: Labor Migration and Employment in Mexico* (Ithaca: Cornell University Press, 1988); Wayne A. Cornelius, *Labor Migration to the United States: Development Outcomes and Alternatives in Mexican Sending Communities* (Washington, D.C.: Commission for the Study of International Migration and Cooperative Economic Development, 1990); Lourdes Arizpe, "Relay Migration and the Survival of the Peasant Household," in Helen Safa, ed., *Toward a Political Economy of Urbanization in Developing Countries* (New Delhi: Oxford University Press, 1982), pp. 19–46; and Jorge A. Bustamante, *Migración de indocumentados de México a Estados Unidos* (Tijuana: Colegio de la Frontera Norte, 1988). On the eventual employment experiences of the migrants once they reach the United States, see Wayne Cornelius, *The Changing Role of Mexican*

Labor in the U.S. Economy (La Jolla: Center for U.S.-Mexican Studies, University of California, San Diego, 1992).

NAFTA

For critical analysis of NAFTA, see Ricardo Grinspun and Maxwell A. Cameron, eds., *The Political Economy of North American Free Trade* (New York: St. Martin's Press, 1993); North American Congress on Latin America, "The New Gospel: North American Free Trade, *NACLA Report on the Americas* 24, (May 1991), pp. 9–38; and the monographic issue of *Frontera Norte* 3 (July–Dec. 1991), edited by Gustavo del Castillo, which features articles in both English and Spanish.

Popular Movements

For background on the kinds of popular urban mobilizations in which Lupe and Conchita are involved, see Joe Foweraker and Ann L. Craig, *Popular Movements and Political Change in Mexico* (Boulder, Colo.: Lynne Rienner Publishers, 1990); Juan Manuel Ramírez Saiz, *El movimiento urbano popular en México* (México, D.F.: Siglo Veintiuno, 1986); María Consuelo Mejía Piñeros and Sergio Sarmiento Silva, *La lucha indígena: Un reto a la ortodoxia* (México, D.F.: Siglo Veintiuno, 1987); and Adriana López Monjardín, *La lucha por los ayuntamientos: Una utopia viable* (México, D.F.: Siglo Veintiuno, 1986). Specifically on Lupe's movement, see Ramón Tirado Jiménez, *Asamblea de Barrios: Nuestra Batalla* (México, D.F.: Editorial Nuestro Tiempo, 1990); and on Conchita's experiences, see Eduardo Muciño Coleote and Elías López Guerra, "San Miguel Teotongo: una experiencia en la construcción de organizaciones autónomas de masas," in Jorge Alonso, ed., *Los movimientos sociales en el valle de México, Vol. II* (México, D.F.: Colección Miguel Othón de Mendizábal, 1986), pp. 191–223.

Clearly related to these movements is the crisis in housing in Mexico City, Tijuana and elsewhere in Mexico. On this subject, see Alan Gilbert, ed., *Housing and Land in Urban Mexico* (La Jolla: Center for U.S.-Mexican Studies, University of California, San Diego, 1989). On local movements in support of opposition political forces, see Jorge Alonso and Silvia Gómez Tagle, *Insurgencia democrática: Las elecciones locales* (Guadalajara: Universidad de Guadalajara, 1991).

Labor

For a general look at the Mexican labor movement see Ruth Berins Collier, *The Contradictory Alliance: State-Labor Relations and Regime Change in Mexico* (Berkeley: International and Area Studies, University of California at Berkeley, 1992); Kevin J. Middlebrook, ed., *Unions, Workers, and the State in Mexico* (La Jolla: Center for U.S.-Mexican Studies, University of California, San Diego, 1991);

Dan La Botz, *Mask of Democracy: Labor Suppression in Mexico Today* (Boston: South End Press, 1992); and Ian Roxborough, "Organized Labor: A Major Victim of the Debt Crisis," in Barbara Stallings and Robert Kaufman, eds., *Debt and Democracy in Latin America* (Boulder, Colo.: Westview, 1989).

On the teachers' movement, see Maria Lorena Cook, "Organizing Opposition in the Teachers' Movement in Oaxaca," in Foweraker and Craig, and Susan Street, *Maestros en Movimiento: Transformaciones en la burocracia estatal (1978–1982)* (México, D.F.: Colección Miguel Othón de Mendizábal, 1992). For a study of women's activism in the garment industry, see Teresa Carrillo, "Women and Independent Unionism in the Garment Industry," in Foweraker and Craig, pp. 213–33.

The Political System

For general analyses of the Mexican political system see Daniel Levy and Gabriel Szekely, *Mexico: Paradoxes of Stability and Change* (Boulder, Colo.: Westview, 1983); Judith Adler Hellman, *Mexico in Crisis* (New York: Holmes and Meier, 1988); Neil Harvey, ed., *Mexico: Dilemmas of Transition* (London and New York: The Institute of Latin American Studies and British Academic Press, 1993); Wayne A. Cornelius, Judith Gentleman, and Peter H. Smith, eds., *Mexico's Alternative Political Futures* (La Jolla: Center for U.S.-Mexican Studies, University of California, San Diego, 1989); Wayne A. Cornelius and Ann L. Craig, *The Mexican Political System in Transition* (La Jolla: Center for U.S.-Mexican Studies, University of California, San Diego, 1991); Philip Russell, *Mexico Under Salinas* (Austin, Tex.: Mexico Resource Center, 1993).

Specifically on the problem of corruption, see Stephen D. Morris, *Corruption and Politics in Contemporary Mexico* (Tuscaloosa: University of Alabama Press, 1991), and ch. 6 of Alan Riding, *Distant Neighbors* (New York: Vintage, 1986).